D0839356

Theories of Multiculturalism

Theories of Multiculturalism

An Introduction

George Crowder

polity

Copyright © George Crowder 2013

The right of George Crowder to be identified as Author of this Work has been asserted in accordance with the UK Copyright, Designs and Patents Act 1988.

First published in 2013 by Polity Press

Polity Press
65 Bridge Street
Cambridge CB2 1UR, UK

Polity Press
350 Main Street
Malden, MA 02148, USA

All rights reserved. Except for the quotation of short passages for the purpose of criticism and review, no part of this publication may be reproduced, stored in a retrieval system, or transmitted, in any form or by any means, electronic, mechanical, photocopying, recording or otherwise, without the prior permission of the publisher.

ISBN-13: 978-0-7456-3625-2 (hardback)
ISBN-13: 978-0-7456-3626-9 (paperback)

A catalogue record for this book is available from the British Library.

Typeset in 10.5 on 12 pt Sabon
by Toppan Best-set Premedia Limited
Printed and bound in Great Britain by Clays Ltd, St Ives plc

The publisher has used its best endeavours to ensure that the URLs for external websites referred to in this book are correct and active at the time of going to press. However, the publisher has no responsibility for the websites and can make no guarantee that a site will remain live or that the content is or will remain appropriate.

Every effort has been made to trace all copyright holders, but if any have been inadvertently overlooked the publisher will be pleased to include any necessary credits in any subsequent reprint or edition.

For further information on Polity, visit our website: www.politybooks.com

Contents

Preface

This book is intended to serve three functions. First, I hope to provide an accessible introduction to the issues and debates in the political-theory literature on multiculturalism. That literature began in earnest in the late 1980s, and since that time an immense number of books and articles have appeared on the subject, representing a wide array of rival positions. The time is ripe, I think, for a book-length survey of the territory that will help to guide students and non-specialists through a complex terrain.

I have chosen to tackle multiculturalism by thinker rather than theme in order to highlight and to try to do justice to the different perspectives that have emerged. In addition, I group the leading thinkers together in rough 'schools' or tendencies, each chapter concentrating on an identifiable pattern of this kind, to help to bring out persistent themes and preoccupations. Inevitably I have had to be selective in deciding which writers to discuss, and no selection will please everyone. I myself regret some omissions and truncations due to lack of space. However, I have tried to focus on those writers and tendencies that seem to me to have been the most influential and stimulating in the field.

The second purpose of the book is to defend certain responses to the main points in dispute. I have tried to be as just to all the various multiculturalists and their critics as possible but I cannot, of course, agree with them all, if only because they disagree so strongly with each other. I do have views and reach conclusions of my own, and it is only fair to warn readers of these in advance.

To begin with, I argue in favour of a broadly universalist approach to ethics in contrast with various species of relativism, although the kind of universalism that I adopt leaves plenty of room for legitimate ethical divergence among cultures. The limits of that legitimate divergence, I believe, are marked out by the boundaries of liberal politics, in particular by the modern doctrine of human rights. Consequently, I conclude against non-liberal forms of multiculturalism.

Within liberalism, moreover, I align myself with that stream of liberal thought that emphasizes the value of personal autonomy, or the capacity to choose one's own way of life through critical reflection, rather than the kind of liberalism that stresses toleration, which is often interpreted to mean toleration of practices that constrict personal autonomy – the withholding of education from women, for example. I do not see my position in this respect as distinctively or ethnocentrically 'Western' or European for reasons I shall come to in due course.

However, whether one should accept what I call 'multiculturalism proper' – that is, the active state recognition and promotion of minority cultures within a society – or whether it would be better to take a more 'hands-off' approach to cultures, perhaps encouraging mutual toleration or respect but going no further, is a more difficult question to answer. On this matter I recommend a contextual or case-by-case approach.

So far, what I wish to argue is controversial but not especially original. The book's third purpose, however, is to give some indication of how such a view might be argued in a way that is not so familiar – namely, on the basis of the notion of 'value pluralism' associated with Isaiah Berlin, the idea that fundamental human values are universal but also irreducibly plural, conflicting and incommensurable. This is not to say that no one has previously approached the issues of multiculturalism by way of value pluralism – in Chapter 7 I examine several theories of this kind. But I believe that I can claim some degree of originality, for good or ill, in the way I combine the pluralist outlook with the particular conclusions I reach.

This project has taken much longer than I thought it would, in part because the literature has kept expanding as I have gone along. At times it has felt as if I were trying to catch a bus that kept pulling away just as I was reaching it. At any rate, I wish to acknowledge the help I have received from several sources along the way.

First, I owe a special debt of gratitude to my former student, Ian Haddock, whose work on his PhD thesis, 'Liberal Multiculturalism: Liberalism, Cultural Equality, and Individual Rights' (Flinders University, 2004) encouraged me to embark on this project. Ian helped with some of the initial research and drafting of the book, and his engagement with the ideas stimulated my own.

I am also grateful to Polity's two anonymous readers for their shrewd comments and generous judgements on the whole manuscript. Further comments on particular parts of the work were kindly provided by Daniel A. Bell, Rick DeAngelis, Lina Eriksson, Martin Griffiths, Chandran Kukathas, Geoffrey Brahm Levey, David Miller, Lionel Orchard and Jane Robbins. I also appreciate the questions and comments of audiences at various seminars and conference events over the years, especially those at successive annual conferences of the Australasian Political Studies Association where I first tried out many of these explanations and arguments. None of these generous souls is responsible for the flaws that no doubt remain. At Polity, John Thompson has been an enthusiastic supporter of the project from the beginning, Jennifer Jahn remained patient with its glacial progress for several years, and Elliott Karstadt shepherded it through its final stages.

Parts of Chapters 5, 6 and 7 were first published in my chapter, 'Multiculturalism, Liberalism and Value Pluralism', in Peter Balint and Sophie de Latour, eds, *Liberal Multiculturalism and the Fair Terms of Integration* (Palgrave Macmillan, 2012), and I thank the publisher for permission to reproduce that material.

As always, my greatest debt is to my partner, Sue.

Introduction

Multiculturalism is one of the most controversial ideas in contemporary public affairs.[1] For some people it has highly positive connotations: an attractive diversity of ways of life, mutual respect among citizens from different backgrounds, free expression and creativity, colourful dances, exotic customs, culinary variety. For others it suggests social fragmentation, a stultifying political correctness, inegalitarian privileges for certain groups, the abandonment or denigration of the core ethical standards and achievements of Western civilization and even of science and reason.

Is multiculturalism a triumph or a disaster, or something in between? In this book my primary purpose is to introduce and evaluate some of the answers given to this question by leading moral and political theorists.

I shall also argue for my own conclusions. Briefly put, these begin with the principle that the accommodation of multiple cultures within a single society is a laudable ideal, but only if qualified by the principles of liberal democracy. In particular, I emphasize the importance of personal autonomy, the capacity of individuals to choose their own way of life and to take a critically reflective view of their own culture. It is a further question whether cultural accommodation should take the form of what I shall call 'multiculturalism proper', the public recognition of minority cultures, or whether it would be better to take a more non-interventionist approach with cultures. On this issue I argue that different responses may be appropriate in different contexts.

These may seem unsurprising and unadventurous conclusions, but they run counter to some of the most influential thinking on the subject in the academy. In addition, I reach my conclusions by 'a road less traveled', namely that of 'value pluralism', in contrast with more familiar forms of ethical argument in this field.

The Debate

Many societies have been multicultural in the sense that they have in fact contained people from diverse cultural backgrounds, but multicultural*ism* 'is a normative response to that fact' (Parekh 2006: 6). Multiculturalists not only observe but also approve of the presence of multiple cultures within a single society and accord public recognition and support to those cultures. Policies along these lines date from the 1970s, emerging in liberal democracies including Canada, Australia, the United States and parts of Western Europe, notably the United Kingdom and the Netherlands. The best-known political theories of multiculturalism have been formulated in response to those policies.

Multiculturalism has always had its supporters and detractors, the weight of influence appearing to fall now on one side, now on the other. Indeed, the dispute is often presented as a narrative of the rise and fall of multiculturalism, or at least its advance and retreat. This pattern has been detected in all of the countries mentioned, with the possible exception of Canada, where multiculturalism has always been at its strongest.[2]

To begin with the 'rise' of multiculturalism, multiculturalist policies were first formulated in the wake of increased migration from developing countries to the developed societies of North America, Western Europe and Australasia, an increase that began after the Second World War and gathered pace in the 1960s and 1970s. Along with the new migration came a change of attitude in the host countries, where the traditional policies of assimilation – the insistence that immigrants adopt the majority culture – came to be seen as neither necessary nor desirable. Unlike previous waves of immigrants, the new arrivals were thought to be too 'different' to be easily assimilated. While for some policy makers this was immediately a major problem, for others it was something to be welcomed. As the British Home Secretary, Roy Jenkins, expressed it in 1966:

> I do not think we need in this country a 'melting pot', which will turn everyone out in a common mould, as one of a series of carbon copies

> of someone's misplaced vision of the stereotyped Englishman . . . I define integration, therefore, not as a flattening process of uniformity, but cultural diversity, coupled with equality of opportunity in an atmosphere of mutual tolerance. (Jenkins 1970: 267)

The valuing of cultural diversity in balance with equality of opportunity and mutual tolerance – here, immediately, are some of the central themes of multiculturalism.

In pursuit of these goals new policies were instituted, first in Canada and Australia in the early 1970s, and in many other liberal democracies soon after. In different degrees in different places these included some or all of the following:[3]

(1) public affirmation of multiculturalism as official policy;
(2) adoption of multiculturalism in educational curricula;
(3) representation of ethnic minorities in public media or media licensing bodies;
(4) exemptions from legally required dress codes or trading hours;
(5) dual citizenship arrangements;
(6) funding of ethnic cultural activities;
(7) provision or funding of bilingual or mother-tongue education;
(8) affirmative action for disadvantaged groups.

One should add to this list various provisions recognizing the special status and claims of indigenous peoples (Ivison, Patton and Sanders 2000).

Multiculturalism has always had critics, and these have become more numerous and vocal over the years. In part the critics have been alarmed by a number of sensational cases in which multiculturalism has been implicated by popular or media opinion: for example, the threats against the novelist Salman Rushdie, the murder of the Dutch film-maker Theo van Gogh, the 'Danish cartoons' controversy and the London bombings of 7 July 2005. Such events have often been said to demonstrate a 'failure of multiculturalism'. In fact, however, it is questionable whether any of these occurrences had much to do with multiculturalism, since none of them was endorsed or directly encouraged by multiculturalist policies. In each case the anti-multiculturalist outcry was really directed at the sheer presence in the host country of groups with divergent beliefs, but that alone is not equivalent to multiculturalism, as I shall explain shortly.

Less dramatic but more pervasive factors in generating opposition to multiculturalism are the broad social, economic and political patterns that have influenced popular thinking on the subject, whether rightly or wrongly. Multiculturalist policies have in general been created by policy elites rather than by popular demand. Ordinary people have often seen such programmes as elitist impositions that have made their lives more difficult in times that are difficult already. As Ali Rattansi argues, the advent of multiculturalism has coincided with a period of 'triple transition': widespread questioning of nation-states and national identities, a shift in developed countries away from manufacturing towards a 'post-industrial' economy, and the 'restructuring' – some would say decimation – of the welfare state (Rattansi 2011: 143–7). It is easy to see how the dislocations and anxieties caused by these changes have been turned against policies of increased immigration, hence against the multiculturalism that seems to justify and encourage this.

The critics bring several charges against multiculturalism. Perhaps the most common is that the multiculturalist emphasis on cultural diversity and distinct identities undermines the cohesion and shared identity that any society needs. In Australia, for example, multiculturalism has been accused of being 'used to hollow out what it means to be and to become an Australian citizen, depriving citizenship of its cultural base in a distinctive Australian nationality' (Galligan and Roberts 2004: 80). The British Prime Minister, David Cameron, has even linked what he sees as the 'weakening of our collective identity' that he attributes to multiculturalism with the rise in the UK of Islamist extremism (Cameron 2011).

Other complaints include a sense that multiculturalist provisions privilege some communities at the expense of others and that they depart from liberal-democratic commitments to the equal treatment of all citizens and to individual rights and liberties (Barry 2001). There is often a concern about accommodation of illiberal cultural traditions that set a low value on the rights of women in particular (Okin 1999). Some commentators have seen in multiculturalism a betrayal not only of liberal democracy but also of Western civilization (Bloom 1987; Huntington 1996; Sandall 2001). Finally, there is a perception that multiculturalism is part of a contemporary movement towards ethical and cognitive relativism that is itself a form of unthinking prejudice (Bloom 1987).

Under the weight of this intellectual and popular opposition, multiculturalism is now, according to many observers, in decline or even finished altogether. Christian Joppke sees 'a seismic shift' in several European societies from multiculturalism to 'civic integration', which emphasizes the uniform entitlements of individuals rather than the differentiated claims of groups, and which is consequently more assertive of overarching liberal principles (Joppke 2004: 248–52).

Similarly, Hans Entzinger writes of the Netherlands as adopting 'a renewed emphasis on citizenship and shared values', and Anne Phillips refers to a reaction against multiculturalism in university curricula and admissions policy in the United States in favour of 'the supposedly core values of freedom, democracy, and a Christian God' (Entzinger 2003: 59; Phillips 2007: 3–4). In Australia multiculturalism has been declared by some to be 'effectively gutted as a national policy' (Galligan and Roberts 2004: 94).

Yet an equally frequent assessment is that reports of the demise of multiculturalism have been exaggerated. In some cases the rhetoric may have changed but this has made little difference to policy. Australia, for example, dropped the word 'multiculturalism' from the title of the Immigration Department in 2007 but retained most of the associated policies and practices. Geoffrey Levey concludes that 'if we are witnessing a retreat from "multiculturalism", it appears to be a measured one' (Levey 2008: 19). Rogers Brubaker describes a turn away from strong 'differentialism' but adds that this 'does not amount to a return to the bad old days of arrogant assimilationism' (Brubaker 2003: 51). For Ali Rattansi, multiculturalism is both under fire and also to some degree 'embedded' (Rattansi 2011: 148). Even among those who want to see multiculturalism amended, there is still widespread support for Nathan Glazer's famous remark that in general 'we are all multiculturalists now' (Glazer 1997). Perhaps the safest conclusion is that the debate over multiculturalism is far from settled.

Defining Multiculturalism

Might it be that at least some of the prevalent disagreement over multiculturalism stems from confusion over what the concept means? The debate in the popular media and even the academic literature often gives the impression that the multiculturalism that the critics attack is not the same as the multiculturalism that its supporters defend.

The problem is that what multiculturalism is or should be is part of what is in dispute. First, is multiculturalism a moderate or a radical idea? There are claims and counter-claims as to whether there is now consensus on the basic multiculturalist principles or whether these remain controversial or idealistic. On the one hand, the leading multiculturalist Will Kymlicka believes that he is merely justifying what is already to a large extent existing practice in liberal democracies, and furthermore that the kind of justifications he offers are a subset or natural development of mainstream liberal-democratic thought (Kymlicka 1998b; 2001: 3–4). On the other hand, the well-known critic of multiculturalism, Brian Barry, sees all multiculturalists, including Kymlicka, as betraying the norms of liberalism and egalitarianism and returning to the pre-Enlightenment moral world of irrational distinctions and privileges (Barry 2001). I shall discuss Kymlicka and Barry in detail in Chapters 2 and 3 respectively.

A second point of disagreement, closely related to the first, is whether multiculturalism is really more about integration or about separation. Roughly speaking, moderate multiculturalists are drawn more towards the integration of cultures within a society, while advocates at the more radical end of the multiculturalist spectrum tend to emphasize the distinctness of cultures. This is speaking only roughly because there is no sharp dividing line between these views: all multiculturalists share both of them to some extent. For example, Kymlicka is more integrationist in his prescriptions for immigrant groups but more separatist when it comes to 'national' or indigenous minorities (see Chapter 2).

At any rate, the integrationist and separatist faces of multiculturalism seem to show themselves by turns. Even the most integrationist form of multiculturalism involves an insistence that the distinctness of cultural identities be respected, indeed valued. In 1966 Roy Jenkins had in mind improved policies for the integration of new immigrants. But the central requirement, he believed, was the replacement of assimilation by the retention, to some extent, of existing cultural identities. The more cultural distinctness is emphasized, the more it seems to pull away from integration. This is especially so in those countries, Canada and Australia in particular, where multiculturalism is advanced not merely as an instrument for settling newcomers within an overarching national identity but as itself a central feature of that identity. In the Australian case this has given rise to the objection that, while multiculturalism was initially 'a humane policy for accommodating migrants from non-English speaking backgrounds', the expanded vision of multiculturalism as a centerpiece of national identity is an empty conception that 'includes everyone but engages no one' (Galligan and Roberts 2004: 75, 80).

A third level of dispute concerns justification: is multiculturalism underpinned by universalist or by relativist ethics? Again this is related to the previous points at issue. The more moderate, integrationist approaches to multiculturalism (like Kymlicka's) are usually justified by arguments based on the standard rights and liberties of liberal-democratic citizenship backed by the idea of human rights. That is, moderate multiculturalists usually appeal to universalist arguments. In their liberal version, such arguments make the well-being of the human individual primary. Cultures may be instrumentally valuable to the extent that they contribute to individual well-being – to the liberty or equality or fair treatment of individuals – but cultural practices may also be criticized by the same standard. Hence, on this view, the legitimate claims of cultures are limited by liberal political principles (see Chapters 2, 3 and 9).

By contrast, the more radical, 'separatist' kinds of multiculturalism tend to rest on the notion that cultures are valuable not merely instrumentally but intrinsically – valuable for their own sake. From this it seems to follow that they are equally valuable, so that all cultures must be equally respected. Views of this kind are usually based on cultural relativism, the theory that moral rules are never universal in application or authority, but only relatively valid from some particular cultural perspective. On this view each culture is its own moral authority, so all must be equals. Such an approach implies a strong or unqualified form of multiculturalism that regards liberal democracy as only one cultural form among others (see Chapter 5).[4]

I cannot resolve all these disputes immediately. Distinguishing and evaluating the many different approaches to multiculturalism will occupy the rest of the book. However, it is possible to sketch a working definition of multiculturalism that will frame the subsequent discussion. This needs to be both specific enough to make the investigation relevant and manageable, and wide enough to include at least most of those political theories commonly referred to under the heading of multiculturalism.

I propose the following three-part definition.

(1) Multiculturalism starts with the observation that most contemporary societies are 'multicultural' – that is, they do in fact contain multiple cultures.
(2) More distinctively, multiculturalists respond to that fact as something to approve of rather than oppose or merely tolerate.
(3) More distinctively still, multiculturalists argue that the multiplicity of cultures within a single society should be not only generally approved of but also given positive recognition in the public policy and public institutions of the society.

The combination of (1) and (2) is enough for multiculturalism at its broadest, the idea that the presence of several different cultures within a single society is desirable. However, it is only with the addition of (3) that we arrive at the more specific idea of 'multiculturalism proper', and it is this latter idea that I shall usually be referring to as 'multiculturalism' in the remainder of the book.

It is also worth noting what my definition excludes and what it leaves open. It excludes from theories of fully fledged multiculturalism purely descriptive theories of contemporary diversity, the mere celebration of that diversity and the advocacy of toleration and other public responses that fall short of positive recognition. It leaves undecided the precise focus and limits of public recognition, and the manner in which, and the extent to which, recognition is justified. These are matters that I shall examine in due course.

Culture

Let me now briefly expand on aspects of the three elements in my definition. First, multiculturalists accept that under contemporary conditions any single political society is likely in fact to contain more than one culture. But what is a 'culture'? This concept is itself a major crux of debate, and I shall have more to say about competing views of culture, and the implications of those competing views, in the chapters to follow.

However, some working definition is again in order, and for this purpose I propose the following: a culture is a set of beliefs and values that is held in common by a group and that identify it as a group.[5] By extension a culture may also be a group that identifies itself in this way. For a culture to exist, there must be, as Ronald Dworkin puts it, 'a shared vocabulary of tradition and convention' (Dworkin 1985: 231). Conventions are accepted ways of doing things, and traditions are conventions transmitted across generations. Such conventions and traditions are likely to differ from one group to the next, so the shared vocabulary is one through which a group identifies itself as a particular group distinct from others.

Some people would want to go further and specify that the relevant beliefs and values must generate an 'encompassing' or 'comprehensive' identity. The initial thought is that everything said about cultures so far could be said of families, or of micro-cultures – clubs or businesses, for example – but the literature of multiculturalism is concerned with beliefs and norms that guide a person's conduct not just in one area, such as sport or business, but throughout life more generally.

But critics would argue that in the modern world there are hardly any comprehensive identities. A central theme of the 'cosmopolitan' thinkers in particular (Chapter 4) is that people identify themselves in many different ways – as parents, children, spouses, students, workers, nationals and citizens – and each of these identities may have various and multiple cultural sources. No single culture is likely to define the entire identity of a modern individual. Some cultures may seek to be more encompassing than others, and some individuals may prefer a more encompassing identity, but on the whole it may be safer to say not that cultures are comprehensive but that they contribute to personal and collective identity to some significant extent.

A connected point concerns the relation between cultural identity on the one hand and ethnic, religious and national identities on the other. Briefly put, these overlap but are not identical. Two groups may, for example, be ethnically identical yet culturally divergent, as in the case of pre-war Australia and Britain. A single national culture can be shared by different religious groups, as in the United States, and co-religionists can be divided by culture, as borne out by a comparison between Muslims in Iran and Indonesia. People with the same ethnicity and culture may still come into violent conflict on the level of nationalism, as shown by the Serbs and Croats during the break-up of Yugoslavia in the 1990s. Nevertheless, while it is important to be aware of different dimensions of identity, it would be idle to pretend that they did not interconnect.[6] Culture is not equivalent to religion but cultures are often deeply influenced by religious beliefs and values. While, strictly speaking, Islam is a religion and not a culture, there is clearly a family resemblance among Muslim cultures.

Another issue concerning the definition of culture intersects with the question of multiculturalist justification raised earlier. Understandings of culture, it may be said, vary along a continuum between two extremes. At one extreme are the 'universalists', who emphasize the commonalities of human nature, conduct and evaluation, and regard cultures as at best secondary phenomena, transient and even ephemeral patterns of life with little or no moral weight compared with the ethical rules that bind all humanity. The other pole is occupied by the 'culturalists' or 'cultural relativists', who see cultures as complete, self-contained, bounded and even incommensurable, each generating its own locally authoritative ethical point of view.

As noted before, this division is highly significant for the politics of multiculturalism. On more universalist views the claims of culture are more qualified; on views tending towards the relativist end of the spectrum they are correspondingly assertive. I shall return to this dispute in Chapter 1.

The Fact of Cultural Diversity

Given my preliminary understanding of culture, the next step is to observe that, for the multiculturalist, nearly all modern societies contain multiple cultures as a matter of fact. Indeed, the fact is unavoidable. In the socio-economic realm, cultural diversity within Western societies has been increased or intensified by immigration and globalization. Levels of migration to the Western liberal democracies have in general increased enormously since the Second World War – although in the case of the United States the acceleration of immigration dates to the nineteenth century. The major causes of this movement of populations includes displacement brought about by the war, economic migration in the aftermath of decolonization and to some extent the freer movement of people under economic and technological globalization. The upshot has been the creation of very substantial minority communities within liberal-democratic societies.[7]

Nor is this change a matter of numbers alone. Many of those migrating have moved from developing nations and belong to cultures and religions with traditions and values very different from those of the majority in their new homes – Muslims, Hindus, Sikhs and Buddhists, for example. It might be argued that liberal states should take this in their stride because liberal democracy is dedicated to the toleration of different religious views and diverse ways of life. The reality, however, is that until recent times Western states had to deal only with religious diversity among rival Christian denominations, and even that proved hard enough to accommodate. Jewish communities were tolerated, on and off, over the centuries, but their presence was accepted only grudgingly by the Christian majority and was frequently rejected in the most violent terms. The new post-war diversity has introduced cultural differences in Western societies very much greater than those between rival Christians, and between Christians and Jews. Indeed, the new situation has a new term to describe it: 'super-diversity' (Vertovec 2007).

Moreover, the new migrant minorities have started to assert their identities more strongly and to agitate for special rights to ensure that their culture is recognized and its integrity protected.[8] They have been joined in this by indigenous communities, now better educated, often justly resentful of past mistreatment, and aware of the United Nations Covenants in regard to the right of self-determination of 'peoples'.

The effect of globalization on cultural diversity has also been significant, although complex and disputed. The principal dimensions of globalization are informational, technological and economic. The increasingly rapid flow of information around the world has led to an accelerated spread of technology and the creation of global markets unconstrained by distance, borders or state authority (Waters 2000). Some observers see this as culturally homogenizing, tending to the global diffusion of the values of capitalism and liberal democracy: materialism, consumerism, individual liberty and human rights (Fukuyama 1992; Tomlinson 1995). Others see globalization as a force for greater diversity, generating new, 'hybrid' forms of culture as novel ideas and outlooks are introduced into previously insular societies (Scholte 2000: 23–4). There is some degree of truth in both views but rather more in the latter. Even if globalization is homogenizing to a degree, that in itself tends to provoke culturalist reactions (Barber 1995; Huntington 1996).

Much the same point has been made in the political sphere in relation to culturalist reactions against the nation-state. It may be that the supposed cultural homogeneity of Western societies before the post-war age of migration was always an invention, even an illusion, created by the nation building of the nineteenth century (Gellner 1983; Anderson 2006; Hobsbawm 2012). At any rate, the dominant nation-states began to be more loudly questioned in the latter part of the twentieth century by native minorities such as the Scots, Welsh, Basques and Bretons in Europe, and indigenous groups in North America, Australia and New Zealand. Many of the new immigrant groups have also lent their voices to this chorus to argue for public recognition of their identity and to reject the old norm of assimilation. This process received added impetus from the ending of the Cold War. For forty years the polarization of the world between rival capitalist and communist blocs had overshadowed and led to the suppression of other differences. With the fall of communism at the end of the 1980s, waves of nationalist and ethnic feeling were suddenly released, most dramatically in the dismantling of Yugoslavia.

Responses to Diversity

Contemporary political societies, then, can hardly avoid being multicultural. But multiculturalism requires the second step mentioned earlier, from fact to approval. Many societies have been 'multicultural' in the sense that they have, as a matter of fact, contained multiple cultures – the Roman and Ottoman empires are often given as examples. But a multicultural society is not necessarily a society animated by multiculturalism. It all depends on how far the society, especially through its political norms and institutions, responds positively to the fact of diversity.

Historically, the great majority of responses to cultural diversity within a society have fallen short of approval. The presence of cultural minorities has sometimes met with violent opposition, as in the case of the Nazis or of those societies that have practised 'ethnic cleansing' in more recent times. Even where cultural difference has not provoked outright violence, many societies have pursued policies and practices of more or less forcible assimilation, the coercive subsuming of minority groups into a dominant national identity. This is not to say that all assimilation is coercive, since sometimes it is very much desired by those assimilated – by immigrants, for example (Kukathas 2003: 154). But where assimilation is a goal of public policy, or even where it is backed informally by public sentiment, an element of coercion is often present.

Another possibility, often overlapping assimilation, is 'toleration'.[9] Here minority cultures are not approved, but not actively discouraged or assimilated either: the policy is basically one of non-interference. Examples include the toleration of minority religious and cultural groups within the Roman and Islamic worlds. At this point we are getting closer to multiculturalism, but we are not there yet. Crucially, toleration requires no element of approval or even respect for the beliefs or practices tolerated. Indeed, toleration implies non-interference despite disapproval: 'I don't care for the way you live, but I won't interfere with it either.'

The same is true of a further step towards multiculturalism, namely the policy typical of liberal states that the law should prevent unfair discrimination among citizens on the basis of race, religion, gender or culture in fields such as employment and education. This kind of policy takes us beyond toleration, since it demands more of the state. Nor, however, does it yet amount to genuine multiculturalism.

Multiculturalism proper requires the addition of the third element on my list. Beyond the idea of cultural diversity as a fact to be registered, or a situation to be tolerated, beyond even the celebration of cultural diversity as in general a good thing, multiculturalism requires that multiple cultures within the same polity be given positive recognition at an official or public level. There have been many societies in which minority cultures are widely admired but receive no official support from the state – indeed, that was the liberal-democratic norm until recently. Such a society is more accurately described as multicultural rather than truly multiculturalist. Multiculturalism requires that the value of cultural diversity be recognized in public policy, the political voice of the society as a whole.

Public recognition of the value of cultural diversity may take various forms. At its weakest, recognition may be purely rhetorical or inspirational. This may involve no more than an assertion that the presence of minority cultures in the society is desirable or that certain minorities, usually indigenous, have a special place in a country's history and identity. Such declarations can be quite powerful, however, especially when they enter into the institutional symbolism of the society – its 'official emblems, anthems, flags, public holidays, and the like' (Levey 2008: 16) – or when they take the form of special one-off government announcements. An example of the latter is the Australian government's official apology for past injustice to the Aboriginal and Torres Strait Islander peoples made by the Prime Minister in parliament in 2008.

Public recognition of minority cultures may also involve adjustments to the law. One common form of cultural recognition is exemption from legal obligation: members of a group may be exempt from a law that applies to everyone else. In this connection a favourite example in the literature is that of Sikh men who are exempt from compliance with British law requiring motorcyclists to wear helmets, on the ground that their religion requires them to wear a turban.[10]

A stronger form of minority recognition is the provision by the state of various kinds of special opportunity not available to other citizens. These special rights are typically justified not as superior privileges but as compensation for certain kinds of disadvantage. For example, in Australia people from indigenous backgrounds are entitled to special university scholarships ('Abstudy') not open to others, on the ground that indigenous people have historically received fewer such opportunities than other Australian citizens.

Finally, the strongest form of special minority accommodation is group self-determination. In some countries, certain minority groups, usually indigenous peoples, are recognized as having the right to govern themselves, in accordance with their traditional norms, within some designated jurisdiction. Self-determination itself can take several forms, ranging from (at the weaker end) advisory institutions such as the Australian Indigenous Council, to semi-sovereign polities like the Canadian Inuit and Native American nations. Beyond 'accommodation' altogether there is the possibility of complete secession, where the self-determining group forms a state of its own.

Plan of the Book

Is multiculturalism desirable? If so, in what form? These are my basic questions. More specifically still, I shall be asking how far, and in what form, multiculturalism can be defended in relation to liberal democracy, the dominant ideology of our time and the political form within which multiculturalist policies have so far arisen. These issues have provoked many different responses, in turn raising further questions. To organize and discuss these, I proceed as follows.

Chapter 1 introduces some of the basic ethical orientations for the theories to follow, focusing on the debate between universalism and relativism. Multiculturalism is for many people associated with cultural relativism, which arose in reaction against the dominant universalism of Western ethical thought. Among the various weaknesses of traditional universalism, culturalists typically emphasize its ethnocentrism – it tended to project as universal norms that in reality were specific to a particular culture or society. Consequently, universalism has been superseded, for some thinkers, by cultural relativism, which holds that each culture has its own legitimate morality. However, cultural relativism too has its problems, since cultures have often endorsed practices – slavery, sexism, racism, xenophobia – that are ethically questionable and contrary to the spirit of multiculturalism or respect for cultural diversity. I go on to look at a contemporary middle way between universalism and relativism, the 'human capabilities' theory of Amartya Sen and Martha Nussbaum. This in turn raises the issue of value pluralism, to which I return in Chapter 7.

The first explicitly multiculturalist theory I examine is Will Kymlicka's seminal account of cultural rights, discussed in Chapter 2. I start with Kymlicka because he is such a dominant figure in the field, occupying a position akin to John Rawls's in current thinking on justice: a central agenda-setter whose work has inspired or provoked much of the writing in the field. In fact Kymlicka's work is to some extent an extension of Rawls's, since he presents it as a consistent working out of the basic egalitarian-liberal principles associated with Rawls and others. Consequently, I begin by setting out the liberal background to Kymlicka's view, distinguishing the traditional liberal toleration-based or 'privatization' approach to culture from the multiculturalist recognition that Kymlicka advocates. I then set out Kymlicka's case, which advocates special rights for cultural minorities within a liberal framework, based on the conditions for autonomy, equal treatment and an emphasis on 'national' minorities. The final section presents a preliminary critical discussion of Kymlicka, focusing on two issues: first, the role of personal autonomy in his theory, which is disputed by the supporters of Rawlsian 'political' liberalism; second, his willingness to use the state to liberalize illiberal cultures, which is opposed by the libertarian or classical liberal Chandran Kukathas.

Further criticism of Kymlicka emerges in Chapter 3, which deals primarily with the work of two liberal critics of multiculturalism, Brian Barry and Susan Okin. Barry approaches the matter from an egalitarian-liberal perspective, rejecting special cultural rights on the basis of equal treatment and a concern for state-sponsored social justice. Okin is a liberal feminist who sees multiculturalist recognition as protecting and preserving traditions that are fundamentally patriarchal. Barry's and Okin's views are in turn criticized by fellow-liberals and others who believe they have gone too far. In this respect I briefly examine the views of Nancy Fraser as a counterweight to Barry's, and those of Ayelet Shachar as a response to Okin.

Another issue raised by Kymlicka's work is that of the relation between multiculturalism and nationalism. For Kymlicka, it is 'national' groups that have the strongest minority rights, but some critics see this as discriminating unfairly against other kinds of cultural identity, such as those of immigrants. In general, nationalists and multiculturalists both endorse the value of cultural belonging, but there are tensions between them as well. Must national belonging override other identities? To what extent is nationalism consistent with cultural diversity? In Chapter 4 I discuss the varying responses to these questions given by John Stuart Mill and the recent 'liberal nationalists', David Miller and Yael Tamir. I then go on to consider the criticisms and alternatives offered by the nationalists' 'cosmopolitan' rivals, including Jeremy Waldron, Anthony Appiah and Amartya Sen.

Up to this point I have presented the debate over multiculturalism as largely a family disagreement among liberal thinkers. In Chapter 5 the discussion broadens to include writers who, in varying degrees, question the liberal framework itself. Charles Taylor, James Tully and Bhikhu Parekh all tend to see liberalism as the political expression of one cultural outlook among others, with no legitimate claim to moral superiority and no convincing title to being regarded as an adequate political container for human cultural diversity. Liberals respond that these anti-liberal or 'difference' versions of multiculturalism rely either on untenable forms of relativism or on implicit liberal assumptions after all.

Increasingly, theorists of multiculturalism, whether liberal or anti-liberal, argue that cultural minorities will be adequately recognized only when they are in some strong sense democratically self-determining. Accordingly, in Chapter 6 I discuss several theories stressing the role of democratic values and processes in multiculturalism. These include Iris Marion Young's advocacy of group representation, Parekh's account of 'intercultural dialogue' and Seyla Benhabib's argument for deliberative democracy. The chapter closes with Young's proposed revisions of the deliberative model.

In Chapter 7 I return to the concept of value pluralism, introduced briefly at the end of Chapter 1. Pluralism in this sense is the idea that there are many distinct human goods, and that different combinations of these generate a multiplicity of genuinely valuable ways of life. Consequently, one would expect that multiculturalism and value pluralism would be mutually sympathetic points of view, the major point of overlap being an emphasis on the value of cultural diversity. I examine this claim in the work of Isaiah Berlin, John Gray, Parekh (again), William Galston and Joseph Raz, finding that there is little agreement among these writers either on the relation between pluralism and multiculturalism or on that between pluralism and liberal democracy. The discussion does, however, suggest some salient points that I pick up in Chapter 9.

Chapter 8 deals with issues of multiculturalism at a global level. In particular, I focus on influential accounts of the relation between 'Western' and other 'global' cultures, starting with Samuel Huntington's claim that the central and permanent pattern here is a 'clash of civilizations'. I test out this claim with especial reference to liberal democracy on the one hand, and to Islamic and Confucian norms on the other. On the whole I argue that Huntington's thesis should not be accepted. While it is true that there are considerable gaps between liberal-democratic values and those of Islam and Confucianism in their currently dominant forms, Huntington's thesis that this points to a permanent clash of civilizations presupposes an essentialist view of global cultures that has been rightly discredited.

Chapter 9 draws together the central issues that have emerged from the previous chapters and outlines the value-pluralist answer I endorse. I argue that the best response to cultural diversity will begin with a modified universalism that emphasizes the incommensurability of basic values. The general political stance that fits best with a pluralist outlook is that of liberalism, in particular a liberalism that stresses the value of personal autonomy. Further, the idea of pluralism implies that all cultures embody genuine human values to some degree and so are to that extent worthy not merely of toleration but positive evaluation. However, to endorse multiculturalism proper, involving public recognition of multiple cultures, is to address a complex balancing of benefit and cost that will have to proceed contextually. The balance sought will also take into account the claims of national identity, democracy and 'civilizational' heritage, although all of these will be strongly qualified by liberal-pluralist considerations.

1

Universalism, Relativism and Culture

'Multicultural thinking', writes Paul Scheffer, 'represents a continuation of cultural relativism by other means' (Scheffer 2011: 197). It is easy to see why someone might believe this. Cultural relativism is the idea that truth or morality is relative to culture, that each culture has its own unique standards of truth or moral rightness, and that consequently all cultures are equal in moral and intellectual status. If that is so then it seems to follow that all cultures should be accorded equal respect. Where multiple cultures are present in the same society none is more authoritative than any other and all should be recognized equally.

However, Scheffer's comment is seriously misleading. It is true that some forms of multiculturalism rest on something like the reasoning just sketched out. This applies to what may be called the 'strong' or perhaps 'popular' multiculturalism of the kind found in the curriculum wars in American schools and universities in the 1980s and 1990s. But a great deal of multiculturalist thought does not take this form. Indeed, not one of the leading multiculturalist thinkers I shall discuss is an outright relativist, although some flirt with relativism from time to time. That is because cultural relativism suffers from a number of difficulties that make it problematic in general and that undermine it as a basis for multiculturalism in particular.

These difficulties are well known. Nevertheless, the popular understanding of multiculturalism is so influential, among both supporters and detractors, that it is important to begin this inquiry by examining the notion of cultural relativism. I hope thereby to challenge immediately certain assumptions that some readers may bring to this investigation. The first step is to consider what relativists react against, namely ethical universalism, before looking in more detail at relativism: its core claims, varieties (including postmodernism) and problems. In the final section I set out a view that could be said to occupy a middle ground between traditional universalism and relativism – namely, the theory of human capabilities advanced by Martha Nussbaum and Amartya Sen. The critical discussion of capabilities theory will briefly introduce the idea of value pluralism that I shall return to in Chapter 7.

Universalism

Ethical universalism is the view that there are certain moral rules that are binding on all human beings in all places at all times. Such universal rules override the norms of particular cultures, which can be judged as more or less acceptable by the criterion of universal morality. Universal accounts of morality have been dominant in Western thought, at least until recently. They have, by and large, been dominant in other world philosophies too, but I shall be focusing on Western thought, since this is, perhaps ironically, the context for explicit theories of multiculturalism. I say 'ironically' because multiculturalist theories so often condemn Western thought for its 'ethnocentrism'. This condemnation is itself a distinctive expression of certain strands of Western thought. Throughout the history of Western philosophy, ethical universalism has frequently been challenged, these challenges amounting to a sceptical and relativist counterpoint that is as old as universalism itself. But it is universalism that has struck the dominant chord.

The most prominent contemporary expression of ethical universalism is the concept of human rights, the idea that all persons have fundamental entitlements simply by virtue of their humanity.[1] This notion can be traced to the seventeenth- and eighteenth-century idea of natural rights advocated by thinkers such as John Locke, Tom Paine and Thomas Jefferson. The idea of natural rights, in turn, has its origin in the concept of natural law, developed most systematically by St Thomas Aquinas from roots in the ancient Greek philosophers. The basic notion of natural law is that universal rules of conduct can be identified by studying human nature (d'Entrèves 1951). Thus, Aquinas argues that we can deduce universal rules of conduct by using our reason to identify the natural 'inclinations' of human beings and to decide how those inclinations should be facilitated and regulated (Aquinas 1959: 123).

According to Locke's late seventeenth-century interpretation, the natural law generates a doctrine of natural rights. Under the natural law, fundamental obligations, such as the duty to preserve human life, imply fundamental rights, notably individuals' rights to their 'life, health, liberty, or possessions' (Locke 1689 [1970]: section 6). These are basic entitlements that trump public opinion, the policies of particular governments and the local norms of particular cultures. Lockean rights became the basis for justifying the great political revolutions of the modern era, beginning with the Glorious Revolution (1688) that established the supremacy of Parliament over the Crown in England. They reappeared among the 'self-evident truths' of Jefferson's Declaration of Independence (1776), and were restated by Paine and the French revolutionaries as 'the rights of Man' – the ancestors of the 'human rights' listed in the United Nations Declaration of 1948.

The idea of a universal morality implicit in human nature is thus one of the most powerful streams in Western thought, and foundational for modern politics, especially liberal democracy. Locke's assertion of respect for natural rights as the test of legitimate government marks something like the birth of the liberal tradition that I shall have more to say about in the next chapter.

From the beginning, however, ethical universalism provoked the obvious question, what exactly are the rules that are said to be universal? Moreover, in the case of the central natural-law tradition, what exactly are the features of human nature that imply the universal rules, and how do they do so? Over the centuries these questions have received many conflicting answers. For example, Aristotle's view that slavery was ethically permissible, indeed justified by natural differences among human beings, was flatly contradicted by the moral egalitarianism of Christian readings of the natural law, culminating in the natural rights advocated by Locke and his successors. Again, Locke's interpretation of human nature is distinctly more optimistic, and consequently the task of government in his view is distinctly more limited, than that of Thomas Hobbes, who pictures human nature as fundamentally selfish, aggressive and in need of strict political control in order to avoid continual conflict.

Such disagreements have been endemic in the history of ethical universalism. Moreover, they have been exacerbated by a series of developments in the history of modern Western ideas that have tended to undermine confidence in a single moral truth and to promote various kinds of moral scepticism and relativism. These developments began with the Reformation of the fifteenth and sixteenth centuries, which saw the break-up of Western Christianity into rival Roman

Catholic and Protestant factions, each asserting and attempting to enforce equally dogmatic claims to the possession of God's truth. The whole notion of divine authority was in turn eroded by the Scientific Revolution of the sixteenth and seventeenth centuries, with its secular explanations of the natural world, and subsequently by the eighteenth-century Enlightenment, some streams of which attempted to apply modern scientific method to the explanation and improvement of the social world. The gradual disappointment of Enlightenment hopes for a natural science of morality only added to doubts about the possibility of identifying a single, coherent body of moral knowledge to rival the achievements of the natural sciences, despite efforts to model such a science on disciplines such as mathematics and evolutionary biology.[2]

Marxism, too, was in part a sceptical or relativizing influence, to the extent that it regarded morality as a secondary, 'superstructural' phenomenon, determined by the more fundamental processes of the economic 'base' (Cohen 1978; Lukes 1985). On a Marxist view, Locke's natural rights merely express the 'bourgeois' morality of capitalist society; non-capitalist societies generate quite different moralities. This is not to say that Marxism departs entirely from mainstream Western universalism. At a deeper level Marx's account of historical progress is underwritten by a vision of human nature as fundamentally distinguished by a capacity for spontaneous and collective creative activity, partly developed by capitalism, partly obstructed by it, and destined to be fully realized only in a post-capitalist future. Still, Marxism remains a key source for recent 'poststructuralist' and 'postmodernist' understandings of morality as relative to interests or power.[3]

In these various ways, then, modernity has been characterized by a retreat from the moral certainties of the premodern world. This is not to deny that there was moral scepticism in ancient and medieval times, still less that ethical universalism has been wholly abandoned – indeed, the modern concept of human rights probably commands a more widespread international consensus than any previous form of universalism. But the sceptical and relativist counterpoint is also more insistent now, and certainly more reputable in the academic world, than ever before. The Reformation, Scientific Revolution, Enlightenment and Marxism have all had a hand in this development. But perhaps the most important factor of all has been the increased proximity and interaction, in modern times, of different cultures, and the subsequent emergence of the idea of cultural relativism.

Relativism

At its broadest, relativism is the idea that judgements of value or truth are not universal or objective, but valid only from some particular perspective (Wong 1993). For a relativist, 'X is morally right' or 'X is true' means X is right or true only from some particular point of view. That point of view is neither more nor less fundamental or authoritative than others, and so the judgement that X is right (or true) is necessarily correct if it sincerely and accurately expresses the perspective in question. Such perspectives vary, and all are equally valid. Relativism, therefore, especially in its stronger forms, is opposed to universalism. Strong forms of relativism deny that any moral judgements are universally valid, or even that any truth-claims are universally valid.

There are different kinds of relativism corresponding to how one answers the question: relative to what? Some relativists believe that value and truth judgements are relative to the person making them. This is 'subjectivism': a moral claim merely expresses the beliefs or feelings of the individual who makes the claim (e.g. Ayer 1936: ch. 6). More important to multiculturalism is a second kind of relativism, 'cultural relativism', in which the validity of claims depends on the beliefs and values not of individuals but of whole cultures or ways of life. According to cultural relativism, 'X is morally right' means X is right from the perspective of a particular culture. It is the cultural kind of relativism that I shall be concerned with in the remainder of this section.

Within cultural relativism another important distinction needs to be drawn – that is, between its 'ethical' and 'cognitive' branches (Lukes 2008: ch. 1). The ethical dimension of cultural relativism asserts that there are no universally valid moral rules, only the codes and practices of particular cultures. On this view moral judgements are always made from the perspective of some cultural code or other. Therefore, there is no culturally neutral or objective standpoint from which to compare and judge the divergent practices of different cultures, and so no way of legitimately criticizing a culture's morality from any perspective other than its own. We are often tempted to judge other ways of life on the basis of our own cultural values. But this is 'ethnocentrism', the illegitimate judging of one culture according to standards imported from another. A cultural relativist can consistently criticize a culture's practices, but only on the ground of that culture's own norms – for example, where the culture's basic values are not adequately expressed or respected by its actual practices or institutions. This is called 'immanent critique' or criticism 'from within', because it appeals to standards immanent in the culture itself rather than external to it (Held 1980: 183–7; Walzer 1988: 26).

But even if different cultures do, as a matter of fact, have different moral codes, might some of these be more rational or reasonable than others? This is where 'cognitive' relativism comes in. Some philosophers argue that not only morality but also rationality, reasonableness and truth are culturally relative too. According to the cognitive relativist, different cultures have such divergent ways of seeing things that they inhabit different conceptual worlds. None of these is objectively more authoritative than any other. One archaeologist, for example, argues that the findings of modern science are no more valid than the creation narratives of the Zuni Indians, who believe that their ancestors emerged from inside the earth into a world created by supernatural beings. The Zuni beliefs are 'just as valid as the archaeological viewpoint of what prehistory is about' (quoted by Boghossian 2006: 2).

If we accept the cognitive relativist view, we must again recognize strong limits on the extent to which we are entitled to criticize other cultures. On this view, when we judge other cultures' practices to be irrational according to standards other than those of the cultures concerned, we are again being ethnocentric, projecting our own standards onto others.

The idea of cultural relativism, like that of universalism, can be traced back to the ancient world. Among the Greeks, the dominant universalism of Plato and Aristotle was opposed by sceptical thinkers like Protagoras, for whom 'man is the measure of all things' (Guthrie 1960: 68–9). Similarly, Herodotus, in the *Histories*, recounts an anecdote in which the Persian king Darius questions the Greeks and the Callatiae about their funeral practices. The former prefer to cremate their dead, the latter to eat them, and each is revolted by the other. 'One can see by this what custom can do,' writes Herodotus, 'and Pindar, in my opinion, was right when he called it "king of all"' (Herodotus n.d. [1972]: 220).

By and large, however, these relativist sallies were for centuries submerged in the development of Western thought by several pro-universalist factors, including the prestige of Plato and Aristotle, the emergence of Christianity and the development of natural-law thinking. The centuries-long dominance of natural law in European thought is nowhere more evident than in attitudes to alien cultures. When Europeans were confronted by unfamiliar ways of life, the basic ethical question was always: how far do these cultures conform to the natural law?

Sometimes the answer was quite complimentary to the culture in question, which was judged to be superior, at least in certain respects, to its European rivals – more rational, or more 'natural'. Montesquieu's *Persian Letters* (1721 [1973]), for example, adopts the perspective of a sensible Persian visitor to a strange, often absurd, contemporary Paris – although Montesquieu was probably more interested in satirizing his own society than in commending Persia. Rather more explicit, if no less imaginative, celebrations of alien cultures emerge from the cult of the 'noble savage', commonly associated (although perhaps mistakenly) with Enlightenment figures such as Rousseau and Diderot.[4]

More often, however, critical comparisons between European and other cultures in natural-law terms worked to the detriment of the non-European. Such cultures were often judged to be inferior because they plainly did not follow the natural law, as Europeans interpreted this, in various respects. One dramatic example was cannibalism: the modern European horror of this ancient practice was famously captured in Defoe's *Robinson Crusoe* (1719 [1985]). Another example was human sacrifice, as discovered by the Spanish conquistadors among the Aztecs, and by the British conquerors of India in the Hindu tradition of *suti*, the voluntary immolation of widows on their husband's funeral pyre (Davies 1981).

The European condemnation of such practices intensified as the 'age of discovery' was succeeded by an age of colonization and imperialism. The settlement of Australia, for example, was justified, in part, by the doctrine of *terra nullius*, the claim that the land was unoccupied (Connor 2005; Rowse 2001). For the British settlers, the presence of the indigenous population did not count as genuine occupation because the Aboriginal people merely ranged across the land without using proper – that is, European – methods of cultivation. This, too, was regarded as a failure to follow natural law, which, as Locke had argued, made legitimate property rights in land contingent on the land's properly productive use (Locke 1689 [1970]: ch. 5).

Overlapping the project of colonial settlement was the imperial project. 'Lesser breeds without the Law', as Kipling put it, would be guided towards the moral light by more advanced European civilizations (Kipling 1897 [2003]). Here, too, the concept of natural law played a central role, although in the nineteenth-century heyday of European imperialism it was often transmuted into the more 'scientific' languages of utilitarianism and Darwinian evolution. The liberal utilitarian John Stuart Mill, for example, was a prominent defender of British rule in India on the ground that the most advanced values of personal liberty would take root there only if encouraged by British example and guidance (Mill 1859 [1974]: 69).

Cultural relativism re-emerged in modern Western thought as a reaction against these universalist judgements. Against the orthodox view that alien cultures were inferior – immoral and irrational – because they violated universal norms, some thinkers began to reassert the idea that different cultures had their own moral codes and that these were no less rational and valid in their own way than one's own. Two intellectual movements in particular stimulated this development: the Counter-Enlightenment, and the emergence of modern cultural anthropology.

In the case of the Counter-Enlightenment, the key name is that of J. G. Herder.[5] Enlightenment thinkers such as Montesquieu and Hume had seen different cultures as variant ways of expressing the universal features – the needs and desires – of human nature. For Herder, it is culture rather than shared humanity that really makes us who we are. (There is also a nationalist dimension to this. Herder's argument is a defence not merely of unique 'peoples' everywhere, but specifically of the German people in their struggle against the universalizing force of the French Enlightenment embodied by the Revolutionary and Napoleonic armies.) Although Herder does have a notion of a common human nature and destiny (*humanität*), this is a very thin, formal idea, and pales into insignificance beside the emphasis he places on cultural particularity.

Herder sees the relation between thought and language as a case in point. The distinctive human capacity for thought is universal, but thought is possible only through language, and languages are the unique creations of particular cultures. Through its language each culture generates its own identifying set of memories, beliefs and norms. There is no 'absolute, unchanging and independent happiness' common to all human beings; rather, human nature is a 'pliant clay which assumes a different shape under different needs and circumstances' (Herder 1969: 185–6). In Isaiah Berlin's influential interpretation, Herder sees cultures as 'incommensurable' with one another: 'all these forms of life are intelligible each in its own terms (the only terms there are)', each representing 'an ideal of indefeasible validity', so that 'we are forbidden to make judgements of comparative values, for that is measuring the incommensurable' (Berlin 2000b: 235, 234, 233).[6]

This conception of cultures as incommensurable wholes, impervious to criticism from the outside, is a staple assumption of cultural relativism. It has been accepted, for example, by many cultural anthropologists, who are concerned to break down the old habits of unreflective ethnocentric judgement and to get people to see that apparently alien cultural patterns have their own underlying norms and rationales. Ruth Benedict in her classic *Patterns of Culture* (1935), for example, describes cultures as not merely 'the sum of their traits', but internally integrated and externally bounded wholes, each with its own unique personality: 'a culture, like an individual, is a more or less consistent pattern of thought and action' with 'characteristic purposes not necessarily shared by other types of society' (Benedict 1935: 33). The implication, again, is that it is unfair, indeed irrational, to judge one culture according to the purposes of another. Cultures are 'equally valid patterns of life' (Benedict 1935: 201).[7]

In particular, anthropologists have challenged complacent judgements that 'primitive' non-Western cultures are inferior to 'advanced' Western societies. Such judgements, they argue, tend to rest either on unthinking ethnocentrism or, in a more sophisticated version, on an evolutionary account of cultures as progressing by stages from the primitive to the advanced, assuming Western patterns to be more advanced (Ivison 2002: 35). In either version, these judgements of superiority and inferiority are disrupted by the Herderian picture of cultures as incommensurable. According to Herder's picture, one culture may have more sophisticated technology than another, but that does not make it less valuable or satisfying as a whole. Such an overall evaluation can be made only in accordance with the culture's own values.

In contemporary thought relativism is often advanced under the banner of 'postmodernism'. For postmodernists such as Jean-François Lyotard (1984), not only ethical systems but also 'truth' and 'reason' themselves are relative to particular perspectives. In Lyotard's explanation the most significant perspectives in this connection are what he calls the 'metanarratives' or 'grand narratives': the major accounts given by the great ideologies and worldviews of human nature and history, which are then invoked to legitimate more specific moral and political claims. In particular, the postmodernists are concerned with the metanarratives of the Enlightenment – liberalism, Marxism and modern science – which all tell stories of progress towards some desirable and liberating end. The characteristic postmodernist response to such grand narratives is one of suspicion, an attitude summed up in Lyotard's famous definition of postmodernism: 'incredulity towards metanarratives' (Lyotard 1984: xxiv).

The postmodernist suspicion of grand narratives has two main dimensions: philosophical and political. Philosophically, the postmodernists attack the claims of liberals, Marxists, scientists and others to be in possession of objective truth. For postmodernists, the 'truth' offered even by modern science is merely the expression of one perspective on the world among others, neither superior nor inferior – hence the remark quoted earlier that archaeology is no more objective than the creation myths of the Zuni. In general, postmodernists view knowledge as inherently and irreducibly fragmented and plural, a matter of multiple and equal or incommensurable knowledges rather than a single end-point.

In its political dimension, the postmodernist attack on the Enlightenment metanarratives sees these as not only lacking the objective authority they claim for themselves, but also as dangerous and oppressive. As Michel Foucault expresses it, all metanarratives are disguised expressions of power: what passes for scientific knowledge, for example, is really the fruit of a certain sort of power relation favouring a certain conception of the person – namely, one guided by a particular kind of reason (Foucault 1977; Rabinow 1984). This is a view that Foucault takes in large part from Friedrich Nietzsche, who had seen all norms as expressions of 'the will to power', a deep-seated human urge to control oneself and others.

Most postmodernists have presented themselves as speaking for the 'progressive' side of politics, including the defence of non-Western cultures and multiculturalism. Although they are suspicious of the dominant metanarratives, they tend to be more welcoming to the 'micronarratives' of hitherto suppressed or marginalized voices. Hence, postmodernism is often presented as implying an ethic that can be summarized as 'fostering otherness' (White 1991: 117). The postmodernist outlook, according to this view, requires or encourages us to be especially sensitive to the claims of historically oppressed or excluded groups such as women, gays and lesbians, indigenous and colonized peoples. The latter in particular are typically central to multiculturalist concerns.

Problems with Relativism

To many people, relativism seems intuitively to be a humane and persuasive outlook. If all perspectives are morally equal, is that not a recipe for toleration and mutual respect? If we look more closely, however, we find that relativism suffers from serious problems.[8] The following discussion refers mainly to cultural relativism, but the principal points also apply to postmodernism, which in addition has difficulties of its own.

Moral and Political Consequences

The most obvious criticism is that cultural relativism does not really provide reliable support for the values and politics endorsed by most of its defenders. On the contrary, it licenses moral and political practices that such people oppose. As we have just noted in connection with postmodernism, most people who are attracted to contemporary forms of relativism think of themselves as occupying positions on the progressive or forward-thinking or radical side of politics, standing up for the interests of the disadvantaged, the excluded, the marginalized. But if we accept cultural relativism, then we have to accept as morally valid any practice that happens to have cultural backing. This covers many practices that seem worthy of strong criticism from a progressive or radical point of view. The standard list includes the following: honour killings, forced marriages, female circumcision, withholding of medical attention from children, ritual scarring and general subordination of women. All of these have been culturally endorsed and are to that extent morally valid on the relativist view. One may add to the list many broader categories of behaviour or policy: imperialism, racism, homophobia, Fascism, Nazism.

Indeed, the fact is that the moral and political implications of cultural relativism, far from being progressive or radical, are basically conservative. If we say that moral right and wrong are wholly relative to culture, we are saying in effect that what is morally right or wrong is simply what a given culture says is right or wrong. This amounts to making existing practices or traditions morally correct by definition: 'it's right because it's what we do here.' I noted earlier that this rules out any legitimate criticism of a culture's practices on grounds other than those accepted within the culture itself. 'Immanent critique' is still possible, but that will be limited in scope; if a practice really is backed by the fundamental values of a culture, then immanent critique has no leverage.

Some people will regard this blocking of cross-cultural criticism as a good thing because it requires us to be tolerant of other cultures. This view is mistaken, for reasons I shall come to in a moment. What is seldom acknowledged is that the logic of cultural relativism blocks criticism not only of other cultures but of one's own culture too (Rachels 1993: 21). According to cultural relativism, cultural endorsement is the moral bottom line, so any practice that can be said to be endorsed by one's own culture is just as sacrosanct as the practices of other cultures. If the relativist's own culture is deeply homophobic or sexist or imperialist, then she has to accept those norms as authoritative.

It follows from these points that the link between cultural relativism and toleration – let alone the positive recognition required for multiculturalism – is much more tenuous than often supposed. What happens when we are confronted by a culture that does not value toleration? Indeed, since all cultures have been intolerant to a degree (both of outsiders and internal dissenters), and many have been highly intolerant, cultural relativism is logically a powerful excuse for intolerance. The impression many people have of cultural relativism as a vehicle for toleration is quite mistaken. It is probably due to their own independent commitment to toleration as a universal value, but if cultural relativism is correct, there are no universal values, not even toleration. Whether we should be tolerant, under relativism, depends entirely on the accident of our cultural affiliation. Naturally, the same limitation applies to attempts to base multiculturalism on cultural relativism; indeed, cultural relativism leaves the case for multiculturalism even weaker than the case for toleration. As explained in the Introduction, multiculturalist recognition is a more demanding norm than toleration. Tolerant cultures have been few and multiculturalist cultures fewer still.

Postmodernism has its own peculiar problems along these lines. I have already noted that postmodernists typically want to 'foster otherness'. But if all norms are merely masks for power relations, then it is hard to see how postmodernists can consistently advocate the fostering of otherness or any other goal. How can one form of power be preferred to another without appealing to values that are themselves reducible to masks for power? The logic of postmodernism undermines any moral code on this basis, including any ethical position the postmodernist herself might favour. So, for example, if someone asserted the claims of a non-Western culture against those of a colonizing power, or the claims of multiculturalism against assimilation, consistent postmodernists would be obliged to say that the non-Western culture and the multiculturalist policy were just as much masks of power as the views they were opposing.

Misdescription

A second major set of problems with cultural relativism concerns its adequacy as a *descriptive* theory. The basic objection is that cultural relativism depends on a false description of cultures and the relation between them – in particular, it depends on an exaggeration of the differences among cultures.

One such exaggeration concerns the extent of intercultural moral disagreement. No one doubts that there is a good deal of this. A practice that is condemned by one culture is often held to be permissible or even desirable in another. However, the fact that cultures disagree about some things does not mean that they disagree about everything. Two cultures that disagree about X may still agree about Y and Z. Certainly there is evidence of ethical divergence among cultures, but there is evidence of overlap too. Indeed, there is evidence of universal overlap. I shall pursue this idea more systematically in the next section, but it is worth noting immediately that simply to point to some, even considerable, cultural diversity in ethics does not rule out the possibility of ethical universals. What may be happening is that different cultures are pursuing or expressing the same universal goods in different ways.

For example, it may seem that there is a vast moral gulf between those societies, like the Inuit, that have practised infanticide and those that have condemned it.[9] But is the gulf as great as it seems? The traditional Inuit practice of infanticide has to be seen in the context of the extraordinarily exigent physical circumstances of the Arctic climate. According to custom, children (and old people) are sometimes left behind when it is clear that keeping them with the group will slow down the group's mobility to a point where everyone will be in serious danger. It is not that the Inuit, unlike other societies, do not value the lives of their children. Rather, a tragic choice between the lives of some and the survival of the whole group is sometimes forced on these people by their circumstances. Indeed, one could argue that the Inuit share a respect for human life with all human societies, and that this leads them to make the hard choices they do. The difference between the Inuit and others, therefore, is a difference of circumstances, not values. This example suggests something of the case for intercultural respect and toleration that attracts many people to relativism, but without supporting the relativist picture of cultures differing radically in their most basic norms.

Moreover, relativists' exaggeration of cultural difference extends beyond their description of ethical divergence to their account of cultural divergence more generally. On the relativist view, ethical difference takes the form of different cultures, each with its unique moral voice, speaking across one another. This view presupposes a certain picture of what cultures are actually like: basically the Herderian model of cultures as incommensurable worlds, each with its own unique outlook. Note two aspects of this picture: first, cultures are assumed to be externally bounded, quite distinct and separate from other cultures; second, they are assumed to be internally univocal, each speaking with a single voice.

This picture is now widely regarded as unrealistic. First, cultures have never – or only rarely – been bounded or separate to the extent assumed by strong relativists. For the most part, cultures have continually interacted with one another, influencing and borrowing from those ways of life with which they come into contact. Second, cultures have seldom been internally univocal. Their norms and traditions have usually been contested from within by rival groups and individuals – men versus women, old versus young, rich versus poor. Rather than the incommensurable entities supposed by the relativist picture, cultures are more 'open-textured' – that is, open to influences from the outside and subject to dispute and conflict on the inside (Ivison 2002: 36). This point is endorsed, at least in principle, by nearly all of the contemporary thinkers discussed in this book. How far their theories remain consistent with it is another matter, as we shall see.

The standard relativist picture of ethical divergence is thus inadequate in two respects: it exaggerates moral differences among cultures, neglecting areas of mutual influence; and it neglects ethical divergence within cultures, exaggerating the extent to which culture-based moral codes are accepted by those whose codes they supposedly are. In general, strong cultural relativists derive a lop-sided picture of moral diversity from a distorted picture of culture.

Facts and Values

Suppose, however, that cultures really were radically distinct to the extent asserted by strong relativists. A further problem is that there remains a gap between the fact of cultural difference and the conclusions that relativists typically draw from that fact. One such conclusion, as we have seen, is that each culture is morally authoritative in its own sphere. But this does not follow simply from asserting that cultures disagree or diverge. From the fact of disagreement it does not follow that all parties to the disagreement are equally correct. People who think the earth is flat disagree with those who think it is round, but that does not mean that both views are valid. Similarly, just because different beliefs are held in different cultures it does not follow that all such beliefs must be accepted as correct (Rachels 1993: 18–20).[10]

A similar point has been vigorously made by Brian Barry, who points out the emptiness of cultural relativism as a system of justification (Barry 2001: 252–8). Strong cultural relativism asserts that a sufficient reason for any practice is simply that the practice is backed by the culture. Since a 'culture' is simply the sum of such practices, this is no justification at all, but rather equivalent to saying 'we do this here because we do this here'.

Logical Incoherence

The cognitive form of relativism suffers from a further problem. If, on inquiry, a culture-based practice seems to rest on mistaken beliefs or faulty reasoning, the cognitive relativist may reply that different rationalities or standards of truth are at work and that one must not impose on other cultures one's own, necessarily relative standard of reason and truth. But this view is incoherent. If cultural outlooks were so completely incommensurable, then we would have no conception of other cultures even counting as 'cultures' comparable with our own, and so would not even be able to formulate the notion of 'cultural' difference (Benhabib 2002: 30–1). An outlook wholly incommensurable with our own would be one with which we had nothing at all in common, even in its basic structure. How, then, could we recognize it as a culture at all?

Postmodernism, in particular, has a deeply paradoxical character. According to postmodernists, there is no objective perspective, only the relative viewpoints that are underpinned by particular metanarratives. What happens when this doctrine is applied to postmodernism itself? Postmodernism must also be one relative viewpoint among others, no more objective than its rivals. To put it another way, postmodernism is, in its own terms, another metanarrative, a grandiose account of intellectual history masquerading as the truth when it is really just another mask for power – in this case the power of those academics and others who support it. Postmodernism cannot be true, because it rejects truth, but in that case it is no more authoritative than the Enlightenment positions which it holds in suspicion.

At this point enough has been said to cast serious doubt, at the very least, on cultural relativism. Its central flaw is its characteristic claim that cultural norms cannot be questioned, that to recognize a practice as culturally endorsed is necessarily to accept it as ethically valid, that 'morally justified' and 'whatever cultures allow' mean the same thing. Bernard Williams rightly calls this 'possibly the most absurd view to have been advanced even in moral philosophy' (Williams 1972: 34).

However, to reject cultural relativism is very far from saying that the moral norms and practices of cultures may never diverge legitimately. Ethnocentric forms of universalism of the kind propagated by Victorian imperialism remain deeply mistaken. The trouble is that the attempt to correct ethnocentrism by way of cultural relativism is also seriously mistaken. In effect the relativists try to counter the imperialists by going to the opposite extreme: where the imperialists had supposed that alien cultures were always inferior to their own, the relativists assert that cultures can do no wrong. Both sides go too far. Rather, we should be seeking a middle ground in which some degree of universality and diversity are combined, making possible both respect for cultures where merited and criticism of cultures where warranted. One prominent candidate for this middle ground is human capabilities theory.

Universalism Revised: Nussbaum and Sen

The theory of human capabilites is associated in particular with the work of Martha Nussbaum and Amartya Sen. Originating in their concern to find objective and realistic measures of human well-being in response to orthodox economic theory, the idea of human capabilities has been expanded, especially by Nussbaum, into a more explicitly political theory of universal justice and rights. The basic idea is that certain capacities are essential to a good life for any human being – a fundamentally universalist view, and something of a restatement of the old notion of natural law. On the other hand, the capability theorists are keen to strike a balance between ethical universalism and legitimate cultural variation.

The starting point for the capabilities approach lies in Nussbaum's and Sen's interest in measuring people's 'quality of life' (Nussbaum and Sen 1993). They react against two tendencies that remain influential, if not dominant, among economists. The first is to measure quality of life – or more properly 'standard of living' – in accordance with Gross National Product (GNP) per capita. The trouble with this, they point out, is that it takes no account of how this wealth is distributed: a country with high GNP can still contain groups living in poverty. A second influential measure of well-being, utilitarian preference satisfaction, fares little better. The problem here is the possibility of 'adaptive preferences', where people are satisfied only because they have lowered their expectations in the face of intransigent obstacles. This phenomenon is sometimes referred to as 'sour grapes': 'I can't get X, so I don't really want it.'

In place of these thin economists' measures, Nussbaum and Sen propose a more realistic, and more demanding, test of well-being. Their basic question is: what are people really able to do or to be (Sen 1992: 37; Nussbaum 2000: 71)? People may have resources and opportunities, but are they able to use these to do the things and to build the life that they want?

Sen sums up this idea under the heading of 'freedom' (Sen 1992: chs. 2 and 4; 2001; 2009). Freedom is sometimes understood in a narrowly 'negative' way, meaning simply the absence of coercion: I am free in this sense if no one deliberately prevents me, by force or the threat of force, from doing what I want. But someone could be free in this negative sense and still be unable to do what she wants because, for example, she lacks the necessary economic or educational resources. In the classic example, I can be negatively free to dine at the Ritz Hotel, because there is no law against it, yet lack the 'effective' freedom to dine there because I cannot afford it. Sen is on the side of those who argue that genuine freedom must be more than merely negative, it must be 'effective'.[11] Indeed, he sees effective freedom as the key measure of human well-being: a person's real quality of life depends on his degree of effective freedom.

Nussbaum agrees with Sen that quality of life is not adequately measured by GNP or preference satisfaction or negative liberty (Nussbaum 2000: 60–3). Nor, however, does she accept that human well-being is a matter of effective freedom alone, or that effective freedom embraces or outranks all other goods. Rather, a good life for human beings involves several distinct dimensions – several different 'human functionings' – which cannot be reduced to or summarized by freedom, even effective freedom. Corresponding to these functionings are what Nussbaum calls the 'human capabilities': in each case the capacity to function well (Nussbaum 2000: 70–86).

What is the content of the human capabilities? Nussbaum provides a ten-point list, the most recent version of which reads (in abbreviated form) as follows: life; bodily health; bodily integrity; senses, imagination and thought; emotions; practical reason; affiliation; relations with other species; play; control over one's environment (Nussbaum 2000: 78–80).[12]

Each item on the list is distinct from, and not reducible to, the others. Each is essential to human well-being, so that a life that lacks any one of the capabilities cannot, according to Nussbaum, be rightly called a good human life. This becomes a political principle, involving claims of justice and rights. A society that does not do its best to secure the capabilities of all its members is to that extent unjust and in violation of their rights as human beings.

How is Nussbaum's list of capabilities justified? In particular, what makes it genuinely universal in scope and validity? One answer she gives is that the list has been arrived at through 'years of cross-cultural discussion' (Nussbaum 2000: 76). It is 'based on the commonness of myths and stories from many times and places' that reveal 'what it is to be human rather than something else' (Nussbaum 1990: 217).

Nussbaum also offers a philosophical defence of her list: the items all reflect 'the core idea' that a good life for a human being must be a life of human dignity (Nussbaum 2000: 72). For Nussbaum, a 'truly dignified human being' is 'a dignified free being who shapes his or her own life in co-operation and reciprocity with others, rather than being passively shaped or pushed around by the world in the manner of a "flock" or "herd" animal'. Human dignity is centrally about being an autonomous, self-directing being.

Nussbaum fills out this idea by acknowledging its sources in Immanuel Kant and the early Marx. For Kant, to be autonomous is to be directed by one's own reason, and not 'pushed around' by one's passions or inclinations. For the early Marx, the great obstacles to the truly dignified life are the necessities of mere physical survival and the inequalities of capitalism. Nussbaum's list tries to capture these various dimensions of human dignity interpreted as self-direction.

Another related dimension of human dignity is more implicit in Nussbaum's thought than spelt out. This is the idea of self-direction as resistance to being pushed around by the conventions and traditions of one's own culture. As J. S. Mill notes, it is not only laws and physical coercion that can diminish a person's autonomy but also 'the tyranny of the prevailing opinion and feeling' or 'the despotism of custom' (Mill 1859 [1974]: 63, 136). That idea is also implicit in Nussbaum's position, especially in her rejection of the 'argument from culture' that subordinates human rights to existing cultural norms (Nussbaum 2000: 41–9). For Nussbaum, such a view tends to simplify what a given culture stands for, swallowing uncritically the account of the culture's values given by its self-appointed elite or by romanticizing foreigners, and ignoring currents of internal dissent.

Behind the argument from culture is often to be found the idea of cultural relativism – 'that normative criteria must come from within the society to which they are applied' – which is also roundly rejected by Nussbaum (2000: 48–9). Cultural relativism is untrue as a descriptive thesis, since cultures have always borrowed ideas and values from one another. Consequently, it also fails as a normative thesis, since in the modern world 'the ideas of every culture turn up inside every other. The ideas of feminism, of democracy, of egalitarian welfarism, are now "inside" every known society' (Nussbaum 2000: 49). Why, moreover, 'should we follow the local ideas rather than the best ideas we can find?'

However, Nussbaum's rejection of uncritical cultural relativism does not mean that she is insensitive to legitimate moral diversity across cultures. On the contrary, the recognition of such legitimate variety, consistent with her account of universals, is one of her major concerns. She argues that the capabilities theory accommodates cultural diversity in several ways. One has already been noted – namely, that the list of capabilities is the product of reflection not just on one culture but on the patterns of evaluation present in all cultures. Second, the list is explicitly presented as 'humble', open-ended and subject to revision: an invitation to dialogue rather than the final word (Nussbaum 2000: 77). Third, each item on the list is capable of 'multiple realizability' – that is, it can be interpreted and realized differently in different cultures.[13]

In general, then, Nussbaum tries to strike a balance between universality and diversity. Universal principles of real moral weight and political consequence are qualified by the recognition that particular moral commitments should be respected in the various ways listed above. This is an intelligent and moderate approach to cross-cultural ethics, and one that has attracted a good deal of support. But the balance struck by capabilities theory is a delicate one, suspended between two difficulties.

On the one hand, any list of capabilities or goods that purports to be valid universally must tend towards the highly generic, and highly generic principles have little critical force. Only if the capabilities are formulated in a very general way, open to many interpretations, can they fairly be claimed to be multiply realizable – that is, part of *any* good life. But the more generic the capabilities are, the less critical bite they have, precisely because they are more easily satisfied by any society.

For example, the first capability on Nussbaum's list, 'life', is defined as 'being able to live to the end of a human life of normal length' (Nussbaum 2000: 78). All human societies can claim to satisfy that requirement. What counts as 'normal' length is subject to such a variety of interpretations, bringing in variations of circumstance, belief and value, that it would be hard to argue that any society has clearly fallen short of its obligations in that regard. An imperative so easily satisfied has little critical leverage.

On the other hand, a more specific requirement, with correspondingly stronger bite, is open to the objection that it is not truly universal – either not universally accepted or not universally acceptable. On the whole, Nussbaum's list of capabilities tends to err rather more in this direction than towards excessive generality. A frequent objection to her position is that its ostensible universality is undermined by a set of assumptions that express a distinctively Western or individualistic view of the person (see e.g. Fabre and Miller 2003: 8–9).

For example, 'practical reason' involves 'being able to form a conception of the good and to engage in critical reflection about the planning of one's life' (Nussbaum 2000: 79).[14] Critical reflection means being able to stand back from one's own way of life and assess it independently. This reflects the 'core idea' at the centre of the whole theory, which explicitly conceives of human dignity as involving a capacity for strong individual self-direction.

But the claim that human dignity is fundamentally about self-direction is highly controversial. A frequent objection is that such a view is too close to the distinctively liberal value of personal autonomy celebrated by writers like Mill. On the contrary, the critics say, a dignified life may take many forms, of which the autonomous life is only one.[15] Many cultures, according to this kind of view, associate human dignity with values alternative to, even exclusive of, self-direction, values such as solidarity and respect for tradition. Nussbaum herself has tried to distinguish the 'practical reason' she identifies as a human capability from the individual 'autonomy' she associates with a more specifically liberal outlook – although how successful she is in separating these ideas is another matter.[16] This question of the universality of individual autonomy is one of the central issues in the literature of multiculturalism, and I shall return to it in several places.[17]

The general point to make here is that capabilities theory faces a major challenge in trying to maintain a critical edge while avoiding the charge of cultural bias. Hostile assessments of the theory often allege that it errs in one direction or the other – usually in the direction of individualist bias. A more generous judgement would allow that this kind of tension is unavoidable in any account of ethical universals, and that the balance struck by Nussbaum is a reasonable one.

However, a further problem with Nussbaum's view should be noted here for later reference. Nussbaum is clear that the various capabilities do not form a hierarchy: each is independently valuable and none is inherently more important than any other. 'We cannot satisfy the need for one of them by giving a larger amount of another one' (Nussbaum 2000: 81). In that case, what should we do if the promotion of one capability comes into conflict with the promotion of another? Nussbaum's answer is that this is a 'tragic' situation, involving serious loss whichever option is taken, and that the best we can do is try to avoid such situations arising in the future (Nussbaum 2011: 37–9). This problem of conflicting incommensurable values is the central issue addressed by the theories of value pluralism discussed in Chapter 7.

Summary

Universalist approaches to ethics have been dominant in Western thought, but in contemporary thinking they labour under the suspicion that norms advanced as universal are really the ethnocentric values of some cultures to the exclusion of others. A popular response has been cultural relativism, which denies universal values altogether and asserts that each culture is lord of its own ethical domain. However, cultural relativism has serious problems, beginning with the realization that cultures often get it wrong: they are not infallible but are themselves subject to moral assessment. A sensible way forward would then seem to be a restatement of universalism in a form more sensitive than many universalisms of the past to legitimate cultural variation. Nussbaum's and Sen's capabilities theory is a strong candidate in this respect, although it too has its critics.

2

Liberal Rights to Culture: Kymlicka's Theory

In the last chapter I argued that, contrary to popular opinion, cultural relativism is a poor basis for multiculturalism. Human capabilities theory, although more promising, is a work in progress to which I shall return in Chapter 7. What alternatives are there? Here we should turn to the thinker widely acknowledged to be the leading theorist of multiculturalism, the Canadian writer Will Kymlicka.[1] Kymlicka's seminal status in the literature has already been noted in the Introduction. He is also important because, as a self-consciously liberal theorist, he constructs a direct link between multiculturalism and liberal democracy, the political system in which multiculturalist principles and policies have in fact emerged over the last forty years. Kymlicka's position is to some extent a rationalization of those principles and policies. It might even be said to represent something of a dominant or 'consensus' view both politically and philosophically (Kymlicka 1998b) – hence, again, a useful point from which to orientate contrasting and opposing views.

It follows that in order to understand Kymlicka it will help to place his theory in the context of liberal thinking about cultural accommodation more generally. For that purpose I begin by setting out the central commitments of liberalism in general, outlining the principal ways in which liberal theorists have dealt with multiple cultures in the past, especially through principles of toleration and neutrality. I will then be in a better position to highlight the distinctive features of Kymlicka's multiculturalist argument before turning to the critical issues it raises.

Liberalism, Toleration and Neutrality

The liberal political tradition is both a natural ally of multiculturalism and in tension with it. Although dedicated to accommodating different ways of life, liberalism does this within a framework that also places limits on cultural accommodation. Whether this means that liberalism is in the end more of a friend or more of an enemy of multiculturalism is a question that will recur throughout the rest of this book.

Liberals disagree with one another about many things, but they have in common the following broad themes.[2] First, they place an especial emphasis on the value of individual liberty. Athough the precise meaning of liberty is given a range of interpretations by different liberals, the basic idea is that people live well when they are free to decide for themselves how to live. As J. S. Mill writes, 'it is the privilege and proper condition of a human being, arrived at the maturity of his faculties, to use and interpret experience in his own way' (Mill 1859 [1974]: 122).

Second, the most fundamental reason why liberals stress the importance of individual liberty is that they see human beings as *capable* of making their own decisions about how to live. All normal adults possess a fundamental capacity for moral autonomy – in Kant's version they are capable of using their reason to discover and follow the moral rules that enable them to live in co-operation with others. Further, all normal human beings possess this capacity equally: liberals believe that among human beings there is a fundamental equality of moral worth. Consequently, a basic liberal principle that applies to the treatment of all human beings everywhere is what is often called 'respect for persons'. To take Kant's version again, one should treat a person 'never simply as a means, but always at the same time as an end' – that is, as a being capable of moral autonomy (Kant 1785 [1956]: 96). It is not ethically permissible to use people merely as the instruments of our purposes in the way slaves, for example, are treated as 'animate tools' (Aristotle n.d [1962]: 31). Rather, we must always treat normal adults as capable of forming their own legitimate purposes.

From the liberal commitment to liberty and equality of moral worth follows a third basic principle: 'limited government'. If the moral status of persons has to be acknowledged by respecting their liberty, then government or the state, although necessary for social order, cannot be absolute in its authority. The state's authority must be 'limited' in the sense that it recognizes and respects its people's basic freedoms. These are often (although not always) conceived as individual 'rights', or claims to a certain minimum standard of acceptable treatment that is binding on everyone concerned, including the state, whatever current politics or public opinion may say. In the phrase made famous by Ronald Dworkin, rights are 'trumps' (Dworkin 1984). Rights include human rights, claimed by people in virtue of their common humanity rather than citizenship of any particular country.

Where exactly the line falls between legitimate state authority and the rights and liberties of individuals is a controversial question on which even fellow-liberals disagree. The disagreement becomes a major parting of liberal ways in relation to a fourth liberal theme, private property. All liberals accept the institution of private property as a legitimate expression of individual liberty. For most, this entails, under modern conditions, a shared commitment to capitalism, or private property in industry and commerce. However, liberal opinion divides over the question of how strong the defence of property must be in relation to other goals, such as the relief of poverty. On the one hand, 'classical' liberals – such as Adam Smith (1776), Friedrich Hayek (1944) and Robert Nozick (1974) – hold that property rights are sacrosanct. People are entitled to conduct and profit from their own business affairs as they choose, unimpeded by government interference (laissez-faire) and taxed only at a level necessary to maintain public security and defence (the 'minimal state').

On the other hand, 'egalitarian' liberals – who include T. H. Green (1881), L. T. Hobhouse (1911), John Rawls (1971) and Ronald Dworkin (1981) – argue that genuine freedom for the individual requires more than laissez-faire and the minimal state. Real liberty is not merely 'negative' non-interference but also a 'positive' (or effective) capacity to act, one that may require access to resources beyond those that one is able to acquire through market competition.[3] Success in the market is in large part a matter of good or bad fortune, since people are often disadvantaged for market competition by factors beyond their control, including accidents of birth, lack of family resources, unemployment, ill health and poor education. A just state that genuinely respects the equal moral worth of its citizenry will be prepared to provide the less fortunate with opportunities they would not have through the market alone, opportunities funded by taxes levied on those who are luckier in the natural and social lottery. This, of course, is the thinking behind the modern welfare state. The divide between the larger- and smaller-state, or higher- and lower-taxing liberals, is an abiding feature of contemporary liberal-democratic politics.

What is the relation between liberalism thus understood and culture? More precisely, to what extent is a liberal society able to accommodate multiple cultures, and to satisfy the demands of multiculturalism?

There are good reasons why liberalism seems well suited to this task. Historically, liberal thinking originated in Europe as a response to the sixteenth- and seventeenth-century Wars of Religion in which Catholics and Protestants each tried to force their version of Christianity on the other. In the wake of the wholesale destruction and suffering caused by these conflicts, thinkers such as Pierre Bayle (1702 [1991]) and John Locke (1689 [1991]) championed a move towards religious toleration, arguing that in matters of religion people inevitably disagree and that enforcement of belief is not only cruel but also futile. The more sensible and humane course is to leave individuals to decide their religious affiliations for themselves and to authorize the state to enforce only those rules of conduct on which agreement can reasonably be expected. A distinction thus arises between a 'public' realm in which the state is entitled to enforce its rules, and a 'private' sphere in which individuals are free to pursue their own beliefs and values.

Originating in the field of religion, the liberal regime of toleration was gradually extended to other areas of morality in which right and wrong are subject to reasonable disagreement. By the mid nineteenth century J. S. Mill was advocating the principle that there should be no state or public interference with the actions of individuals unless they are causing 'harm' to others (Mill 1859 [1974]: ch. 1). Mill defended a 'sphere of liberty', including freedoms of thought, expression and association, as entitled to absolute protection.

It would seem no great step to argue that not only religious and personal but also cultural differences should be included within this private category. When there is reasonable disagreement over the merits of different cultural practices, there would appear to be a prima facie case for liberal toleration.

In practice, liberal toleration 'privatizes' minority cultures (Barry 2001: 24–32). The majority or dominant culture is typically expressed in the public institutions of a society through the choice of an official language, public holidays and ceremonies and so on. Minority languages, beliefs and values are not interfered with as long as they are kept within the home or maintained by private associations or clubs.

The accommodation of cultural difference is taken a step beyond privatization by one of the standard themes of contemporary liberal thought, 'state neutrality'. This is the idea 'that government must be neutral on what might be called the question of the good life' (Dworkin 1981: 191). The state should be impartial in its treatment of different conceptions of how one ought to live, including not only religious conceptions but also personal and cultural accounts.

Much of the theory of state neutrality can be traced to John Rawls (1971; 1993). For Rawls, the merits of rival conceptions of the good are reasonably disputed by different groups, and modern societies usually contain a plurality of such groups. Consequently, no modern society can justly be governed according to a single, substantial conception of the good, since that will always be reasonably rejected by those who disagree with it. Rather, the modern pluralist state should enforce only a 'thin' framework of rules that Rawls labels 'the right', which all reasonable citizens can accept. The right is 'prior to the good' both in the sense that it overrides the good when the two conflict and in the sense that the right must be defined independently of any particular substantial conception of the good. Consequently, reasonable people can and ought to accept the right as a neutral framework of rules within which their various notions of the good can coexist peacefully. The content of the right is filled in by Rawls's famous theory of 'justice as fairness', where the principles of justice are chosen by the parties to a hypothetical 'original position' that models impartiality.

As a scheme for accommodating differences liberal neutrality goes beyond toleration or privatization. Toleration is consistent with a society's being dominated politically by a single culture or conception of the good, usually that of the majority, as long as this does not interfere with minority beliefs and practices pursued in private. This was in fact the pattern of most liberal societies until the advent of multiculturalism, and to some extent it remains the norm even today. Neutrality, by contrast, requires that no particular culture or conception of the good be politically dominant. In Rawls's language, the right should be independent of the good. The state and its framework of basic rules will be completely even-handed among different cultures, even that of the majority.

However, two issues arise immediately. First, is liberal neutrality the same thing as multiculturalism? Second, is liberal neutrality possible?

Many critics of liberalism would answer no to both these questions, and for the same reason. Some cultures, they would argue, cannot be accommodated by any form of liberalism because such cultures reject fundamental liberal values and assumptions. All four items on my list of basic liberal commitments – the primacy of individual liberty, equal respect for persons, limited government and private property – would be disputed by one culture or another. No recognizably liberal system, however 'thin', can accommodate all such cultural views. Moreover, if that is true then strict state neutrality would seem to be impossible because any genuinely liberal framework will always reflect a distinctively liberal understanding of human nature and the human good. As some critics put it, the neutral right turns out to depend on a substantial good after all.[4]

How can liberals respond to this problem? In the course of this book I shall consider several replies. One is worth broaching straight away, however, because it raises basic issues to which I shall be returning. This is that liberalism might accommodate illiberal cultures or cultural practices by making exceptions in their favour. To take an example mentioned in the Introduction, a Sikh who has to wear a turban for religious or cultural reasons might be exempted from laws requiring that helmets be worn by motorcyclists.

Some liberals would not be happy with this solution because, they would say, it flies in the face of the basic liberal commitment to equality (see e.g. Barry 2001). If persons are to be respected equally, then it seems to follow that the state ought to treat them equally. Further, equal treatment seems to require that people be treated identically. For example, all citizens should have exactly the same rights to vote and to due process of law. There should be no privileges for certain classes of people and no arbitrary disqualifications, as there are in aristocratic or racist societies.

But must equal treatment mean identical treatment in every case? Suppose that a disabled person in a wheelchair wants to use the local library. Does equal treatment require that she enter the building by using the same steep set of steps as everyone else? Surely not. The deeper meaning of equal treatment is that people should be treated 'as equals' – that is, they should be treated as having the same moral status as others, and as entitled to the same degree of consideration. They are entitled to 'equal concern and respect' (Dworkin 1977: 180). To treat people with equal concern and respect is not necessarily to treat them identically; it may mean treating them differently if the circumstances require it.

To put it another way, although the goal of equal treatment may raise a presumption in favour of identical treatment, that presumption is rebuttable. The basic idea of equal treatment is not that people must always be treated in the same way no matter what; it is that people should be treated in the same way unless there is good reason to treat them differently. When it comes to public library access, for example, there is no good reason to treat whites differently from blacks or men differently from women, but there may be good reason to make special arrangements for the disabled person who has difficulty with the steps.

The principle that differentiated treatment may be justified is a standard feature of egalitarian liberalism, and it provides an entry-point for multiculturalism. The egalitarian defence of public welfare entitlements is based on the claim that people's circumstances are different, entitling those who are unfairly disadvantaged by their social and economic situation to be compensated through a tax system funded by those who are not. If so, might there not be similar public obligations when people suffer unfair disadvantage because of their cultural circumstances? This is one line of inquiry taken up by Kymlicka.

Kymlicka's Case for Cultural Rights

Kymlicka's key innovation is to construct, most notably in *Liberalism, Community, and Culture* (1989) and *Multicultural Citizenship* (1995a), a systematic case for multiculturalism on a liberal basis. Like all liberals, he emphasizes universal values of individual liberty, the equal moral worth of all human beings, human rights, limited government and private property. Further, in the tradition of egalitarian liberalism, he interprets these values as requiring the active intervention of the state for their advancement rather than a laissez-faire reliance on individual enterprise. A just society will attempt to compensate people for the worst effects of undeserved disadvantage. Thus far Kymlicka is an orthodox egalitarian liberal in the mould of Rawls and Dworkin.

Where he parts company with these predecessors is in his insistence on a more active role for the state in sustaining minority cultures. The traditional liberal policy of passive toleration should be replaced or supplemented by a more active policy in which the state accords minority cultural groups positive recognition and assistance. He justifies this view by appealing to the two fundamental values of egalitarian liberalism: equality and liberty.

On equal treatment, Kymlicka develops the line of thought opened up at the end of the last section. Just as equal treatment requires compensation for undeserved *economic* disadvantage, Kymlicka argues that so too does equal treatment demand compensation for undeserved *cultural* disadvantage.

In making this case, Kymlicka sees himself as correcting some long-standing prejudices in liberal thought. Traditional liberal thinkers, even within the more egalitarian stream, have tended to be hostile to treating cultural groups differently for two reasons (Kymlicka 1989: 140–1). First, liberals have tended to equate 'group' rights with 'collective' rights, which immediately threaten to undermine the rights of the individual. Second, the liberal tradition has been wary of importing cultural and ethnic particularity into political thinking because this has so often been associated with irrational and unjust discrimination, such as the racial segregation practised in the past in the southern United States and apartheid South Africa.

For Kymlicka, these traditional liberal suspicions are too sweeping, and amount to throwing the baby out with the bathwater. Liberals are justified in being concerned about attributing rights to groups as such, since a group 'has no moral existence or claims of its own' (Kymlicka 1989: 140). A group or community is valuable only so far as it benefits its members. But by the same token, Kymlicka argues, a group that benefits its members is valuable to them in that instrumental sense. Consequently, although a group itself has no rights, it makes sense to say that its individual members have rights to the survival of the group if it serves their well-being. Kymlicka's 'group rights' are the rights of individuals, and are thus consistent with traditional liberal concerns.

As for the worry that politicizing group differences is synonymous with inequality and injustice, Kymlicka argues that this is not always so. On the contrary, there are cases where recognition of cultural difference, far from denigrating a group, is necessary to compensate its members for undeserved disadvantage. Moreover, to make this point is not to depart from the fundamental liberal concern for equality but to express that concern more fully, since it takes into account circumstances that are highly relevant to questions of respect and fairness.

> To give every Canadian equal citizenship rights without regard to race or ethnicity, given the vulnerability of aboriginal communities to the decisions of the non-aboriginal majority, does not seem to treat Indians and Inuit with equal respect. For it ignores a potentially devastating problem faced by aboriginal people but not by English-Canadians – the loss of cultural membership. (Kymlicka 1989: 151)

Not all differential treatment of citizens is bad; it depends on the reasons for the different treatment. For Kymlicka, this basic point nullifies the traditional liberal hostility to all special claims made on the basis of group affiliation. As long as such claims are backed by good reasons, they are quite consistent with, indeed required by, liberal equality.[5]

The other fundamental liberal commitment that Kymlicka reinterprets in the direction of cultural rights is individual liberty. To the basic liberal concern for freedom egalitarian liberals add an insistence on the economic conditions for freedom, and to that insistence Kymlicka adds attention to the cultural conditions for freedom. For Kymlicka, individual freedom is most fundamentally the capacity people have 'to choose their own plan of life' (Kymlicka 1995a: 80). This is a strong sense of freedom, often called 'personal autonomy', in which people are able not only 'to choose a conception of the good life' but also 'to reconsider that decision, and adopt a new and hopefully better plan of life'. Autonomous people are capable not only of choosing how to live but also of reflecting critically on that choice and revising it. This is the kind of freedom celebrated, for example, by Mill in his notion of 'individuality' (Mill 1859 [1974]: ch. 3).[6]

Why is freedom in this sense so valuable? Kymlicka argues that it is necessary if we are to be sure that we are leading a truly good life, or as sure as we can be that we are living the kind of life we really want to live. The best life for a human being is one that we lead 'from the inside' – a life we live because we really want to live that way (Kymlicka 1995a: 81). But we have to recognize that our beliefs in this respect are 'fallible and revisable': we can get things wrong, and if that is so we want to put things right so far as that is possible. To live well, then, we need freedom, the kind of freedom that enables us to choose and to revise our choices. Further, there is a link here with self-respect: to respect ourselves, we need to be sure our goals are worth pursuing. Since freedom as autonomy enables us to confirm whether this is so, autonomy is essential to self-respect (Kymlicka 1989: 164).

To enjoy individual autonomy, we have to enjoy the conditions for it. Fundamental to these conditions for freedom is membership of a flourishing, or at any rate viable, culture. It is our cultural heritage that enables us to make sense of the choices before us, and to choose among them in a way that makes sense to us. 'Our language and history are the media through which we come to an awareness of the options available to us, and their significance; and this is a precondition of making intelligent judgements about how to lead our lives' (Kymlicka 1989: 165; see also 1995a: 82–4). Our cultural inheritance is a kind of map with which we can navigate through the various opportunities and challenges with which life confronts us.

Cultural membership is valuable, therefore, because it provides us with a necessary context for our choices. As a necessary condition for freedom as autonomy, cultural membership is also essential to self-respect. Indeed, cultural membership is, for these reasons, a 'primary good' in Rawls's sense – it is an essential means to any good life (Kymlicka 1989: 166).

If culture is valuable because it provides a context for choice and a basis for self-respect, we might ask whether it matters *which* culture people take as their context, and consequently whether it matters if their society promotes only one such cultural context. In other words, how does Kymlicka's account of the value of cultural membership amount to a multiculturalist view: why is it not consistent with monoculturalism?

Kymlicka's answer is that, for most of us, it is our own culture – the culture we are brought up in – that matters most in this way. Most people do not change their cultural affiliations readily (Kymlicka 1995a: 84–5). Changing one's culture is not like changing one's job; people tend to remain within the culture that formed them. It is true that some 'people do genuinely move between cultures. But this is rarer, and more difficult', and even then one's own culture is always, at least, a starting point (Kymlicka 1995a: 85). More common is the experience of revising and selecting among different streams or aspects of one's culture, but this presupposes rather than denies the need for one's own culture. If people generally do best within their native culture, then it is likely that a modern society, containing people from different cultural backgrounds, will need to accommodate or encourage more than one such culture.

This explains why Kymlicka does not rely on an argument for multiculturalism that many liberal-minded people find immediately attractive: that there is value in cultural diversity itself. The reason often given for that claim is that the presence of multiple cultures in our society adds to the richness of our lives by increasing the options we can choose from when we are deciding how to live.[7] But if Kymlicka is right, we should be wary of talking about cultures as if they were supermarket items among which we can choose at will. He concludes that, although 'there is some truth' in the cultural diversity argument, 'it is a mistake to put too much weight on it' (Kymlicka 1995a: 121).[8]

To sum up, Kymlicka's argument from equality is that equal treatment may require special compensation for minority cultural groups, and his argument from liberty is that cultural membership, and more specifically membership of one's own culture, is essential to individual freedom and therefore to well-being.

The next question is, how are these goals to be secured? Kymlicka believes that this is a task for the state. Just as, on the standard egalitarian-liberal view, the state has a duty to ensure the economic conditions for real individual freedom, so too the state has an obligation to guarantee, as far as possible, the cultural conditions for that freedom. But someone might object that although it may be true that cultural membership is important, it does not follow automatically that cultures must be protected by the state. Conceivably, it might be argued, the importance of cultures is consistent with the traditional liberal toleration or privatization view, which simply calls for the state to leave people alone to make their own decisions in this regard.

Kymlicka calls this the 'benign neglect' approach, and he argues that it is inevitably harmful to vulnerable cultural minorities such as indigenous groups. Simply to say that groups like these should compete in 'the cultural market-place' along with other groups is unfairly to ignore their real circumstances, since these groups are automatically at a disadvantage in such a competition. In the Canadian case, for example,

> unlike the dominant French or English cultures, the very existence of aboriginal cultural communities is vulnerable to the decisions of the non-aboriginal majority around them. They could be outbid or outvoted on resources crucial to the survival of their communities, a possibility that members of the majority cultures simply do not face. As a result, they have to spend their resources on securing the cultural membership which makes sense of their lives, something which non-aboriginal peoples get for free. (Kymlicka 1989: 187)

Members of the dominant culture get their culture for free, as it were, simply because of its dominance – they see their beliefs and values reflected in all of the institutions and practices around them (media, entertainment, public holidays and so on). Indigenous cultures have to swim against this tide just in order to survive.

Hence the need for state intervention on behalf of cultural rights. Hence, too, Kymlicka's answer to the common objection that special minority rights are inegalitarian privileges. The disadvantaged position of indigenous groups is the result not of their choices, but of unchosen circumstances for which they are not responsible. 'Rather than subsidizing or privileging their choices, the special measures demanded by aboriginal people serve to correct an advantage that non-aboriginal people have before anyone makes their choices' (Kymlicka 1989: 189).

What exactly are the 'special measures' that form the substance of these rights? The general rationale is that these are measures designed to provide minority groups with redress for unfair disadvantage. What form of redress is appropriate will depend on the nature of the disadvantage in the particular case. For example, monetary compensation is unlikely to be adequate, since 'having money for the pursuit of one's ends is of little help if the price involves giving up the context within which those ends are worth pursuing' (Kymlicka 1989: 193). Kymlicka mentions many more promising possibilities, including 'territorial autonomy, veto rights, guaranteed representation in central institutions, land claims, and language rights' (Kymlicka 1995a: 109).[9]

Two Qualifications

A significant development in Kymlicka's thinking occurred with the publication of *Multicultural Citizenship* in 1995. In the earlier *Liberalism, Community, and Culture*, he seemed to regard all cultural minorities as suffering from much the same kind of disadvantage, and consequently as entitled to the same rights. This position was criticized for failing to acknowledge the special circumstances of indigenous minorities compared with immigrant groups (Danley 1991).

Subsequently, in *Multicultural Citizenship*, Kymlicka introduces a key distinction between two kinds of cultural minority: 'national' and 'ethnic'. 'National' minorities prominently include indigenous peoples and regional groups like the Québécois and the Basques. Such minorities have been incorporated into modern states 'through conquest, colonization, or federation', but they have never relinquished their claims to a 'societal culture' of their own (Kymlicka 1995a: 79). A 'societal' culture involves 'not just shared memories or values, but also common institutions and practices' that embody those memories and values across 'most areas of human activity' – 'in schools, media, economy, government, etc.' (Kymlicka 1995a: 76). Where such cultures have been absorbed into larger societies they have often struggled hard to preserve their distinct existence, with the result that in many places 'their status as self-governing "domestic dependent nations" is now more firmly recognized' (Kymlicka 1995a: 79).

By contrast, 'ethnic' minorities are immigrant groups whose members have chosen to become part of a new society. In doing so, they usually bring their beliefs and values with them, embedded in 'their language and historical narratives', but they tacitly agree to leave behind the institutions and 'social practices which this vocabulary originally referred to and made sense of' (Kymicka 1995a: 77). That is, they leave behind their fully societal culture. They may no longer be

> expected to assimilate entirely to the norms and customs of the dominant culture, and indeed are encouraged to maintain some aspects of

> their ethnic particularity. But this commitment to "multiculturalism" or "polyethnicity" is a shift in how immigrants integrate into the dominant culture, not whether they integrate. (Kymlicka 1995a: 78)

While 'assimilation' implies a more or less complete identification with the dominant culture, 'integration' suggests a more relaxed approach in which a group fits into the dominant pattern, but in its own way. Nevertheless, the acceptability of integration in the case of ethnic minorities contrasts strongly with the entitlement of national minorities to lead, in some substantial sense, an independent existence.

It follows that national and ethnic minorities are entitled to different kinds of rights. The rights of national or indigenous minorities are much stronger: rights to the preservation of the full societal culture, the institutions and practices that they never agreed to abandon. These are essentially rights of self-determination, including, as appropriate to the case in hand, group representation and various forms and degrees of self-government.[10]

Ethnic or immigrant minorities have much weaker entitlements, which Kymlicka labels 'polyethnic rights', essentially designed to assist their integration. These claims are not negligible, since they may include anti-discrimination measures, legal exemptions (for example, for Jews and Muslims from Sunday closing laws and humane slaughter requirements), and support for, or at least toleration of, education in the group's mother tongue (Kymlicka 1995a: 96–7). Still, Kymlicka's polyethnic rights are clearly in a very different and subordinate category compared with the self-determination rights he ascribes to national indigenous minorities.

Kymlicka's heightened emphasis on national (including indigenous) claims sharpens an issue that will concern many people about his whole enterprise – indeed, the whole notion of special group or cultural rights. What justification can there be for preserving groups whose values and practices are deeply illiberal? In traditional cultures, such as those of indigenous groups, liberal ideals such as individual liberty and equality of moral worth tend not to be highly valued. Such cultures typically endorse restrictive and inegalitarian attitudes to moral and religious requirements, the source and scope of political authority, forms of punishment, distribution of knowledge, freedom of expression and the nature and social role of women and children.

Nor are these norms confined to indigenous societies; they are common to many cultures that remain deeply influenced by local traditions or by the more fundamentalist or conservative versions of the world religions (Okin 1999: 21). Yet these are often the very groups on whose behalf claims for special minority rights are made within liberal democracies. Is it not the case that to recognize such special rights is in effect to accept and endorse the continuation of illiberal, patriarchal and harmful traditions and practices?

Kymlicka is well aware of this problem. His answer is to introduce another major qualification into his theory of cultural rights: 'as a general rule, liberals should not prevent illiberal nations from maintaining their societal culture, but should promote the liberalization of these cultures' (Kymlicka 1995a: 95). Special cultural rights will not protect illiberal cultures – or at any rate the illiberal components of cultures. On the contrary, Kymlicka's case for cultural rights implies that the liberal state is entitled to intervene in illiberal cultures in order to liberalize them: to protect the basic civil and political liberties of a group's members, and to promote their capacity for personal autonomy.

The reason for this is that Kymlicka's central justification for cultural rights, according to Kymlicka, is the value of cultural membership as a context for autonomous choice. That justification reaches its limit in cases where a culture ceases to support but rather undermines the conditions for personal autonomy. Cultural rights should protect minority groups from the 'external' decisions of majorities, but not from the 'internal' dissent of their own members (Kymlicka 1995a: 35). To allow internal dissent, and still more to authorize liberalization by the state, is to allow and even encourage a culture to change, but change is not the same as destruction. We should distinguish the protection of 'the community as such' from people's 'particular preferred version of what sort of *character* the community should have' (Kymlicka 1989: 168).

Kymlicka gives the example of the Pueblo Indians in the United States, who have 'in effect, established a theocratic government that discriminates against those members who do not share the tribal religion' (Kymlicka 1995a: 40). For example, housing benefits are denied to those members of the Pueblo community who have converted to Christianity. Kymlicka rejects Pueblo majority claims that prohibiting members from changing their religious affiliation is necessary in order to safeguard the future of their culture. Cultural rights should protect minority cultures from the dictates of powerful individuals and groups outside of the community; they should not prevent people within the community from acting in accordance with their conscience and changing their religious affiliation. Freedom of religion does not destroy the culture, but merely allows it to change in accordance with the desires of its members (Kymlicka 1989: 196).

In general, Kymlicka argues, it is misleading to divide the world into essentially 'liberal' societies on the one hand and 'illiberal' on the other, as if liberalization were appropriate only to the first and not the second. Rather, the extent to which any culture counts as liberal is a matter of degree, and can change over time. Today's liberal societies were not always liberal. 'The task of liberal reform remains incomplete in every society' (Kymlicka 1989: 94).

Critical Issues

Kymlicka's theory of minority cultural rights has attracted a wide range of criticism.[11] Some of the major issues will be postponed to later chapters. These include Kymlicka's notion of equal treatment (Chapter 3), his emphasis on national identity (Chapter 4) and his acceptance of a liberal framework (Chapter 5). In this section I consider two main topics: his treatment of illiberal minorities, and his appeal to individual autonomy.

Illiberal Groups

As noted already, one of the most difficult problems for Kymlicka's theory (or any liberal theory) is how to deal with minorities that have substantially illiberal characteristics. Some critics complain that Kymlicka concedes too much to such groups, allowing them to tyrannize over their own people, as we shall see when we discuss Brian Barry and Susan Okin in the next chapter. Others fault him for treating illiberal groups too restrictively, making them over in the image of liberals like himself.

Chandran Kukathas falls very definitely into the second camp. Writing from a classical liberal or libertarian perspective, Kukathas generally advocates minimal state intervention and maximal negative liberty for individual citizens. For Kukathas, Kymlicka's approach is excessively and unnecessarily interfering. This is true 'both from a liberal point of view and from the perspective of someone concerned with the interests of cultural minorities' (Kukathas 1992: 120).

From the perspective of non-liberal cultural minorities, Kukathas argues, Kymlicka's liberalizing policy gives such cultures too little. The insistence on the universal value of individual autonomy leads to unacceptable state interference with the cultures concerned, since many do not value autonomy highly. As a result, Kymlicka's policy would amount to the imposition on these cultures of an ideal that is alien to them and likely to undermine them, or at least to subject them to a 'reshaping' that is contrary to 'the terms set by their own practices' (Kukathas 1992: 122). Kymlicka gives with one hand and takes away with the other.

From a liberal point of view, according to Kukathas, Kymlicka's special rights are simply unnecessary for the adequate accommodation of cultural minorities. There is no need to go beyond orthodox conceptions of 'individual liberty or individual rights' to do justice to cultural minorities (Kukathas 1992: 107). Moreover, these liberties and rights should be interpreted in the strictly negative sense favoured by classical liberals, as individual entitlements to non-interference. The classical liberal ideal of individual freedom of association – and its corollary, the freedom to exit from a group – is all that is required. If individuals feel that they are being treated oppressively by their group, they can simply leave.

In this connection Kukathas emphasizes that cultural groups are, contrary to the claims of defenders of cultural preservation (as he sees it) like Kymlicka, fluid and constantly changing. They 'may be regarded as voluntary associations' in the sense that their survival depends on the extent to which their members continue to 'recognize as legitimate the terms of association and the authority that upholds them' (Kukathas 1992: 116). 'The basis of the community's authority is not any right of the culture to perpetuation, or even existence, but the acquiescence of its members' (Kukathas 1992: 117). Liberals should not respect cultures themselves, but only people's decisions either to stay in their cultures or to leave. Cultures just are the embodiment of all these decisions.

In short, for Kukathas, the duty of the liberal state towards cultural groups (whether minority or majority) is nothing more or less than to leave them alone. His view may be summed up as 'cultural laissez-faire'. This involves neither interference nor protection; the sole task for the state will be to secure individuals' freedom to associate and to exit from their associations. Seen from this perspective, Kymlicka's special rights look like artificial and futile devices intended to regulate what need not and ought not to be regulated, and to secure what individuals can already secure for themselves.

Kukathas takes this view a step further in *The Liberal Archipelago* (2003), which elaborates his positive vision of the desirable multicultural society. Such a society consists 'of different communities operating in a sea of mutual toleration' (Kukathas 2003: 8). The state has no overriding function or authority at all. It is merely one island among others, one community with which people may partially identify, just as they may identify with others. Its sole function appears to be to enforce freedom of association – or more accurately, dissociation. Goals of social unity and national identity, often used to justify stronger states, are regarded by Kukathas as greatly overrated, neither necessary nor desirable in the formation of a political society. Rather, the good society is akin to international society: 'a society of multiple authorities operating under a de facto regime of mutual toleration' (Kukathas 2003: 27). The good society is one in which groups simply leave one another alone.

Kymlicka is not short of replies, however. First, he would argue, as before, that some state intervention is necessary not to preserve cultures unchanged but to sustain them as dynamic contexts for choice. The alternative is the 'benign neglect' that leaves vulnerable groups alone with their undeserved circumstances of disadvantage.

Second, Kymlicka would insist that his requirement of liberalization need not be as damaging to minority cultures as Kukathas claims. For one thing, liberalization need not be coercive, and in most cases coercion would be unwise. Alternatives range from simply 'speaking out' against intra-group injustice, to 'offering various incentives for liberal reforms', and promoting 'international mechanisms for protecting human rights' (Kymlicka 1995a: 168, 169). This is not wholly convincing, since Kymlicka also rightly notes that there are certain basic rights violations that a liberal state cannot countenance – murder, arbitrary arrest and so forth (Kymlicka 1992: 142). The use of coercive measures to correct these fundamental injustices would seem an unavoidable last resort.

Even so, Kymlicka can again make the point that not all social change is destruction: the 'character' of a culture can be distinguished from 'the community as such', and changes in the former do not necessarily mean the dismantling of the latter. This argument is perhaps more convincing in some cases than in others. British culture no doubt remained recognizably British after the decriminalization of homosexuality in the 1960s, but whether the Pueblo culture could be said to survive the introduction of freedom of religion is another matter. Kymlicka himself concedes, as we saw, that such cases raise difficult choices that must be faced honestly.

His stronger reply to Kukathas is that, whatever its costs may be, liberalization is necessary because the alternative is to leave the members of illiberal groups vulnerable to those groups' internal restrictions. A liberal state must stand up for the civil and political liberties of all its citizens.

Further, Kukathas's reposte that individuals are adequately protected from their groups by a right of exit is highly questionable. Such a right might be sufficient for the purpose if it was demanding enough – if it guaranteed that people were really able to leave their groups. But Kukathas believes, in line with his libertarian background, that a genuine freedom to exit requires only negative liberty, or the absence of coercion, together with the existence of a free market society for people to exit into (Kukathas 1992: 134). Kymlicka sees this as 'a bizarre view of what gives individuals a substantial right to leave', since it is consistent with their being 'deprived of literacy, education, or the freedom to learn about the outside world' (Kymlicka 1992: 143). Without an effective right of exit, Kukathas's model society promises to be not so much an archipelago of liberties as a 'mosaic of tyrannies' (Green 1995: 270).[12]

One way of summing up the dispute between Kymlicka and Kukathas is in terms of conflicting values: Kymlicka champions individual autonomy, Kukathas favours toleration. Since autonomy and toleration both appear to be basic liberal goods, one might conclude that Kymlicka and Kukathas simply represent different aspects of the liberal tradition that are ultimately in tension with one another.

This interpretation would be resisted by both parties. Each would claim that his preferred value is more fundamental to the liberal outlook. Kukathas sees liberalism as ultimately about toleration, or not interfering with the way other people choose to live. Kymlicka would respond that a distinctively *liberal* form of toleration rests on the value of personal autonomy. That is because liberal toleration is specifically about 'individual freedom of conscience', the idea that *individuals* should be free to go their own way (Kymlicka 1995a: 156). This contrasts with the kind of group-based toleration advocated by Kukathas. This has a precedent in the 'millet system' of the Ottoman Empire, in which different religious groups were allowed, with some qualifications, to govern themselves. The trouble is that millet-style toleration of groups is compatible with the suppression of individual conscience and dissent within the group. 'The millet system', Kymlicka writes, 'was, in effect, a federation of theocracies. It was a deeply conservative and patriarchal society, antithetical to the ideals of personal liberty endorsed by liberals from Locke to Kant and Mill' (Kymlicka 1995a: 157). For Kymlicka, Kukathas's group toleration is a contemporary version of the millet system, it is not a liberal form of toleration at all. A genuinely liberal form of toleration involves an appreciation of the importance of group membership to individual well-being, but it also presupposes the value of personal autonomy and justifies the defence of individuals against attempts by groups to restrict that autonomy.

The Role of Autonomy

The role of personal autonomy in Kymlicka's theory is a target for several critics besides Kukathas. One line of objection questions Kymlicka's account of the relation between autonomy and culture. Recall that, according to Kymlicka, cultural membership is valuable because a person's autonomy is made possible by her cultural context. Some critics charge that this gets things the wrong way round: for liberals it should be personal autonomy that determines cultural membership rather than culture that conditions autonomy (Levey 1997; Gill 2001). Some cultures will not provide any contextual support for personal autonomy because they do not value it. We should choose our cultural affiliations, or at least these should be subject to critical revision.

Kymlicka does not altogether disagree with this point. He tries to accommodate it, but it does complicate his position. On the one hand he agrees that a person's identity is not simply determined by the culture in which she is brought up, and that she can question its orthodoxies through critical thinking. On the other hand, he still wants to say that a person's original culture plays a special role in providing a context for her autonomy, and that is one of his principal arguments for cultural rights. Combining these thoughts is tricky. Presumably, one's original culture is a necessary starting point from which to make sense of one's choices, but that does not explain how one becomes autonomous in the first place (since some cultures are not encouraging in this way), or why it should be so important to maintain a cultural context that an autonomous person may well repudiate.

Another issue is whether Kymlicka is wise to appeal so strongly to the value of individual autonomy in the first place. The dispute between Kymlicka and Kukathas on this matter is part of a wider debate about the foundations of liberalism. Another important contribution to that debate, suggesting a criticism of Kymlicka by implication, is made by John Rawls in his later work. In *Political Liberalism* (1993), Rawls argues that modern societies are characterized by the coexistence of a plurality of rival conceptions of the good life about which people may reasonably disagree. Liberal political thought should attempt to accommodate this reasonable pluralism instead of taking up a belligerent position within it. Rather than presented as a 'comprehensive' conception of the good, provoking reasonable disagreement, liberalism should be interpreted as a position that people can accept for purely 'political' purposes, in the public realm, while maintaining their own conception of the good in private.

In these terms Rawls would categorize Kymlicka's theory as harmfully comprehensive, since it is explicitly grounded in a controversial account of the good life based on personal autonomy. This kind of liberalism is too 'sectarian', according to Rawls (1985: 246), because the fact of modern pluralism is such that many citizens of liberal democracies belong to groups that value personal autonomy much less than allegiance to religious or traditional authority. In order to reach out to these non-liberal citizens, liberals must justify their principles and institutions only for the limited purposes of political consensus rather than as expressing the truth in all spheres of life. Kymlicka fails to limit his claims in this desirable way.

Kymlicka responds that Rawlsian political liberalism is incoherent. 'The problem is to explain why anyone would accept the ideal of autonomy in political contexts unless they also accepted it more generally' (Kymlicka 1995a: 160). Rawls imagines that the same people who reject autonomy in their private lives, because they see themselves as inextricably identified with their beliefs, can also affirm the possibility and value of autonomy when they are acting as citizens. 'For Rawls, people are communitarians in private life, and liberals in public life.' But people cannot realistically be expected to divide up their moral sensibilities in this way. Either they will accept personal autonomy comprehensively or not at all. If liberals want to defend civil and political rights, that defence must be comprehensive.

Kymlicka illustrates this point with the much-cited US case of *Wisconsin v. Yoder*, involving the Old Order Amish community. The Amish are an ultra-conservative Christian religious minority who prefer to live apart from mainstream American society. In *Yoder*, they were drawn into the legal system because of the decision of Amish parents to withdraw their children from school at the age of fourteen years rather than sixteen as required by state law. The purpose of this early cessation of education, according to Kymlicka, was to limit the children's knowledge of what takes place in the world beyond the confines of their own community, and thereby to reduce the possibility of the children's choosing to leave the community (Kymlicka 1995a: 162). But the US Supreme Court decided in favour of the Amish parents and against the state on the ground of freedom of religion.

Kymlicka rejects that decision, since the Amish policy was designed to prevent the critical questioning and revision of beliefs – that is, it diminished personal autonomy. His point against Rawls is that, although political liberalism would require that education for autonomy be respected by the community in the public forum – since in that context this is a 'political value' that overrides the community's comprehensive values – the community is unlikely to do so if it does not respect autonomy as valuable in other spheres of life. Rawls's purely political approach, although in principle it would defend autonomy in this case, is unworkable. If autonomy is to be secured within the Amish community, it must be accepted comprehensively; merely to propose it as acceptable for political purposes against the grain of community sentiment is bound to provoke resistance.[13]

In general, then, Kymlicka sees Rawls's political liberalism as a half-measure that will neither satisfy the non-liberal groups it is designed to placate nor adequately defend the liberal ideals it is supposed to uphold. People who do not accept personal autonomy comprehensively are unlikely to accept it politically. Conversely, if people are expected to accept autonomy politically, they need to be persuaded of its comprehensive value. The traditional liberal task of arguing the case for personal autonomy is a difficult one, and inevitably brings liberals into intellectual conflict with non-liberals. But the task must be faced.

Summary

The traditional liberal approach to minority cultures is one of toleration or 'privatization', in which the state guarantees minority groups the freedom to practise their own culture in private. Subject to the maintenance of basic civil liberties, the traditional liberal state neither impedes such cultures nor assists them. Kymlicka departs from this policy by arguing that special rights for minority cultural groups are justified as a logical development of the egalitarian-liberal principle that people ought, where possible, to be compensated for undeserved disadvantage. Membership of a viable culture is one of the primary goods that contribute to individual well-being because people's culture provides a necessary context for their autonomous choices. Minority groups are in a weaker position than the majority when it comes to maintaining their culture. This is not such a problem in the case of migrant groups, which have effectively chosen to integrate into a new society, but it points to a major injustice towards indigenous and other 'national' minorities, whose absorption is typically involuntary. While migrants can still claim 'polyethnic' rights to help with their integration, national groups are entitled to much stronger rights of self-determination. However, Kymlicka also places a major qualification on these conclusions, which is that no group is entitled to deny its members their basic civil and political liberties or to stifle dissent within the group. On the contrary, the same argument that grounds group rights – namely the value of cultures as contexts for individual autonomy – also justifies state-sponsored liberalization of illiberal practices. The many critical issues raised by Kymlicka's view include complaints that his approach is unnecessarily interventionist and that his appeal to the value of individual autonomy is too sectarian. Further issues will emerge in subsequent chapters.

3

Liberal Critics of Cultural Rights

This chapter deals with three liberal responses to multiculturalism that contrast with Kymlicka's.[1] The first two, those of Brian Barry and Susan Okin, are united by a strong hostility to cultural rights and by a belief that liberalism, as they understand it, already has the resources for a satisfactory response to the fact of modern cultural plurality without recourse to such special, group-differentiated claims. Barry appeals to what he sees as the traditional Enlightenment ideal of equal citizenship, backed up by a strong welfare state. Okin writes from a liberal-feminist perspective, looking forward to the reform, even radical transformation, of traditional cultural practices that she believes have restricted the development of women.

The third writer I discuss, Ayelet Shachar, is more sympathetic to special cultural rights provided that vulnerable individuals, especially women, have the freedom to choose whether their treatment will be governed by the law of the group or that of the liberal state. She shares Okin's concerns about patriarchal traditions, and so may be broadly classed as a 'feminist' writer, but she also wants to allow women a way of balancing emancipation with the benefits of continued group membership.

Equal Treatment: Barry

Brian Barry, in his entertainingly intemperate *Culture and Equality* (2001), is convinced that multiculturalism represents a wrong turn in egalitarian-liberal politics. The opening section of his book is entitled 'Losing our way'. There Barry argues that the defeat of communism, although welcome, has opened up a political void that has been filled by two disturbing developments. First, the universality of communism has been replaced by a new emphasis on various dimensions of 'difference'. 'The spectre that now haunts Europe is one of strident nationalism, ethnic self-assertion and the exaltation of what divides people at the expense of what unites them' (Barry 2001: 3). Second, laissez-faire forms of liberalism have greatly increased their influence at the expense of public services and the redistribution needed to sustain them. Indeed, Barry believes that the two points are connected. 'Claims for special treatment are advanced by groups of all kinds while material inequality grows and the post-war "welfare state" shows increasing signs of strain' (Barry 2001: 3). Multiculturalism is an obstacle to the more traditional, and more legitimate, economic conception of social justice.

At an intellectual level these developments are underpinned by a 'flight from the Enlightenment', a loss of faith in the eighteenth-century ideals of a common human nature and the basic rights, possessed by all individuals equally, which that nature implies (Barry 2001: 9). Of course, the right-wing Counter-Enlightenment of Edmund Burke, Joseph de Maistre and other conservative thinkers had always rejected universalism and equality and defended particularism and privilege, but now the same path is taken by thinkers who present themselves as belonging to the left. Similarly, other notions formerly the preserve of the Counter-Enlightenment, such as the reification of 'culture' and the promotion of essentialist notions of groups, are now revived by supposedly progressive multiculturalists (Barry 2001: 11).

Among those multiculturalists Kymlicka is the first to be mentioned. Barry presents no concerted treatment of Kymlicka's view as a whole, but he keeps returning to it as one of his favourite critical targets. First, Kymlicka's claim that there is a new 'convergence in the recent literature . . . on ideas of liberal multiculturalism' is, for Barry, true only of those who choose to write on the subject; for those who do not 'there is something approaching a consensus . . . that the literature of multiculturalism is not worth wasting powder and shot on' (Barry 2001: 6). Kymlicka exemplifies the central error of multiculturalism as Barry sees it, which is 'the politicization of group identities' instead of the traditional liberal policy in which group differences are privatized (Barry 2001: 5). Formerly, members of cultural and religious minorities were deemed to possess the same rights and duties as everyone else and left to pursue their ways of life in private, so far as these were consistent with their duties as citizens. But

Kymlicka and other multiculturalists demand that the ways of life be given official recognition in the form of special rights.

Another initial point made by Barry is that Kymlicka and the others assume too readily that significant social groups are identified by a distinctive 'culture' rather than by some other feature such as race, ethnicity or religion. In this connection Barry emphasizes the difficulty Kymlicka has in accounting for the position of African-Americans, whose shared identity has less to do with culture, whether national or ethnic, than with race (Barry 2001: 306, 315–17, 322–4).

Barry also objects to both of the main kinds of group-differentiated right that Kymlicka advocates. The polyethnic rights that Kymlicka would accord to immigrant groups Barry finds unfair and unnecessary. Legal exemptions, for example, are unjustified because if the relevant law has legitimate public goals then there is usually no good reason to excuse any group from compliance with it. On the other hand, if there really is a convincing case for their non-compliance then that probably means that the law was not well conceived in the first place and needs to be abolished or rethought (Barry 2001: 39). While Kymlicka was willing to exempt turban-wearing Sikhs from the laws requiring crash-helmets to be worn on motorcycles, Barry argues that the crash-helmet laws have the legitimate public purpose of preventing serious head injuries. This is not outweighed by considerations of freedom of religion because the laws do not prevent Sikhs from practising their religion – Sikhs do not have to ride motorcycles (Barry 2001: 44–5).

Kymlicka's rights of national self-determination for minority groups are also rejected by Barry. He sees such claims as motivated by Kymlicka's support for the nationalist goals of Quebec. Kymlicka wishes to turn Canada into an 'asymmetrical' federation in which Quebec has exclusive control of its own affairs in addition to being represented in decision making that affects Canada as a whole (Barry 2001: 310). Barry objects that this arrangement would create 'two classes of citizens with unequal rights', since the Québécois would have political rights that other Canadian citizens would not have (Barry 2001: 311–12). A similar objection might be made to self-determination rights for indigenous groups. In addition, indigenous self-determination often raises the issue of whether its effect is to provide legal and political protection for illiberal practices. Barry convicts Kymlicka of this too, remaining unimpressed by the latter's protestations that basic liberal values are universal in principle and that liberals 'can, in his view, "speak out against . . . injustice" and "lend their support" to reformers – if they have not been jailed or executed' (Barry 2001: 140). For Barry, the upshot is merely 'an illiberal theory with a bit of liberal hand-wringing thrown in as an optional extra' (Barry 2001: 140).

Kukathas's position is even more illiberal, according to Barry. Barry agrees with Kukathas in rejecting special rights and insisting on equal treatment as the proper standard. However, Barry interprets equal treatment very differently. For Kukathas, equal treatment means, among other things, equal toleration of all groups, no matter what their internal practices may be. For Barry, this almost unqualified toleration of group norms amounts to a licensing of groups to mistreat their members that is more wholehearted than anything in Kymlicka – there is no hand-wringing at all. Groups are then free to kill apostates, enforce female circumcision and withhold life-saving blood transfusions from their children (Barry 2001: 142).

The defence offered by Kukathas, as we saw, is that individual group members have the negative liberty to exit. But that kind of exit right is condemned by Barry, as it is by Kymlicka (Chapter 2), as wholly inadequate because it fails to recognize that coercion is not the only way of preventing people from leaving a group. For Barry, there is no real freedom to exit unless the state is prepared to alleviate 'costs that the state both can and should do something about' (Barry 2001: 150). These costs include not only coercion but also, for example, a case where a person who leaves a religious group is dismissed from his job as a result, even though doing the job does not really require being a member of the group. The upshot is that although Kukathas's rules are uniform, they 'permit groups to harm their members with impunity' (Barry 2001: 141). In Kukathas's hands, 'public tolerance is a formula for creating a lot of private hells' (Barry 2001: 143).

In his own approach Barry may be seen as trying to steer a middle way between what he sees as Kymlicka's inegalitarian and meddling special group rights and Kukathas's uniform but illiberal cultural laissez-faire. On the whole, he sees himself as returning to the classic liberal policy of privatization of culture: intervention in cultural matters is limited to the minimum necessary to ensure the maintenance of core liberal values. Foremost among these are liberty and equality, respectively interpreted as freedom of association and equality of opportunity.

On freedom of association, Barry seems initially to take a view very close to Kukathas's: 'groups should have the utmost freedom to handle their affairs in accordance with the wishes of their members' (Barry 2001: 148). Moreover, he states explicitly that 'it is no part of liberalism, as I understand it, to insist that every group must conform to liberal principles in its internal structure' (Barry 2001: 147). The liberal ideal of freedom of association means 'that individuals should be free to associate together in any way they like', even if the internal rules of the association turn out to be authoritarian, or sexist, or unenlightened in other ways.

However, it soon emerges that, unlike Kukathas, Barry makes freedom of association subject to certain significant provisos. First, 'all the participants must be adults of sound mind' (Barry 2001: 148). Second, even though the state is not entitled to make the internal structure of groups fully liberal, it nevertheless has a duty to provide their members with protection from the most basic offences against the person, such as 'physical injury and marital rape' (Barry 2001: 149). Third, group members must have 'real exit options' open to them, by which Barry means that they are not only negatively free but also genuinely capable of exit, and that the state is prepared to intervene if necessary to relieve them of exit costs as far as possible (Barry 2001: 150–4). Barry's state is thus distinctly more interventionist than Kukathas's, although less so than Kymlicka's, which is entitled to 'liberalize' non-liberal groups comprehensively.

Barry's notion of equal treatment is the most complex part of his theory. In general, he aspires to a political order that is 'neutral' in the sense of 'even-handed', or consistent and fair in its dealings with individuals from whatever group they come (Barry 2001: 29). Barry sees this as implying that individuals will be governed by the same rules, within which they will be free to make their own choices. The ideal is equality of opportunity: each person will have a fair chance to live as they wish, subject to limitations that are, again, fair to everyone.

How does this kind of equality bear on cultural minorities? The mere fact that a rule has a different impact on different individuals or groups does not, in Barry's view, make it unfair. He rejects what is sometimes called 'neutrality of effect' (Mulhall and Swift 1996: 30). Laws against theft have a different effect on those who steal compared with those who do not. Equal treatment cannot require that cultures achieve exactly the same advantages under the rules; inevitably, some will be disadvantaged relative to others because people are different. That is not necessarily unfair.[2]

Furthermore, people are not entitled to special treatment if they already have the same opportunities as others, and for the most part the members of minority groups do have the same opportunities as others. To have an opportunity is not necessarily to take advantage of it. The existence of an opportunity is an objective state of affairs, but various subjective factors may prevent us from taking that opportunity. Jews and Muslims have the opportunity to eat pork but do not do so because of their religious or cultural beliefs. Culture can, in a sense, 'prevent' our taking an opportunity, but that does not cancel out the opportunity itself. So, if our cultural commitments can in this way place us at a 'disadvantage', that is nevertheless consistent with our having the same opportunities as others. Sikhs have the same opportunity as everyone else to ride a motorcycle; it is their own choice if they do not do so because of their religious or cultural beliefs. In general, according to Barry, cultural identity does not disadvantage us in a way that calls for redress in the form of special treatment.

At this point it may seem that the issue between Barry and the defenders of special group rights turns on the question of whether cultural or religious beliefs are chosen or unchosen (Mendus 2002). It is common ground among egalitarian liberals like Barry that people deserve compensation only for disadvantage arising from circumstances for which they are not responsible rather than for disadvantage caused by their own free choices – for the latter the responsibility is theirs alone. No one believes that a person should receive extra resources to satisfy expensive tastes that they affirm freely: there should be no state assistance to enable people to holiday in the Bahamas. On the other hand, few people would object to compensating someone suffering from a physical disability caused by an accident over which they had no control. So, perhaps Barry is saying that cultural or religious beliefs are more like expensive tastes than physical disabilities – that is, that they are freely affirmed rather than simply given by circumstances. In that case, in line with general egalitarian-liberal intuitions, members of cultural and religious groups must take responsibility for the consequences of adhering to their beliefs, and not expect special accommodation or assistance.

If that is Barry's view, then it is open to the objection that cultural and religious beliefs are, at least in many cases, more a product of circumstances than deliberately chosen. Thus Bhikhu Parekh writes that 'in some cases a cultural inability can be overcome with relative ease by suitably re-interpreting the relevant cultural norm or practice; in others it is constitutive of the individual's sense of identity and even of self-respect and cannot be overcome without a deep sense of moral loss' (Parekh 2006: 241). Kymlicka would say something similar: although people are capable of personal autonomy, the culture in which they are brought up is usually the given context within which that autonomy is achieved rather than itself autonomously selected. And if cultural and religious beliefs are not so much chosen as given by circumstances beyond our control, then should we not be compensated for disadvantages arising from them?

However, Barry retorts that this whole line of objection is irrelevant. He agrees that beliefs are generally given rather than chosen (Barry 2001: 35–6). Nevertheless, 'the crucial question is not the origins or revisability of norms and beliefs, but the justifiability of the range of alternatives with which people are confronted' (Barry 2002: 216, also 219). If a cultural minority is disadvantaged by a law or practice that has no 'legitimate public objective' or for which there is 'no objectively good reason', then that minority can justly complain of mistreatment (Barry 2002: 213). So, for example, an employer should not be allowed to prohibit the wearing of culturally or religiously required headscarves at work if the scarf does not prevent the wearer from doing her job (Barry 2002: 216). But when the law in question is justified by a legitimate public objective, Barry is inclined to insist that the minority group comply. Sikhs should comply with the motorcycle helmet law because it has the legitimate purpose of preventing deaths on the road.

This seems admirably decisive, but two matters remain unclear. First, Barry sometimes gives the impression that if a law or practice serves a desirable goal, then that judgement immediately trumps any countervailing consideration. But elsewhere he hints that things may not be so simple. True, preventing deaths on the road is a legitimate public goal, but should we not also consider the *costs* of the helmet policy, which include the costs of complying with it incurred by the Sikh community (Miller 2002)? As we have seen, Barry is sensitive to the question of costs when it comes to the issue of exit from groups, so in consistency should he not also acknowledge that otherwise justified laws may have serious costs, peculiar to cultural minorities, that call for special accommodation?

Indeed, Barry does allow some cases of this kind. For example, he accepts that it would be unreasonable to demand immediate compliance with hard-hat regulations by the approximately 40,000 Sikhs currently working on building sites in the UK if that meant that they would lose their jobs (Barry 2001: 49–50). There is also 'a pragmatic case' for existing exemptions to continue when removing them would be interpreted as an attack on the minority concerned (Barry 2001: 50–1). And again, Barry takes the side of a Sikh schoolboy who was prevented from entering a private school because it banned the turban as part of its policy on uniforms (Barry 2001: 61). In this last case Barry's reasoning is not transparent, but presumably he accepts that the uniform policy is justifiable in general yet the cost of its imposition in this case is too onerous for the Sikh schoolboy, who is presented with a choice between a better education and the abandonment of a religious or cultural practice central to his identity. None of these cases shows that the balance must always be struck on the side of cultural accommodation, but they do seem to show that, even for Barry, cultural considerations can enter into our assessment of the applicability of rules and practices after all.

Barry's view raises a second question. If cultural beliefs can be taken into account when we assess the justification of laws or practices, how exactly should that be done? Barry's general claim is that 'minority cultural claims should be subject to democratic deliberation' or to 'the ordinary process of political decision making' – that is, the weighing of these competing considerations should be open to public discussion (Barry 2002: 213, 214, 321). However, there are certain areas where Barry believes that rights enforceable by the courts are more appropriate than political debate. He mentions access to education and employment (Barry 2002: 216, 219).

How these political and judicial categories are to be distinguished is obscure. According to Barry, cases suitable for democratic resolution involve 'questions in which conflicting considerations have weight and . . . ought therefore to be discussed on their merits, not decided by judges' (Barry 2002: 217). But it is hard to see how issues of education and employment, which Barry assigns to the courts, are not also 'questions in which conflicting considerations have weight'. It seems that Barry's views are in the end not as different from some of those he criticizes as may first appear, since he hints that there may be cases where cultural minorities ought to be accommodated by special rights, like Kymlicka's, and other cases where the accommodation should be the product of a democratic process, as advocated by the thinkers discussed in Chapter 6.

Recognition vs Redistribution?

So far we have seen Barry argue that multiculturalism licenses illiberal practices and betrays the Enlightenment principle of equal treatment. In the final chapter of *Culture and Equality* he adds a further indictment: multiculturalists undermine the most important policy goal of egalitarians, economic redistribution. The problems that should concern contemporary egalitarians are the problems of poverty and lack of opportunity. Cultural recognition is no more than a distraction from these ills, at best irrelevant and at worst a direct impediment.

The 'one pervasive flaw' in all multiculturalist thinking, according to Barry, is its assumption that all groups are defined by 'culture', leading to the conclusion that 'whatever problems a group may face are bound to arise in some way from its distinctive cultural attributes' (Barry 2001: 305). But, he asks, is culture the problem? In some cases it is not a problem at all. Italian-Americans have a minority culture, but they have not needed state recognition to enable them 'to eat pasta, practice Roman Catholicism and play *bocce*' (Barry 2001: 318). Nor has their privately pursued minority culture disadvantaged them economically. On the other hand, African-Americans really have suffered from disproportionate and unfair socio-economic disadvantage, but not because of their culture. Rather, the problem has been racism and its legacy of poor opportunities for education and other resources necessary for gaining access to better jobs. Barry quotes Anthony Appiah: 'Culture is not the problem, and it is not the solution' (Barry 2001: 306).

Worse still, the multiculturalist agenda comes into conflict with redistribution, splitting the egalitarian or progressive movement into rival camps competing for the same public funding. Policies of cultural recognition not only fail to address the real causes of poverty, they can reinforce poverty. The field of language education is one example. From a multiculturalist point of view it may be desirable to support the teaching of 'black English' or 'ebonics', since this will preserve a cultural form and may sustain people's self-respect. But if this policy excludes or neglects education in standard English, it ignores the reality that 'being able to speak and write only in a non-standard form of English is a one-way trip to a dead-end job' (Barry 2001: 324).

Moreover, Barry repeats in this context his earlier concern about 'the abuse of culture', which includes culture-based excuses for the mistreatment of women and children. Although he does not draw the connection explicitly, the point can be made that cultural restrictions on women and children may prevent the development of their specifically economic capacities among other aspects of their potential. Further, the view is now widespread that there is a strong correlation between the emancipation of women in particular and increased prosperity for a society overall (Landes 1999: 412–13). Personal, social and economic development may require liberation from 'the despotism of custom', as Mill expressed it (1859 [1974]: 136). The reinforcement of culture can amount to the entrenchment of economic disadvantage.

However, Barry leaves an opening for multiculturalists by attributing to them the exaggerated view that cultural factors are responsible for '*whatever* problems a group may face' (my emphasis). A moderate multiculturalist can reply that although the problem is not always culture, it sometimes is. Perhaps culture is not the key issue for African-Americans, but it may be for Québécois or for some indigenous peoples.

The theoretical literature on the relationship between redistribution and recognition is now very considerable and it contains a range of different positions.[3] Barry's view stands at one extreme. Towards the opposite extreme are those theorists, like Axel Honneth, who argue that redistribution has been wholly or largely (and rightly) eclipsed by recognition, since the latter is more fundamental or encompassing (Fraser and Honneth 2003). In the middle ground is the view that redistribution and recognition are equally important and that an adequate account of justice must combine them both, a position pioneered by Nancy Fraser (2008).

This middling position comes in two versions (Parekh 2008: 42–3). First, redistribution and recognition may be seen as independently important or 'complementary': each addresses a distinct dimension of injustice and proposes a distinctly appropriate remedy (Parekh 2008: 43). For example, redistribution addresses the poverty and lack of opportunity suffered by some indigenous Australians, but for others – those in the affluent middle class – it may be that (contrary to Barry's view) recognition is more important.

To see redistribution and recognition as distinct goals in this way, however, highlights a practical difficulty: they can come into conflict. The channelling of redistributive assistance to a group may frustrate those of its members who want to be recognized as succeeding through their own efforts. Conversely, to insist on the separate identity of a group may impede that group's claims to redistribution, since people are in general happier about paying taxes for redistribution to the extent that they have feelings of solidarity with the recipients (Miller 1995: 139–40).

It is hard to see how such conflicts can be avoided altogether, but perhaps they can be placed in perspective by attending to the second version of the 'equal importance' thesis. This stresses the degree to which redistribution and recognition may be interdependent on one another. Economic disadvantage and inequality may have cultural causes – for example, the low expectations and lack of self-confidence engendered by the systematic denigration of one's cultural background (Parekh 2008: 48). By the same token, negative images of a culture may arise from its association with poverty and economic inequality. Economic conditions and cultural attitudes can combine in a vicious circle. In such cases measures that tackle material ills are also likely to address cultural disadvantage, and vice versa. Redistribution and recognition are to that extent allies.

But certain kinds of recognition are more in tune with redistribution than others. It depends on what identity is being recognized. This can be brought out by considering the capabilities theory introduced in Chapter 1. Recall that, for Nussbuam and Sen, genuine well-being requires not just resources but also the capability to use them. Capabilities typically have a cultural component. For example, a person's educational capability is only partly realized by the existence nearby of a school or university and the availability of funding to attend. She will not be able to use those resources if she is forbidden to do so by cultural norms – for example, sexist attitudes that confine women to domestic roles. It follows that where recognition takes a conservative form that merely affirms existing cultural limitations on people's opportunities, it will quite likely conflict with redistribution aimed at expanding those opportunities.

Nancy Fraser thus distinguishes between 'affirmative' and 'transformative' forms of recognition, and argues that only the latter is capable of overcoming the tension between recognition and redistribution (Fraser 2008: 28). For Fraser, affirmative recognition, which she associates with 'mainstream multiculturalism', aims at preserving existing cultural identities. Since these include racist and patriarchal elements, they collide with the egalitarian goals of redistribution. On the other hand, 'transformative' recognition challenges conservative notions of identity and so opens the way to patterns of distribution more in keeping with the principles of egalitarians. The woman seeking an education, for example, does not want the affirmative recognition that will keep her at home but rather the transformative recognition that will acknowledge that women's intellectual capacities are equal to men's.

A difficulty with Fraser's view is that she sees transformative recognition as most fully expressed by 'deconstruction' (Fraser 2008: 33–9). This is a species of the postmodernism discussed in Chapter 1, and so suffers from the family curse of extreme relativism. From the perspective of deconstruction, emancipated identities are no more justified than culturally conservative, patriarchal or racist identities. An alternative understanding of transformative recognition, without the hyper-relativism, is provided by the liberal ideal of personal autonomy found in Mill and Kymlicka, for example. On that view, the identity recognized is that which is endorsed by the individual's own critical reflection. While this may turn out to affirm existing cultural patterns, it also may, and often does, lead to the critical revision of cultural commitments.[4]

The upshot is that, contrary to Barry, redistribution and recognition are not necessarily or invariably at loggerheads. There are genuine points of conflict, especially if recognition takes the merely affirmative or conservative form in which existing identities are endorsed, since these may be inegalitarian or limiting. But recognition need not take that form. Indeed, we have already seen a liberal version of recognition championed by Kymlicka, and later I discuss a variety of democratic approaches that emphasize the extent to which recognition involves dialogue (Chapter 6).

Overall, Barry raises some important critical questions about multiculturalist thinking, in particular about the extent to which some versions of multiculturalism satisfy basic liberal concerns for liberty and equality. His critique is often compromised by a tendency to treat all the writers he discusses as saying much the same thing – as if Kymlicka were on the same page as Kukathas and as critics of liberalism such as Iris Young, Bhikhu Parekh and James Tully, whom I discuss later. Certain of these writers are more vulnerable to his objections than others. For example, the worry about groups oppressing individuals than is more of a problem for Kukathas than it is for Kymlicka. Moreover, in various respects some of those he criticizes are closer to his own position than he allows. Nevertheless, there remains an important distinction of broad principle between his old-fashioned privatization approach to cultural minorities and the demand for the political recognition of minorities that is characteristic of multiculturalism proper.

Feminist Concerns: Okin

It has often been noticed that many of the most fraught issues raised by multiculturalism concern the treatment of women and the organization of the family (e.g. Benhabib 2002: 82–6). This subject is discussed in especially forthright terms by Susan Okin. Writing from a liberal-feminist perspective, Okin asks, 'Is Multiculturalism Bad for Women?' (1999). Her answer is an emphatic and almost unqualified 'yes'.[5]

Multiculturalism is basically about the accommodation of cultural or religious minorities. The trouble with this, for Okin, is that the groups accommodated tend to be highly patriarchal. Indeed, 'most cultures have as one of their principal aims the control of women by men' (Okin 1999: 13). This is because the roles women traditionally play in the group, as mothers, educators and guardians of the home, often become central to the group's self-image. To depart from the traditional role is to threaten the whole group's identity. While 'Western liberal cultures' have made a certain amount of progress, by no means complete, in moving away from this pattern, other groups have not. 'Discrimination against and control of the freedom of females are practiced, to a greater or lesser extent, by virtually all cultures, past and present, but especially by religious ones, and those that look to the past – to ancient texts or revered traditions – for guidelines or rules about how to live in the contemporary world' (Okin 1999: 21). In these cases, 'the servitude of women is presented as virtually synonymous with "our traditions"' (Okin 1999: 16).

Examples of the practices endorsed by such groups include clitero-dectomy, polygamy, forced marriage (including rape victims being forced to marry their attacker) and various punishments (including death) for bringing 'dishonour' to the family (Okin 1999: 14–16). Yet the groups that maintain such practices are often the very groups on whose behalf claims for special rights or general toleration are most vigorously pressed. To accommodate such groups is in effect to accept the continuation of illiberal, patriarchal and harmful traditions and practices.

Of course, liberal defenders of cultural accommodation are generally well aware of the problems posed by illiberal groups, and they introduce various qualifications intended to deal with these problems, as we have seen. But Okin finds these moves generally unsatisfactory. In the case of Kukathas's reliance on a right of exit, for example, she complains of its purely negative, formal nature, arguing that the prospect of exit from traditional groups is usually unrealistic. In particular, 'women are far less likely than men to be able to exercise the right of exit' from such groups, which typically place various obstacles in their way, including a degree of socialization that makes exit virtually unthinkable (Okin 2002: 206, 215). Moreover, even if exit is viable, it is not always a satisfying solution. 'Rights of exit provide no help to women or members of other oppressed groups who are deeply attached to their cultures but not to their oppressive aspects' (Okin 2002: 226–7). They want reform rather than exit.

Kymlicka is willing to use the liberal state to reform illiberal minorities, at least in principle, but Okin is not happy with his position either. She recognizes that Kymlicka in effect extends group rights only 'to cultural groups that are internally liberal', withholding rights from 'cultures that discriminate overtly and formally against women – by denying them education or the right to vote or hold office' (Okin 1999: 20, 21). The problem is that 'sex discrimination is often far less overt.' In many cultures, the civil and political liberties of women are formally guaranteed but their freedom and equality is restricted in less formal ways in the 'private' sphere, especially the household. There, the cultural authority of fathers and father-figures, backed by the complicity of older women, often locks younger women and girls into traditional and limiting gendered patterns of behaviour: cooking, cleaning, caring for children, the sick and the elderly. While Kymlicka is right to insist on formal civil and political rights, 'his arguments for multiculturalism fail to register what he acknowledges elsewhere: that the subordination of women is often informal and private, and that virtually no culture in the world today, minority or majority, could pass his "no sex discrimination" test if it were applied in the private sphere' (Okin 1999: 22). Cultural traditions tend to be such strongholds of patriarchy that any measures that might protect them from reform must be questionable.

Even Barry would probably be too accommodationist for Okin. As we saw, Barry insists on the general right of the liberal state to intervene in illiberal groups in order to enforce basic rights of citizenship. But he stops short of extending this kind of intervention to groups whose membership is clearly voluntary – or in other words, groups from which there is a genuine and uncontroversial right of exit, examples including religious bodies like the Catholic Church. Okin is not completely explicit about this, but she seems to advocate an in-principle right on the part of the state to intervene, on behalf of sex equality, even in these cases. So, for example, where Barry would leave the Catholics alone to decide for themselves whether to accept the ordination of women, Okin would argue that the public interest in sexual equality is overriding. In general, Okin offers just two legitimate responses to illiberal groups: either assimilation/integration, or reform. It would be best if such a group 'were either to become extinct (so that its members would become integrated into the less sexist surrounding culture) or, preferably, to be encouraged to alter itself so as to reinforce the equality of women' (Okin 1999: 22–3).

Responses to Okin's argument range from strong expressions of support from like-minded liberals to hostile criticism from more radical multiculturalists. At the more liberal end of the spectrum, several commentators share Okin's basic concern with the oppressive aspects of traditional cultures, and some argue that this should be taken further. Cultural constraints can harm not only women but also other internal minorities including children, homosexuals, the disabled, religious reformers and dissidents of various kinds.[6]

Kymlicka, too, agrees with Okin's concerns about patriarchal traditions, but downplays the extent to which this places feminism and multiculturalism at odds. He allows that many cultural limitations placed on women are of the less overt, more informal kind, imposed within the private sphere, and he agrees that these are as much to be condemned as more formal restrictions. But he describes Okin's wider scepticism towards the whole field of cultural rights as 'regrettable' (Okin 1999: 32). There is, he believes, much common ground between feminism and multiculturalism. Both emphasize the role of social structure as well as formal rules in perpetuating injustice, both point to the relative 'invisibility' of certain groups (identified by gender or culture) in the history of liberal thought, and both propose a new attention to group rights as a remedy for these problems. In short, feminism and multiculturalism should be seen not as opponents but as 'allies engaged in related struggles for a more inclusive conception of justice' (Okin 1999: 34).

Another group of critics, although sharing Okin's concern for women's rights (and for individual liberties more generally), sees her as underestimating the value of cultural identity. Clearly, the claims of the group must be balanced against those of individuals, but group membership itself contributes to individual well-being. 'Culture', writes Bonnie Honig, 'is something more complicated than patriarchal permission for powerful men to subordinate vulnerable women' (Okin 1999: 36). Religion, for example, can provide people with meaning, consolation, moral education, courage in the face of mortality, a sense of community and 'imaginative and emotional fulfilment' (Okin 1999: 106). Cultural identity more generally can have an instrumental value in helping people to survive 'in a hostile or discriminating host culture' (Okin 1999: 77).

The most severe critics of Okin's view are, not surprisingly, those multiculturalists who have the least allegiance to liberalism. Sander Gilman, for example, sees cliterodectomy as merely a non-Western practice that is the functional equivalent of male circumcision, and consequently no more objectionable. Okin's condemnation of cliterodectomy is no more than a biased assault on 'difference', a 'projection of Western, bourgeois notions of pleasure onto other people's bodies' (Okin 1999: 56). Bhikhu Parekh points out that cliterodectomy is accepted as a legitimate practice by many of the women who undergo it. To argue, as Okin does, that these women 'are victims of a culturally generated false consciousness . . . is patronising, even impertinent' (Okin 1999: 73). Similarly, Azizah al-Hibri objects that Okin is speaking from a dominant Western point of view, with the effect that 'the inessential Other . . . is rendered remarkably indistinguishable and voiceless' (Okin 1999: 42).

Okin's response to her critics is lively and, on the whole, effective. The radical critics, in her view, ignore genuine human commonalities and are deaf to the dissident voices *within* cultures. Gilman and Parekh, for example, seem unaware of the physical and psychological harm done by cliterodectomy. Gilman's equation of the practice to male circumcision is grotesquely misleading – the more accurate correspondence would be to 'penidectomy', the removal of the penis (Okin 1999: 124). Parekh's dismissal of socialization as an explanation of the acceptance of cliterodectomy by some women ignores the likelihood of adaptive preferences, and is undermined by his own admission that sometimes women are indeed 'brainwashed' by their cultures (Okin 1999: 126). In reply to the charge of rendering the Other voiceless Okin pointedly asks whether she is 'the silencer of such voices' or whether 'the silencers [are] those feminists who downplay the patriarchy of many variants of their religions' (Okin 1999: 121).

With the more moderate critics she finds more room for agreement, although by and large she maintains her general position. She accepts, for example, that her concerns for women apply also to other vulnerable sub-groups, but notes that the tension between cultural accommodation and gender equality is 'particularly sharp' because 'most cultures are highly gendered' (Okin 1999: 120). She agrees that cultural affiliations are not without value, and consequently that there is a difficult balance to be struck between the claims of culture and those of sub-groups and individuals. Nevertheless, she is more prepared to err on the side of the latter than the former.

This comes out in her reply to Kymlicka, for example. Yes, there are commonalities between feminism and liberal multiculturalism, but these should not blind us to a significant difference: 'The few special rights that women claim qua women do not give more powerful women the right to control less powerful women. In contrast, cultural groups do often (in not-so-obvious ways) reinforce existing hierarchies' (Okin 1999: 131). She concludes that 'what we need . . . is a form of multiculturalism that gives the issues of gender and other intragroup inequalities their due – that is to say, a multiculturalism that effectively treats all persons as each other's moral equals.' There is an implicit concession to cultural accommodation here, but the emphasis on individual liberty and equality remains strong.

Cultural Options: Shachar

An interesting attempt to mediate between Okin's uncompromising liberal-feminist universalism and the concerns of her critics for the value of cultural membership is provided by Ayelet Shachar. In

Multicultural Jurisdictions (2001), Shachar points to what she calls 'the paradox of multicultural vulnerability' (Shachar 2001: 3). By this she means that well-meaning attempts by liberal states to accommodate minority cultures may leave members of those groups 'vulnerable to severe injustice within the group, and may, in effect, work to reinforce some of the most hierarchical elements of a culture' (Shachar 2001: 3). Some members of minority groups tend to be more vulnerable to abuse than others, in effect bearing a 'disproportionate burden' of the costs of multicultural accommodation. Predictably, women are among those most seriously affected in this way, because women play such vital roles – reproductive, caring, educational and symbolic – in the identification and preservation of cultural groups.

Consequently, Shachar opposes 'strong' forms of multiculturalism in which the state authorizes the self-determination of cultural and religious groups even when the group's practices violate the standard liberal citizenship rights of their members. At the level of theory she refers in this connection to the work of thinkers such as Kukathas, James Tully, and Iris Young. However, Shachar does not support a solution in which cultural claims are simply overridden by the norms of the liberal state. Such a 're-universalized citizenship' policy may protect individual rights, but it ignores the value that cultural identity has even for those whose group treats them unfairly (Shachar 2001: 66). Women who continue to identify with their culture under those conditions are not necessarily victims of brainwashing. It may be that for them the group is a source not only of oppression but also of value and meaning; they may reject the norms of the group in some respects but not others.

Can we not do more, Shachar asks, to satisfy 'women and other [minority group] members who legitimately wish to preserve *both* their cultural identities *and* to challenge the power relations encoded within their minority groups' traditions' (Shachar 2001: 71)? One attempt to take this middle way is, of course, Kymlicka's, but Shachar regards his position as incoherent (Shachar 2001: 29–32, also 9 note). According to Shachar, Kymlicka contradicts himself by allowing 'national' groups a power of self-determination unfettered by his usual qualifications in favour of liberal rights. This seems to be a misreading of Kymlicka, for whom national minorities are just as much subject to individual rights as any other group – at any rate in principle. It may be that Shachar has in mind Kymlicka's reservations about *implementing* liberal principles within national minorities, but Kymlicka makes it clear that the implementation of his principles is a separate issue from their validity (Kymlicka 1995a: 164).

Shachar's own solution to the problem is what she calls 'joint governance' (Shachar 2001: ch. 5). This starts with the assumption that people generally have multiple identities rather than a single, dominant identity – they are not primarily either 'citizens' or group members, but both equally and simultaneously. Consequently, the laws or 'jurisdictions' that govern them should be multiple, each coming into play for different purposes, at different times, depending on the details of the situation. No single jurisdiction – neither the state nor the group – will have a monopoly of authority over the individual.

According to Shachar, joint governance may take several different forms, but the one she favours is 'transformative accommodation' (Shachar 2001: ch. 6). Under this system, legal issues will be divided into different 'arenas', such as family law, which will in turn be divided into 'sub-matters', such as marriage, divorce and the distribution of property after divorce. Both the state and the minority group will have rules dealing with some or all of these sub-matters, but neither will claim a monopoly of authority over them. Rather, it will be up to the individual to decide which jurisdiction will deal with her case.

In this way the transformative model will in effect make the state and the group compete with one another for the allegiance of their constituents. This will provide an incentive to traditional groups in particular to adapt their rules in ways that will satisfy their own members. In effect, the system can be used to put pressure on traditional groups to accept reforms on pain of the 'selective' or 'partial' exit (into the alternative jurisdictions) of women and other vulnerable members whose rights are not being respected. Hence, the system is not merely accommodating but 'transformative' – it is intended to provide hitherto vulnerable members of traditional groups with the power to change those groups from the inside. In this way Shachar hopes to combine respect for cultural identity with respect for individual rights.

Shachar's overall stance is optimistic and constructive, inventive and concretely substantiated. Her optimism and constructiveness are seen in her determination to move beyond the familiar critical confrontation between liberalism and culturalism, and to show how women and other vulnerable group members can assert their rights as individuals without sacrificing their cultural identity altogether. Of course, one might question how far this is possible: might the choice between culture and rights not be unavoidable in some cases? This is where her inventiveness comes in, especially her notions of selective exit and incentive to internal reform, although on her own account these ideas are to some extent systematic descriptions of practices already in operation in some places.

Here are some critical questions, though. First, disagreements may arise at various stages of the process. To begin with, disputes can break out between the state and the group when they are negotiating the rules that will govern particular cases: in particular, the initial jurisdictional demarcations (from which individuals can opt out if they choose) and subsequent 'reversal points' – that is, the conditions under which people can opt out. When it comes to defining the reversal points, for example, Shachar proposes the general rule that an individual may opt out if the group 'has failed to offer a meaningful remedy' (Shachar 2001: 135). But of course what counts as 'a meaningful remedy' may well be a subject of intense dispute in negotiations between the group and the state.

Shachar's general principle governing state–group conflicts at the negotiation stage is that a presumption should be raised in favour of group rather than state jurisdiction. This is done to compensate for the fact that in dealings between the state and the group, 'the state is the more powerful entity' (Shachar 2001: 129). But then, in dealings between the group and the individual, Shachar makes it clear that the group is the more powerful entity. So, why should the presumption not be in favour of the state, as the entity best equipped to represent the rights of the individual in the negotiations?

Shachar would probably respond that the pro-group presumption at the stage of rule-making negotiations is offset by what is, in effect, a presumption in favour of the vulnerable individual at the stage of applying the rules in particular cases. On the face of it, the application stage would seem to involve another level of potential disagreement: namely, between individuals – for example, an ex-husband who wants to apply the patriarchal property rules of the group, and an ex-wife, who wants the property settlement to be governed by the more egalitarian laws of the state. When such a reversal point is reached, it appears that transformative accommodation allows the will of the opting-out party (the ex-wife) to prevail.[7]

However, this brings us to a second problem with Shachar's view. Transformative accommodation gives individuals the right to choose, at the application stage, which jurisdiction will deal with their case. But will there not be a danger, especially where the person belongs to a culture in which individual choice is not highly valued, of that choice being manipulated or coerced? For example, how easy will it be for a woman to opt out of group jurisdiction over a post-divorce property settlement when her group strongly believes that this is a realm in which the traditional rules must apply?

Shachar accepts this point as a difficulty for one of the alternative forms of joint governance that she considers – namely, 'consensual accommodation', the chief feature of which is precisely a focus on individual choice of jurisdiction (Shachar 2001: 103–9). In that discussion she lists a number of problems with relying on individual choice, including cases where the person choosing is a child, where there is social pressure and where there is a lack of information. She also suggests that this kind of system mistakenly allows the state to abdicate its responsibility for reform. But if these are valid objections to the consensual model, why are they not valid objections to the consensual component of the transformative model?

A third problem is as follows. Shachar presents the 'transformative' dimension of her view as involving the generation of incentives on the part of groups to reform themselves 'from within' (Shachar 2001: 141–2). The idea is to give the group's leaders reasons to make desirable changes. This is contrasted with attempts by the state to liberalize groups by intervening directly (and perhaps coercively) in their affairs, as envisaged by Kymlicka. However, it might be argued that Shachar underestimates or underplays the extent to which her view will, in practice, require active, and coercive, state intervention in the affairs of groups.

The key to providing groups with an incentive to reform, Shachar says, is that traditionally vulnerable members must be armed with 'a credible threat of exit', even if this is only selective exit (Shachar 2001: 124). It is only when group leaders are faced with the widespread defection of their women members that they will have a reason to change. But the threat of exit will be credible only if the women are 'empowered' to leave, and this is no small matter. As we have seen already, to have a real prospect of exiting from one's culture involves the possession not merely of a formal or negative liberty but a range of capacities. This is confirmed by Shachar. Women can strengthen their 'bargaining position' in relation to the group only if 'they have acquired the basic capacities needed to live effectively outside it' (Shachar 2001: 138). For this the mere existence of 'outside courts' is not enough. They need 'tools, knowledge, and resources', including 'guaranteed access to minimal material protections, as well as to other capacity-enhancing resources (educational, legal, institutional, and so on)' (Shachar 2001: 138–9).

On this point the logic of Shachar's position seems to converge with that of liberals like Kymlicka who make cultural diversity subject to an overarching concern for the value of personal autonomy.[8] That means that the implications of Shachar's view are perhaps more pro-state and less accommodating of cultural minorities than she supposes. This is not necessarily a criticism, however. As Shachar would acknowledge, the proper accommodation of cultural diversity is a matter of striking a desirable balance between three distinct and often contending parties: state, group and individual. The balance struck by Shachar's 'transformative accommodation' model may lean rather more towards the individual and the state than she realizes, but that is not to say that she has not got it right.

Summary

Kymlicka's liberal critics raise questions about cultural recognition that need to be taken seriously. Barry alleges that multiculturalism has betrayed the legacy of the Enlightenment, leaving individuals at the mercy of illiberal group norms, departing from fair standards of equal treatment and distracting egalitarians from their proper business of economic redistribution. Okin warns of the potential in policies of group recognition to reinforce patriarchal traditions that restrict and harm women. But while these criticisms strike telling blows against the kind of 'strong' multiculturalism that relativizes individual rights and liberties, they are less decisive against the liberal multiculturalism for which Kymlicka stands. Moreover, Shachar shows how it may be possible to add to the liberal-multiculturalist repertoire by enabling people to opt into or out of rival cultural-legal spheres.

4

Nationalists and Cosmopolitans

One of the standard objections to multiculturalism is that it undermines the sense of common citizenship that is essential to social cohesion. In particular, multiculturalism is often accused of destroying a shared national identity. At the same time, however, we saw in Chapter 2 that the liberal multiculturalism of Kymlicka is itself a nationalist view of sorts, since it champions the claims of national minorities within larger states.

Two questions arise here. First, why should we pay so much attention to national *minorities* in contrast with the overarching nationalism of the majority in a society? Second, what is so important about *national* identities, of whatever kind, as opposed to other dimensions of identity? If culture as such is valuable, then perhaps 'there is no basis for the theorist to privilege national cultures over immigrant ones' (Benhabib 2002: 66).[1] Indeed, why accord national identity any moral weight at all? Does it not make more sense – especially if we accept the bedrock liberal commitment to the moral equality of all human beings – to regard nationality as simply a matter of accident, and to give ethical priority to our commonality with all other human beings?

In this chapter I examine a range of responses to these questions. First, I briefly consider the relation between cultural diversity and nationalism in general. Second, I investigate a school of thought within the liberal tradition that usually stresses the importance of majority nationalism in contrast with Kymlicka's concern for national minorities: the 'liberal nationalism' foreshadowed by John Stuart Mill and exemplified more recently by David Miller and Yael Tamir. All these writers acknowledge the value or at least the reality of national identity from a liberal perspective, but they differ in the balance they recommend between majority and minority nationalities and between national and other kinds of identity.

Third, I go on to discuss the 'cosmopolitan' alternative that places limits on the importance of national identities in the face of our universal duties to humanity at large. Here I consider both the 'strong' cosmopolitanism of Kant and Jeremy Waldron, in which nationality carries little or no ethical weight, and the more moderate views of Anthony Appiah and Amartya Sen, who allow that nationality is an especially significant form of identity but insist that it should not become overriding. In all cases I shall, of course, be especially interested in the extent to which each position responds to the idea of multicultural accommodation.

Nationalism and Cultural Diversity

A basic understanding of nationalism in general is provided by David Miller, who sees the idea of 'nationality' as consisting of three main components (Miller 1993: 5–6). First, there is the idea that the widespread tendency of people to identify themselves with a particular national group is legitimate and important. Second, national identity has ethical implications, including the notion that people have special obligations towards their fellow-nationals that they do not have towards outsiders. Third, there are political implications too, the most important being that national groups generally have some claim to 'self-determination', often, although not necessarily, in the form of statehood.

Looking more closely at the first of these components, national identity, Miller sees this as having the following main features, which may be present in greater or lesser degrees in particular cases: a dependence on belief – the nation is constructed through a 'daily plebiscite', in Ernest Renan's famous phrase; a sense of historical continuity, in which the national community is seen to stretch backward and forward in time, involving shared memories and goals; an element of active agency – 'nations are communities that do things together, take decisions, achieve results, and so forth'; an affinity with a particular 'homeland', place or territory; and possession of 'a common public culture' – 'there must be a sense that the people belong together by virtue of the characteristics that they share' (Miller 1995: 22–5).

This last element, a common national culture, suggests the key issue that nationalism raises for multiculturalism: how far is nationalism compatible with the accommodation of multiple cultures? For Miller, the common culture required for national identity need not be 'monolithic and all-embracing', but rather may leave room for 'a diversity of ethnic groups' and 'private cultures' to 'flourish within the boundaries of the nation' (Miller 1995: 25–6). However, this is truer of some forms of nationalism than others.

One basic contrast may be drawn between non-liberal and liberal kinds of nationalism.[2] Non-liberal nationalisms tend to regard a given nation as not only valuable to the well-being of its members but valuable in itself, possessing an 'organic' existence separate from, and more important than, that of its individual members. On this view, roughly speaking, the nation has ethical priority over the individual and over other groups. Liberal nationalism, on the other hand, conceives the nation as valuable not in itself but as (at best) instrumental to the well-being of its individual members, its claims therefore subject to individual rights and liberties.

The prospects for multiculturalism are clearly limited under non-liberal nationalism. This is most obvious in the case of those extreme or totalitarian forms of nationalism that have done so much to give nationalism as a whole a bad name: the Fascism and Nazism of the twentieth century. In these ideologies, not only is the nation conceived as an organic entity with an intrinsic value separate from and superior to the value of its individual members, but further, a particular nation is seen as inherently superior to all other nations and groups, and as licensed to rule them by force (Griffin 1995). The nation and the state that expresses it politically are all-encompassing, demanding total loyalty and uniformity of purpose. Clearly there is little if any room for cultural diversity within such a system in principle, and actual totalitarian policies towards minority groups such as Jews and Gypsies show that there was precious little accommodation in practice.

An alternative kind of non-liberal nationalism that at least deserves a hearing is conservative nationalism, as found, in embryo, in the writings of Edmund Burke, for example (Burke 1790 [1970]). Here there is again the organic conception of the nation and the state and a strong sense that these have a reality that is more permanent and morally elevated than that of the individuals who pass through them in their successive generations. But the totalitarian insistence on the complete superiority of particular nations, and on the legitimacy of their self-appointed missions of violent domination is not essential to the conservative view. Rather, the key conservative-nationalist commitment is to the nation-state understood as the principal bearer of a society's tradition. This need not be thought of as superior to the traditions of others, still less as having a mission for world conquest. What is essential is that the authority of the state and of other established institutions be accepted as expressing a moral, social and political order that should be changed, or even questioned, only with the utmost care. These institutions and the values they embody are the repository of the wisdom of generations.

When it comes to responding to cultural diversity, conservative nationalism will no doubt be more accommodating than totalitarianism, but the degree of accommodation will still be very limited. On this model, all citizens will be expected to pledge allegiance to a substantial national identity, involving an uncritical acceptance of its traditional institutions, values and myths, and a corresponding repudiation of alternative cultural inheritances. In such a society immigration will be either discouraged or highly selective of those most likely to fit a relatively narrow cultural or racial profile – the 'White Australia' policy is an example (Jayasuriya 2007). Indigenous groups might be admired in principle for their own fidelity to tradition, but in practice still pressured to abandon this in favour of the dominant national tradition. In short, this approach is strongly assimilationist.

The problem with the conservative approach is that identities are arguably more fluid than conservatives allow. Indeed, conservative thinkers often seem unaware of the degree to which the so-called 'traditions' they defend are really no more than relatively recent inventions – a minor but striking example is the Highland clan tartan, which actually dates only to the nineteenth century (Trevor-Roper 1992: 18–19). Indeed, whole national identities may properly be regarded as 'imagined' in the sense that they are culturally constructed rather than primordial (Anderson 2006). This does not mean that they are necessarily less 'authentic' than other identities or that they have no ethical force at all. It does mean that the conservative view is mistaken so far as it insists on seeing national identities as fixed, unchanging essences; rather, they are fluid and permeable. Their content is consequently open to critical examination rather than closed by uncritical veneration, and subject to negotiation among the different groups that have a stake in them. Immigration, on this view, need not be a problem unless it involves large groups that are wholly unwilling to integrate (Miller 1995: 128–9).[3]

A more fundamental problem common to all the non-liberal forms of nationalism is their tendency to regard the nation (and often the state too) as having an 'organic' existence and value apart from that of the individuals who people it. It may be reasonable to think of the nation or state as having its own personality in a highly metaphorical sense, as a way of emphasizing the idea of historical continuity. But this way of thinking becomes dangerous when it is taken too literally and leads people to allow the supposed purposes of the collectivity to override individual rights. Avoiding this problem is a central concern of liberal interpretations of nationalism.

Liberal Nationalism: Mill, Miller and Tamir

Liberal nationalists combine a commitment to the central importance of national identity with a liberal insistence on the rights and liberties of individuals. The idea that these views can be reconciled was commonplace in the nineteenth century, when national liberation movements in Europe and elsewhere simply assumed that national self-determination was a natural outgrowth of the liberal ideal of individual self-determination (Mazzini 1907 [1966]). In the wake of the extreme nationalisms of the twentieth century, however, nationalism of any kind has fallen out of favour with many liberals. The onus has fallen on those who want to recover a nationalist link to make their case more explicitly.

Within liberal nationalism there are two main lines of argument, separable for analytical purposes although not always neatly separated by particular liberal nationalists. The first, realist or pragmatic line regards national identities as simply 'a brute fact' about the modern world (Margalit and Raz 1995: 86). These identities may be primitive and irrational, indefensible by the best reasoning, but liberal and other enlightened thinkers cannot afford to ignore them. Rather, we must accept their reality and likely survival, and work round them. This view is found, for example, in J. S. Mill, who looks forward to the day when national differences will be transcended, but accepts that this is impossible 'in the present state of civilization' (Mill 1861 [1958]: 232).[4]

The second, 'ethical' stream in liberal nationalism takes a more positive view of national identity, regarding it as not merely a grim fact about the world, but as capable of working to the benefit of individual well-being. For one thing, people fare best when they receive the respectful recognition of those around them, and part of what they want recognized is the group they belong to, including the national group (Taylor 1994; Berlin 2002: 200–3). In addition, some liberals argue that individual autonomy links naturally with collective autonomy: to have control over one's life requires being able to express that control, at least to some degree, in the public realm and therefore politically (Kedourie 1961). Self-rule at the individual level connects with self-rule at the democratic level.

So far it might seem that, in either version, liberal nationalism can easily acknowledge and accommodate cultural diversity. The realists or pragmatists can regard diversity, too, as a fact about the world, and the ethicists can factor sub-group membership into their account of the individual well-being that qualified nationalism is said to serve. However, liberal nationalists have not always been entirely happy with cultural diversity.

J. S. Mill, for example, can be regarded as a precursor to the contemporary liberal nationalists, but he is positively hostile to the multination state. For Mill, as noted above, the powerful role that national identity plays in people's lives is something to be accepted as a reality rather than celebrated as a good. Further, there is a prima facie case for each nation to have its own government – this is simply an expression of freedom of association. But one of the implications of national self-government, according to Mill, is that it is unwise to have multiple nations under the same government. This is especially so where 'free institutions' – individual liberties and democratic structures – are at stake. 'Free institutions are next to impossible in a country made up of different nationalities' (Mill 1861 [1958]: 230). Such institutions depend on a 'united public opinion', by which Mill seems to mean a common culture: the same leaders, sources of information, interests, values and assumptions. Where that commonality is lacking and the population is divided into distinct nationalities, 'their mutual antipathies are generally much stronger than jealousy of the government' (Mill 1861 [1958]: 231). The national groups will be too busy competing with one another to preserve the freedoms of individuals – indeed, the groups may well undermine those freedoms for their own strategic purposes.

Moreover, it may be a good thing from the perspective of universal progress if more 'backward' cultures are assimilated into more advanced or 'superior' nationalities. In a much-quoted passage Mill writes that it is better for a Breton or Basque

> to be brought into the current of the ideas and feelings of a highly civilized and cultivated people – to be a member of the French nationality, admitted on equal terms to all privileges of French citizenship, sharing the advantages of French protection and the dignity and prestige of French power – than to sulk on his own rocks, the half-savage relic of past times, revolving in his own little mental orbit, without participation or interest in the general movement of the world. (Mill 1861 [1958]: 234)

Mill is clearly more of a 'majority' than a 'minority' nationalist – although for him it is not numbers but 'civilization' that counts – and more of a cosmopolitan than either. What matters for him above all is human progress. The kind of liberal nationalism that he represents is lukewarm, pragmatic and expressly antipathetic to strong cultural divisions within the same political society.

A qualification is in order, though. Mill is opposed to strong *national* divisions within a society; it is not so obvious that he objects to other kinds of cultural minority, in particular the immigrant or 'ethnic' identities distinguished by Kymlicka. Indeed, the case he presents for 'individuality' in *On Liberty* suggests that he would support the valuing of such identities as long as individual autonomy was not impeded (Mill 1859 [1974]: ch. 3).[5] Perhaps we should conclude that Mill's view of cultural diversity is mixed: he is hostile to multinationalism but may be more willing to accommodate ethnic minorities – almost the opposite of Kymlicka's position. Moreover, the accommodation he offers would remain within the classical liberal framework of toleration or privatization of cultures rather than the official recognition characteristic of multiculturalism proper.

By contrast, David Miller reverses this emphasis in his version of liberal nationalism, arguing that immigrant communities are adequately accommodated by privatization but showing a willingness to extend public recognition to national minorities. In *On Nationality* (1995), Miller sees nationality as a valid and important component of modern individual identity. National identity is especially important for generating a shared sense of justice, mutual obligation and trust among the members of large, impersonal modern societies. In particular, policies aimed at achieving social justice through programmes of redistributive taxation depend on the kind of bond that only nationality is capable of providing on this scale; in its absence people would be likely to insist on 'strict reciprocity' (Miller 1995: 71–2, 83, 98).

When it comes to drawing out the political implications of nationality, Miller states his basic principle as national self-determination: 'as far as possible, each nation should have its own set of political institutions which allow it to decide collectively those matters that are the primary concern of its members' (Miller 1995: 81). This is only a general principle, and there will be some cases where it cannot or should not be implemented. Further, it need not be implemented in the form of a state; less complete forms of self-determination may be appropriate in particular cases. Nevertheless, Miller follows Mill in registering a general preference for the nation-state. Nations usually need states to protect and express them, and states should usually take as their focus a single dominant national identity.

However, Miller believes that the nation-state can accommodate cultural pluralism. On the one hand he rejects conservative forms of nationalism as too rigid, narrow and exclusive; on the other he opposes the 'radical multiculturalism' of Iris Young as too fragmented and divisive (Miller 1995: 131–40). (I discuss Young's view in Chapter 6.) Between these extremes Miller steers a middle course to a broadly liberal view.[6] The state will be animated by a central national identity, thicker than a merely 'civic' commitment to a set of universally valid institutions and values, but capacious enough to be 'accessible to all cultural groups' within the society (Miller 1995: 141). Such an identity 'is expressed partly through allegiance to a body of principles embedded in the Constitution, but also includes the more concrete ideas of common membership and shared history that are essential to nationality' (Miller 1995: 141–2).

This kind of identity can still be acceptable to people from many different cultural backgrounds. Indeed, a core national identity is positively essential to a multicultural society in order to motivate a shared sense of justice, trust and co-operation across such differences, as mentioned already (Miller 1995: 139–40). Before it can play this role it must be 'stripped of elements that are repugnant to the self-understanding of one or more component groups, while members of those groups must themselves be willing to embrace an inclusive nationality, and in the process to shed elements of *their* values which are at odds with its principles' (Miller 1995: 142). There has to be give and take on both sides. But this is possible, and there are real-world examples to prove it. The United States, for instance, has combined a strong sense of nationalism, which cannot be summed up in terms of its abstract values alone, with a capacity to integrate people from many different cultures. Many of these retain something of their traditional affiliations, becoming 'hyphenated' Americans: Italian-Americans, Greek-Americans and so forth.

So, Miller wants to be accommodating to cultural minorities, but how far is he willing to go? Traditional liberal toleration or privatization is certainly on the menu, but what about multiculturalism proper, meaning positive public recognition? To some extent Miller follows Kymlicka, first by accepting the distinction between national and ethnic minorities, and then by according the former much stronger rights than the latter. That national minorities should have self-determination rights simply tracks the logic of Miller's basic view: if a group counts as a nation, then it has a prima facie case for self-government. For Miller, such rights extend all the way to secession given the right set of conditions, which include irreconcilable differences with the majority, viability as an independent state and the allaying of concerns for new minorities that are created either within the seceding nation or within the rump left behind. Short of these conditions being met, a national minority may be entitled to 'partial autonomy' within the existing state, as in the case of the Catalans and Basques in Spain and the Lapps and Saami people in the north of Scandinavia (Miller 1995: 115–16).

Where Miller departs from Kymlicka, however, is in his resistance to any special rights for ethnic or migrant minorities. The claims at stake include both 'substantive' rights, as Miller calls them – special exemptions, protections and resources – and 'political' rights such as the group representation advocated by Iris Young. The former are rejected by Miller using arguments much like those of Barry – these are claims that conflict with equality of citizenship; the latter, the political rights, he condemns as narrow, dogmatic and divisive (Miller 1995: 146–54).

Miller's strong preference for self-determination rights for national minorities over polyethnic rights for other cultural minorities is logical given his emphasis on nationality, but perhaps ironic too. Like other liberal nationalists, Miller stresses the value of national identity in part because of its unifying potential, in Miller's version linked strongly to social justice goals. Yet extending self-determination to national minorities within a state is arguably a more divisive move than granting polyethnic rights to other groups – or at least a more ambiguous move. So, for example, a self-determining Scotland may be more unified internally, but at the price of foregoing some of the sense of community, and as a result some redistributive programmes, previously shared with the rest of the United Kingdom. By contrast, the main purpose and effect of polyethnic rights is integrative, helping immigrant groups to find their own niche within a new society. Indeed, polyethnic rights can be justified as required for the social justice that Miller says is served by nationalism. So, although Miller's liberal nationalism is closer to multiculturalism than that of Mill, perhaps it should go further still.

Yael Tamir, an Israeli political theorist and active politician, would agree. In *Liberal Nationalism*, which was first published in 1993, Tamir presents a liberal case for nationalism that is much like Miller's. But in a new Preface added in 1995, apparently influenced by Iris Young's 'politics of difference', she departs from Miller in two key respects. First, Tamir would extend special group rights beyond the national groups acknowledged by Miller to include other minorities. The rights in question will not be as strong as self-determination entitlements; on the other hand they may be stronger in some cases than the polyethnic rights ascribed to ethnic minorities by Kymlicka.

Further, it is not only ethnic minorities that will be accommodated in this way. Specifically, Tamir approves of 'Young's demand that institutionalized means be provided for the explicit recognition and representation of oppressed or disadvantaged groups' – which on Young's account include women and the gay and lesbian communities among others (Tamir 1995: xxviii). Tamir's cultural accommodation goes well beyond Miller's and even beyond Kymlicka's.

Tamir's accommodation is by no means open-ended. She immediately insists, against Young, that the special rights be framed and regulated by 'liberal principles as the basis of political discussion and decision making' (Tamir 1995: xxviii). Without such a framework, multiculturalism threatens to disintegrate into an interest-group free-for-all in which the weaker groups will be dominated by the stronger.

This leads to a second contrast with Miller. While Miller believes that the unifying framework must include not only general 'civic' principles but also a substantial national identity (invoking a shared history, for example), Tamir holds that a shared civic identity is sufficient – indeed, all that can be expected or justified in the face of contemporary social diversity. She backs this up with a parallel distinction between national and civic education, arguing for 'a thin layer of civic education, introducing children to the liberal discourse of rights and rationality' (Tamir 1995: xxix). Beyond this, instruction in thicker forms of identity should be in the hands of particular groups. All this is in line with Tamir's more general view that citizenship should be distinguished from nationality, that one's national identity should not determine one's rights as a citizen.[7]

Is Tamir's version of liberal nationalism better than Miller's? Arguably it is more consistent. She has a stronger sense that if national identities are valuable for human well-being, generating feelings of belonging and solidarity, then the same can be said of other group identities too. On the other hand it is one thing to appreciate that identities have value, but another to insist that they be accorded public recognition. Here Kymlicka's distinction between national and non-national claims might be reinforced with a further argument. Unlike other groups, a nation 'at its core, is political' (Moore 2001: 66). To possess a Scottish national identity, for example, is necessarily to belong to a community with claims to some level of self-determination. Claims like these can be properly expressed only through public recognition. When it comes to other group identities, however – religious, ethnic or cultural – it is not so obvious that state recognition is essential. As Barry points out, many such groups have succeeded in valuing their heritage and maintaining their identity without the intervention of the state. This does not mean that special rights for non-national groups are never justified (or that the recognition of national groups is always justified); it means only that the case that has to be made for non-national groups is different from that of national groups and perhaps more demanding. When Miller stops short of Tamir's blanket endorsement of rights for minority groups his position is not unreasonable.[8]

What about Tamir's second departure from Miller, her claim that a thin 'civic' identity is sufficient for citizenship compared with a more substantial identification with, for example, a shared history? Here, too, Tamir's position can be questioned. For most of the liberal defenders of nationality, including Tamir herself, part of its value is that it supplements the universal and abstract principles of liberalism with more particularist and emotional bonds – helping to motivate commitment to redistribution, for example (Tamir 1995: 10, 117–21). That central rationale would seem to be undermined if citizenship is reduced to a set of generic principles.[9] Indeed, the question arises whether in Tamir's hands there is much left of liberal nationalism that is truly distinctive. Once she advocates the recognition of multiple non-national identities while at the same time reducing the overarching citizenly identity to acceptance of a set of generic civic principles, what remains of the original focus on 'the nation'? How far there should be such a focus at all is a question pressed by the cosmopolitans.

Cosmopolitanism

Cosmopolitanism can be analysed into three principal components corresponding to those applied by Miller to nationalism: identity, ethics and politics. First, cosmopolitans emphasize the importance of identification not with the nation or other particular groups but with humanity at large. The word cosmopolitan comes from the Greek *cosmopolis*, the world city, and the concept of cosmopolitanism is usually traced back to the ancient Greek philosopher Diogenes the Cynic. In reaction against the Greek custom of close identification with one's own city or *polis*, Diogenes is reputed to have declared 'I am a citizen of the world.'[10] But that does not mean that all cosmopolitans dismiss all sub-universal identities as irrelevant or unimportant, as we shall see.

Second, cosmopolitans typically hold that to identify with humanity is to give priority to ethical obligations that are universal rather than particular. In contrast with nationalists, cosmopolitanism questions the idea of special duties to one's fellow-nationals that exclude or override duties to human beings whoever and wherever they may be. As Martha Nussbaum writes, it is the community of humanity 'that is, fundamentally, the source of our moral obligations', and 'the accident of where one is born is just that, an accident; any human being might have been born in any nation' (Nussbaum 1996: 7). Again, though, this is not to say that cosmopolitans necessarily reject special duties altogether.

Third, what kind of politics is implied by a cosmopolitan outlook? Appiah notes the possibility of 'ruthless' or 'toxic' forms of cosmopolitanism in which radical or reactionary political programmes are commended and imposed universally, with 'repugnant' results – he cites the radical Islamists of 'September 11' as an example (Appiah 2005: 220). But although the agents of Al-Qaeda are certainly universalists of a sort, it seems odd to describe them as 'cosmopolitans'. That is because cosmopolitanism involves not just a programme for humanity but identification with humanity. This suggests an element of taking people as one finds them, accepting them and their values at some level, respecting them and being prepared to learn from them.

Hence, there appears to be a degree of cultural accommodation built into the very concept of cosmopolitanism. On the other hand, cosmopolitanism is not merely relativism. To adopt the perspective of a 'citizen of the world' is not to accept that any local set of customs or politics is just as good as any other. On the contrary, some local outlooks stand condemned by cosmopolitans if only because they are anti-cosmopolitan – they deny moral obligations or even moral status to anyone but their own people.

Cosmopolitanism, then, takes a universal view of human affairs, but one that claims to be sensitive to, and appreciative of, legitimate differences among nations and cultures. This immediately suggests a possible affinity with liberal forms of multiculturalism, and with liberalism in general. Indeed, one of the most frequently cited names in the cosmopolitan pantheon is that of Kant (1795 [1991]).

The claim that liberal cosmopolitanism provides a satisfying balance between univeralism and particularity will be provocative to those critics who deny that liberalism is an adequate vehicle for multicultural accommodation, and who would see it as, at base, ethnocentric. But I shall postpone discussion of that debate to the next chapter. For the time being, I shall simply assume that when we are talking about cosmopolitanism we are talking about a basically liberal form of politics.

Different versions of cosmopolitanism might be roughly divided between two broad tendencies, stronger and weaker (or moderate).

Stronger versions hold either that identification with humanity is the only morally relevant form of human identity, or that it always overrides local or particular identities, or perhaps that it embraces or subsumes all such identities. Weaker or more moderate forms of cosmopolitanism concede a greater role to sub-universal identifications, in particular to certain especially prominent kinds of identity, such as nationality.

Strong Cosmopolitanism: Kant and Waldron

Kant can serve as an initial representative of the stronger kind of cosmopolitanism. In Kantian thought there is an emphasis on the role in morality of reason in contrast with the passions: to act rightly is to be guided by one's reason, which must control the potentially unruly or distracting desires and emotions (Kant 1785 [1956]). This general theme translates readily into a preference for the universal over the particular: reason is universal, one's emotions are particular. While we may be tempted to satisfy our own particular desires, to do the morally right thing is to act in accordance with a rule that is universalizable – a rule that we can accept under any conditions, no matter whose desires are at stake. So, a Kantian cosmopolitanism looks like asking us to separate ourselves from emotion-laden allegiances, such as those to our nation and culture, to rise above these and endorse as our moral and political model a set of universal rules that are completely impersonal and consistent among different people and groups. On this model, the universal decisively trumps the particular.[11]

Many people would say, however, that Kantian cosmopolitanism is too demanding. At an empirical level most people find it hard to occupy the universal high-ground consistently. People generally believe that they have special relationships with those nearest to them, or with those with whom they share a particular interest or purpose or identity, and such relationships generate special duties. At a more philosophical level contemporary communitarians argue that when Kantians ask us to stand back impartially from our personal and local allegiances they ask us to do what is not only practically but also conceptually impossible. We cannot think of ourselves as 'unencumbered' selves, separate or separable from our particular commitments and identities, because these commitments and identities are constitutive of who we are (Sandel 1982; Taylor 1985; 1989). If the reality is that our personalities are unavoidably constructed by our particular affiliations, then the notion of rising above these would be incoherent.[12]

Could there be a version of cosmopolitanism that meets these objections – that adequately acknowledges the particularity of people's identities – yet remains recognizably at the stronger end of the cosmopolitan spectrum? An interesting candidate is the position set out by Jeremy Waldron in his article, 'Minority Cultures and the Cosmopolitan Alternative' (1995). Waldron's cosmopolitanism acknowledges the importance of particular identities in people's lives, but emphasizes the fact that modern identities are constructed out of a multiplicity of different cultural sources, creating lives of 'kaleidoscopic tension and variety' (Waldron 1995: 94). None of these sources is intrinsically more significant or valuable or authentic than any other – nationality is no more significant than tastes in food or entertainment – and we are capable of combining them in all sorts of ways. Social policy should not attempt to arrest this fluidity, yet that is the tendency of theories that stress ethnic or national particularity. On this basis Waldron is especially critical of Kymlicka's case for minority cultures, but his view might equally be directed against Miller's liberal nationalism.

Waldron agrees with Kymlicka that culture provides an essential context for meaningful choice, but denies that this role must be played by a single overarching culture for each person (Kymlicka's notion of the 'societal culture'). In the modern world people are subject to many different cultural influences, none of which subsumes or overrides all the others. Though a modern person

> may live in San Francisco and be of Irish ancestry, he does not take his identity to be compromised when he learns Spanish, eats Chinese, wears clothes made in Korea, follows Ukrainian politics, and practices Buddhist meditation techniques. He is a creature of modernity, conscious of living in a mixed-up world and having a mixed-up self. (Waldron 1995: 95)

Continued membership of one particular culture, so far as we can even identify such a distinct entity, does not have the importance Kymlicka claims for it. 'To put it crudely, we need culture, but we do not need cultural integrity' (Waldron 1995: 108).

Moreover, to attempt as a matter of public policy to preserve cultures is not only unnecessary but harmful, even on Kymlicka's own terms. Kymlicka's case for cultural preservation is based on the value of culture as a context for autonomous individual choice. But choice of this kind involves not merely reference to a given cultural framework but the evaluation of that framework itself. That in turn involves critical comparison of one's culture with the alternatives. The upshot is that choice is promoted not by 'securing' or 'insulating' cultures from challenge and change, but the very opposite: by opening them up to such challenges (Waldron 1995: 109).

Overall, Waldron regards theories of cultural particularity and preservation as potentially dangerous – he singles out ethnonationalist theories as especially troubling in this regard – or at best as exercises in nostalgia. The reality of the modern world is that traditional, self-sufficient communities are things of the past, and all ways of life are interconnected. Indeed, there is a sense in which small communities are now parasitic on larger societies, so that to insist on special rights for the former 'is like demanding the funds to live in Disneyland and the protection of modern society for the boundaries of Disneyland, while still managing to convince oneself that what happens inside Disneyland is all there is to an adequate and fulfilling life' (Waldron 1995: 101).

Contrary to the more demanding communitarians and multiculturalists, and even to liberal nationalists like Miller, Waldron argues that the life of the traditional community is, under modern conditions, deeply inauthentic. It pretends to a self-sufficiency and moral authority it can no longer possess. Rather, 'the only appropriate response to the modern world in which we live' is cosmopolitanism (Waldron 1995: 100). For Waldron, the cosmopolitan outlook is embodied by the novelist Salman Rushdie (significantly, condemned by religious fundamentalists) and his 'migrant's-eye view of the world'. Rushdie's controversial novel *The Satanic Verses* 'celebrates hybridity, impurity, intermingling, the transformation that comes of new and unexpected combinations of human beings, cultures, ideas, politics, movies, songs. It rejoices in mongrelization and fears the absolutism of the Pure. *Mélange*, hotchpotch, a bit of this and a bit of that is how newness enters the world' (Rushdie quoted by Waldron 1995: 93).

Precisely what policies best express this view Waldron does not say beyond making it clear that he strongly opposes the general direction taken by Kymlicka's case for special group rights. So presumably he would reject the kind of self-determination rights Kymlicka and Miller propose for national minorities – or at least he would accept such rights only on condition that the indigenous and national groups that claim them are willing 'to recognize their dependence on the wider social, political, international, and civilizational structures that sustain them' (Waldron 1995: 103, emphasis omitted). He would have less reason to reject Kymlicka's 'polyethnic' rights, since these do no more than assist groups to integrate into the social mainstream.

Kymlicka's general response to Waldron's critique is conciliatory. He accepts that modern cultures tend to be cosmopolitan, but denies that this prevents them from being distinct. The Québécois who eats Chinese and listens to Italian opera is still identifiably a Québécois; all this shows is that the Québécois belongs to a societal culture that 'is an open and pluralistic one, which borrows whatever it finds worthwhile in other cultures, integrates it into its own practices, and passes it on to [its] children' (Kymlicka 1995b: 8). Similarly, cultural protection need not be thought of as excluding all change. Minority rights do not have to be seen as attempts to perpetuate a culture that is 'authentic' in the sense of fossilized.

What about the objection, mentioned earlier, that the cosmopolitan vision is incoherent because the cosmopolitan self at its heart is impossible: either chaotic to the point of schizophrenia or dependent for its integrity on some implausibly abstract and bloodless conception of the 'unencumbered' self? Waldron anticipates this and replies that it is possible to conceive of the cosmopolitan person 'managing' her commitments and influences in a non-hierarchical way (Waldron 1995: 110–12). What he has in mind is that no particular commitment or identity is inherently weightier or more authentic than any other; nevertheless, people are capable of sorting these out within their own lives. He does not develop this view in detail, but it is in keeping with contemporary liberal understandings of personal autonomy as a process of piecemeal critical reflection rather than the discovery of a pre-existing 'true self' (Benn 1988; Christman 1991).

A final line of criticism is that the ideal cosmopolitan person commended by Waldron, although not logically incoherent or psychologically disturbed, is nevertheless an elitist creature whose habits and values are peculiar to a certain kind of international professional. Rushdie and Waldron might look at the world in this 'migrant's-eye' way as they go back and forth between engagements, accumulating frequent-flyer points, 'yet how many humans travel in this relaxed and reflective manner between cultures, sensing their own hybridity and reflecting on their enriched contingent cosmopolitanism? Very few, one suspects' (Vincent 2002: 219).

Waldron would reply that the cosmopolitan need not be a migrant or refugee or frequent flyer, and could very well live in the same place throughout his life. The key feature of the cosmopolitan is not where he lives but the fact that 'he refuses to think of himself as defined by his location or his ancestry or his citizenship or his language' (Waldron 1995: 95). Point taken, but does this shake the objection? How many people regard these identifying features as no more important than whether they eat Chinese food or listen to Italian opera? Are all identities really on the same level? The suspicion remains that, despite Waldron's refreshing scepticism when it comes to the claims of traditional cultures and his up-to-date realism about the reach of global culture, he does not give cultural and, especially, national particularity their due.

Narrative and Reason in Cosmopolitanism: Appiah and Sen

If Waldron's kaleidoscopic view does not do justice to the status of national identity, is there a form of cosmopolitanism that does? One possibility is the 'rooted' or 'partial' cosmopolitanism advocated by Anthony Appiah in *The Ethics of Identity* (2005) and *Cosmopolitanism* (2006). For Appiah, cosmopolitanism should indeed make room for 'patriotism'. His starting point is the practical example of his own father, who was a leader of the Ghanaian movement for independence from Britain in the 1950s and later a brave critic of Kwame Nkrumah's dictatorship. Joseph Appiah urged his children to be both 'citizens of the world' and Ghanaian patriots, as he was himself, seeing no conflict between these commitments (Appiah 2005: 213–14.).

For Anthony Appiah, cosmopolitanism and nationalism can be reconciled within a moderate cosmopolitanism that acknowledges the ethical force of contingent identities such as personal affinities with nations. Conversely, Appiah asks nationalists to look beyond their local identity to the larger world outside. While they need not – indeed, should not – abandon their more intimate identifications, they should be prepared to try to understand and (within limits) respect and learn from other outlooks (Appiah 2006: 78).

How is this to be done? According to Appiah, the principal task of cosmopolitanism is dialogue, or 'debate and conversation across nations': 'we must rely on the ability to listen and to talk to people whose commitments, beliefs, and projects may seem distant from our own' (Appiah 2005: 246). The main impulse of this conversation is summed up in the idea of 'the primacy of practice' over principle (Appiah 2006: 69). We cannot expect to get agreement or even much understanding by starting with general principles, since these are widely and deeply disputed. In particular, we get nowhere by taking the traditional humanist route that begins with an account of human nature, proceeds to deduce general rules from this and then applies the rules to concrete cases (Appiah 2005: 252–3).

Rather, we should look first for points at which we agree with others in our particular judgements. 'Practically speaking, we need not resolve disagreements of principle about why we should save this child from drowning if, in fact, we agree that the child must be saved' (Appiah 2005: 253). Appiah notes that this approach has affinities with Cass Sunstein's idea of 'incompletely theorized agreements', where people can converge on the same conclusions without agreeing on the same reasons for those conclusions (Sunstein 1995).[13]

A related feature of Appiah's idea of conversation is that it will be concerned more with 'narrative' or story-telling than with reason-giving. Again, the object is to achieve not so much agreement or justification as sympathetic understanding – to 'get used to one another' (Appiah 2006: 78). Moreover, 'our efforts to justify what we have done – or what we plan to do – are typically made up after the event, rationalizations of what we have decided intuitively' (Appiah 2006: 72). Our intuitions, in turn, are largely a matter of habit. Consequently, people are most likely to change their minds as a result not of reasoned argument but of 'a gradually acquired new way of seeing things' (Appiah 2006: 73). What tends to produce this kind of 'perspectival shift' is not argumentative logic but 'narrative logic', or the capacity to 'construct the world to which our imaginations respond' (Appiah 2006: 77; 2005: 257). We make sense of the world through narratives or stories with which we identify or to which we respond in imagination. Stories have the power to influence us through their concrete presentation of experience and value, in contrast with the colder abstraction of argument.[14]

But how far are the commitments of liberalism and cosmopolitanism likely to be served by 'conversation' as Appiah conceives it? In particular, what use is understanding without critical judgement? We may understand another culture or group very well without having much sympathy with it. In some cases this may be justified, as where we may come to understand the motivations and thinking of the Nazis without in any way endorsing their beliefs, values or actions (Berlin 2000a: 12–13). But in other cases the combination of comprehension and disapproval may be less defensible. Appiah himself presents the Victorian orientalist Sir Richard Burton as 'a standing refutation . . . to those who imagine that prejudice derives only from ignorance, that intimacy must breed amity' (Appiah 2006: 8).

Of course, Appiah may reply that understanding, if not a sufficient condition for good judgement, is at least a necessary condition. But this falls short of his own requirement that the patriotic cosmopolitan be prepared to learn from others if there is something worth learning. For that, we need not just understanding but critical thinking. And for this, in turn, we need reasoning and principles. Cosmopolitans should by all means exchange stories with other people – Appiah is right that narratives do have a certain power, and that this has to do with the way their concreteness grips the imagination. But cosmopolitans should also be prepared to argue with other people where necessary, or at least to question the beliefs of others for themselves. Indeed, Appiah endorses a Millian conception of personal autonomy as central to his approach to identity claims in general: identities are not simply to be accepted as authoritative regardless of content, but should be open to critical review and revision (Appiah 2005: ch. 1). He seems to lose sight of this in his discussion of cosmopolitan conversation, where stories rooted in identity rule unchallenged.

A more rationalist counterpoint to Appiah's narrative-based cosmopolitanism is presented by Amartya Sen, who has written a good deal about cultural identity, notably in *The Argumentative Indian* (2005) and *Identity and Violence* (2006). Like Appiah and Waldron, Sen rejects models of the human person that assume a single, 'encompassing' cultural identity. His starting point is an attack on what he calls 'solitarism', the tendency to reduce or 'miniaturize' people into one dimension of their identity, such as their membership of a particular 'civilization' (e.g. Western or non-Western), or nation or religion (Sen 2006: xii–xiii). Solitarism is distorting and also dangerous, since it can be readily mobilized by political and religious leaders in order to pit one group against another. If people see their religious identity, for example, as the only or paramount thing that matters to them, they are more open to ignore all other considerations in situations of perceived conflict. 'Within-group solidarity can help to feed between-group discord' (Sen 2006: 2).

The answer to solitarism, Sen argues, is to remind ourselves that in reality our identities are complex and many-layered. People are 'diversely different' (Sen 2006: xvi). This is not just a fact about jet-setting elites but a feature of human lives everywhere. 'A Hutu labourer from Kigali may be pressured to see himself only as a Hutu and incited to kill Tutsis, and yet he is not only a Hutu, but also a Kigalian, a Rwandan, an African, a labourer, and a human being' – hence Sen's response to identity-driven violence: 'the force of a bellicose identity can be challenged by the power of *competing* identities' (Sen 2006: 4). Yes, I am a Hutu, but that does not override every other way in which I might see myself and my commitments.

This brings in a theme of choice. 'Given our inescapably plural identities, we have to decide on the relative importance of our different associations and affiliations in any particular context' (Sen 2006: xiii). Indeed, we may have to consider 'the cogency and relevance' of particular identities too – that is, not just where to rank these in our lives but also whether certain claims on our allegiance are at all relevant, coherent or desirable. Does it really mean anything significant to say that I am a Hutu? If it does, does being a Hutu necessarily involve hating Tutsis? Identities are not good in themselves regardless of their content. Choice is relevant not only to ranking our allegiances but also to reflecting on them critically and revising or even abandoning them.

To choose in this way is to reason: to ask ourselves *why* we should go in one direction rather than another. This process involves some grasp of the nature of the alternatives at stake, hence a certain level of 'knowledge and understanding of other cultures and of alternative lifestyles' (Sen 2006: 117). It helps to have some idea of how our lives might be other than those laid out for us by the orthodoxies within which we are brought up. Given some notion of the options, we are in a position to ask critical questions, both of our own way of life and of the alternatives. We do not simply 'discover' our identities, since there are multiple possibilities. 'People have to use reasoning to decide on how to see themselves, and what significance they should attach to having been born a member of a particular community' (Sen 2006: 119).

Is Sen placing too much reliance on reason? He acknowledges Jonathan Glover's contention that the Enlightenment's faith in reason has been shown to be naïve by the atrocities of the twentieth century. Rather than appealing to reason to avoid these horrors, Glover argues, we would be better off relying on our humanitarian 'instincts', especially respect and sympathy (Sen 2005: 275, 278). A similar claim is made by Appiah when he recommends the replacement of a reasoned search for shared principles with an exchange of narratives.

In reply, Sen concedes that reason is not everything; respect and sympathy are important too, as Enlightenment thinkers such as Adam Smith and David Hume clearly recognized. He also allows a significant role for narrative.[15] But he insists that reason remains essential. For one thing, it is simply unavoidable: even to question the reach of reason involves reasoning (Sen 2005: 288). More positively, the value of reasoning lies in its capacity to root out mistakes in our attitudes and to reveal underlying causes that explain the true nature of the problems we want to solve. Here he gives the example of the causes of famine, one of his specialist areas as a developmental economist (Sen 2005: 276–7). In general, reasoning and feeling are 'deeply interrelated activities' (Sen 2005: 279). We need reasoning to question, test and guide our raw feelings – and to question, test and guide our narratives, one might add. The need to correct feelings with reason, rather than the redundancy of the Enlightenment, is the real lesson to draw from the events of the twentieth century.

Summary

Nationalism and cosmopolitanism both provide significant responses to cultural diversity, but each comes in multiple versions with correspondingly varying implications for multiculturalism. Many nationalists have been hostile to minority group identities of any kind, and in the past even the more liberal-minded were often reluctant to allow minorities to qualify the dominant national identity that was thought necessary to provide a stable platform for free institutions. But recent liberal nationalists are happy to allow that if national belonging is valuable for human well-being in general, then that is true not only of majority or dominant nationalities but also of minority national identity. Miller, however, would draw the line at special rights for non-national identities, arguing that these are too divisive. Tamir is prepared to extend public recognition to non-national identities as well, but in doing so she seems to lose sight of what is distinctive in nationalist positions, the claim that national identity has something special about it. Cosmopolitans are naturally inclined to be sceptical of that claim, emphasizing that people identify themselves in many different ways and that none of these should be regarded as overriding. This position is consistent with the active state promotion of multiple ways of life, but it does not really require multiculturalism in that sense either. The various cosmopolitan recommendations – intercultural hybridity, narrative-based dialogue and critically reflective choice – are primarily matters of personal conduct and do not explicitly call for public recognition of any particular cultural group. Perhaps surprisingly, multiculturalism proper turns out to have stronger links with nationalism than with cosmopolitanism.

5

Beyond Liberalism?

So far I have been considering responses to multiculturalism that for the most part belong within the broad church of liberalism. The reason for this, as explained at the outset, is that multiculturalist policy has by and large developed within liberal democracies, and multiculturalist theory has on the whole emerged as a development of, or response to, liberal political theory. However, there is a prominent stream of multiculturalist thought that rejects liberalism as a framework for a truly diverse society. I take this up in detail in this chapter.

I shall focus on three principal lines of multiculturalist objection to liberalism. First, Charles Taylor rejects liberal neutrality and argues for a communitarian politics of the common good, which morphs into a multiculturalist politics of recognition. Second, James Tully portrays liberalism as imperialist: it wrongly imposes an 'empire of uniformity' on legitimate cultural diversity, in particular where indigenous peoples are involved. Third, Bhikhu Parekh argues that liberal norms are too ethnocentric – specifically, Eurocentric – to provide a genuinely universal framework for justice to cultures, especially non-European ones.

All of these writers point beyond liberalism to the need for intercultural dialogue as an adequate response to cultural difference, but I shall postpone a detailed consideration of dialogue theories until Chapter 6.

Does Liberalism Neglect Community? Taylor

Charles Taylor's reputation as a critic of liberalism rests principally on his association with 'communitarianism'.[1] In general, communitarians believe that contemporary liberal democracies are too individualistic, too insistent on individual liberty at the expense of other values, especially those of community, and consequently too lacking in shared values. They see this state of affairs as aided and abetted by liberal political theory, which neglects 'community' in two main ways: as a source of value, and as an object of value.

The first of these concerns addresses the question of where our values come from. According to communitarians, liberals falsely suppose that people choose their values freely as if from a supermarket shelf – hence, the excessive liberal emphasis on freedom of choice and personal autonomy. This emphasis is reinforced at the level of theory by views such as Rawls's theory of justice, which begins by imagining people choosing principles of justice from an original position in which their identifying features and conceptions of the good are screened off by a veil of ignorance (Rawls 1971).

Communitarians like Taylor argue that the Rawlsian strategy and liberal neutrality more generally depend on a false and incoherent conception of the human person as (to use Taylor's term) 'atomistic' – that is, as in some sense separable from the particular characteristics that make people who they are (Taylor 1985). The truth is that people are intimately identified with the language, culture and values in which they are brought up and in which they live. The self is not atomistic but rather 'situated' in a community or 'constituted' by its communal identity.

Moreover, Taylor and other communitarians argue that liberal atomism connects with liberal neutrality. If the individual could be conceived independently of any particular conception of the good, then so too could the state. In fact, however, neither is possible. Despite the pretensions of liberals, the liberal state turns out to be identified, like the liberal person, by a distinctively liberal conception of the good focused on values such as personal autonomy.

The second main problem with liberalism is that it neglects community as a value in itself. The individualism that characterizes modern liberal democracies leaves such societies without adequate sources of unity – in particular without a sufficiently substantial set of shared values. Instead of the anomie and moral confusion promoted or condoned by liberalism, we should be pursuing a politics of 'the common good', in which a political society openly affirms a particular conception of the human good as the goal of its public policy (Taylor 1989).

The communitarian critique has been countered by some vigorous liberal responses.[2] First, most liberals would deny that they hold an 'atomistic' conception of the individual self, and they would argue that the communitarian criticism on this score misses the point. The liberal point is not that the self is an isolated metaphysical entity detached from all identifying particulars, but only that we should see individual human beings as having a capacity for personal autonomy – that is, an ability to take a critically reflective view of their own cultural, moral and other attachments. This need not be thought of as involving a person's detaching herself from all of her commitments simultaneously – that really would be inconceivable. Rather, liberals say that people are capable of piecemeal questioning of their own values and commitments by asking themselves how well these cohere with their other values and commitments, which may include universal considerations (Kymlicka 1995a: 91; Dworkin 2000: 220). History and one's own personal experience are full of cases in which people have revised their beliefs, values and identities through critical reflection.

Second, liberals would resist the claim that they fail to appreciate the benefits of communal belonging. For one thing, the basic liberal commitment to freedom of association and expression implies the importance that all liberals attach to communities whose membership is voluntary: churches, sports clubs, professional bodies and so forth. In the case of communities in which membership is usually not chosen – cultural groups, for example – the matter is more complicated, since groups of this kind sometimes restrict the freedom of their members in ways that put them at odds with the fundamental principles of liberalism. But again, it is far too simple to say that liberalism is unable to value this kind of group membership at all, as the example of Kymlicka shows.

More generally, liberals do care about social unity, if only because liberal states rest their legitimacy on their citizens' consent. Liberalism is not founded on moral scepticism but on a reasoned commitment to a core set of values, including individual liberty and toleration. Consequently, liberal theory seeks to justify consensus on the privileging of these values. So, liberals do after all subscribe to a notion of the common good, although this will be founded on, as Rawls puts it, a 'thin' theory of the good that leaves room for people to differ when it comes to the 'thick' details.

Liberals have not only sought to defend themselves against communitarian criticisms, they have also taken the offensive in their turn. One obvious liberal worry about the communitarian politics of the common good is its authoritarian potential, since the claims of the community, or the common good, have often, historically, come into conflict with those of individuals or minorities, including cultural minorities.

Consequently, in the case of Taylor an important question to ask is what weight he attaches to individual rights and liberties. His responses are somewhat equivocal. Sometimes he asserts that rights to life, liberty and expression 'are so fundamental that we can more or less commit ourselves in advance to upholding them in all possible contexts' (Taylor quoted by Abbey 2000: 128). Elsewhere he affirms the view, more in keeping with basic communitarian principles, that the content and extent of rights depend on background understandings of the human good that are embedded in particular cultures (Abbey 2000: 130). A vital question, then, is whether Taylor wants us to think of rights as universal standards for judging particular communities or as merely the judgements of those communities themselves. The answer is unclear.

Another concern, closely connected with the first, is the relativist strain in communitarianism. The starting point in communitarian moral thinking is not universal principle but the de facto beliefs and values of a given community. Since different communities have different beliefs and values, it appears that communitarianism tends naturally in the direction of cultural relativism. The obvious shortcoming of this approach from a liberal point of view is that the consistent communitarian, like the consistent cultural relativist, is obliged to accept as legitimate whatever the relevant community believes to be legitimate, no matter how unjust or unethical this may be from the perspective of human rights and freedoms.

Finally, when we refer to 'the relevant community', which community do we mean? The idea of community is highly ambiguous between different kinds and levels of commonality. Different visions of community are upheld by rival communitarian thinkers, yielding competing communitarian ideologies: traditional communities are commended by conservatives; egalitarian and participatory communities by Marxists and other radicals; and pluralist communities by liberals or centrists (Miller 1999).

This ambiguity points to a link between communitarianism and multiculturalism. In the context of multicultural societies, an especially important instance of the tension among different kinds of community is between larger communities and the sub-communities within them. While the goal of the communitarians of the 1980s was usually to promote the unity of whole political societies, it soon became clear that the logic of respect for community could equally support the claims of internal minority groups.

In this respect the work of Taylor has served as a bridge from communitarianism to multiculturalism. The key text is his essay, 'The Politics of Recognition' (1994). There he stresses the need to recognize the unique claims of particular groups, as opposed to treating all citizens identically as required by traditional liberal policies of toleration or neutrality.

Part of the background for Taylor's view is his support for the political autonomy of his native Quebec in relation to the rest of Canada. However, his starting point is the general claim that having one's identity accurately and positively recognized by others is an essential part of individual well-being. The withholding of such recognition, or the imposition on people of negative or distorted identifications – racist, sexist, homophobic and so on – can be very harmful to people's sense of self-worth. Taylor has in mind here what he calls 'the dialogic self' – that is, the idea (originating in Hegel) that the individual personality is formed through dialogue and negotiation with others. A person's sense of identity is difficult to maintain unless it is affirmed and reflected back to her by those around her, especially those 'significant others' who matter to her (Taylor 1994: 32–3).

Recognition has taken different forms in different historical periods. In premodern societies, characterized by fixed hierarchies, people were recognized on the basis of 'honour', or the position they held, generally inherited, in the stratified social order (Taylor 1994: 27). This kind of recognition was automatic, in the sense that it attached inevitably to one's position regardless of personal conduct, and it was also inherently unequal. Those in positions of privilege did not view others in terms of equality; on the contrary, it was through social inequality that their own identity was asserted.

It was only with the eighteenth-century Enlightenment that a new, egalitarian form of recognition emerged, heralding a new notion of 'the inherent "dignity of human beings", or of citizen dignity' (Taylor 1994: 27). Kant and others started to view human beings as more than rank-holders in a stratified community. Rather, they were moral beings 'endowed with a moral sense, an intuitive feeling for what is right and wrong' (Taylor 1994: 28). This led to the liberal notion of equality of moral worth introduced in Chapter 2: if human dignity attaches to the capacity for moral autonomy, and this is seen to be universal, then human beings matter equally, and they do so in respect of their universal characteristics. The classic expression of this outlook is the US Civil Rights legislation of the 1960s that prohibited discrimination between people on the basis of their colour, religion or gender. The politics of equal dignity produces a society that tends to discount the differences among people.

However, Taylor claims that in the contemporary world the difference-blind politics of equal dignity has given way to a new form of recognition: the politics of difference. Recognition understood as requiring uniform treatment has been superseded by recognition conceived as requiring differential treatment. This transition has not occurred because the whole concept of equal dignity has been abandoned. On the contrary, the demand for differential treatment has grown out of the logic of equal dignity. If each individual has an equal claim to fundamental recognition as a dignified being, the argument goes, then that recognition should extend not only to the universal but also to the particular or unique aspects of a person's identity (Taylor 1994: 38).

There is also a collective aspect to the politics of difference. To recognize the unique identity of an individual is, for Taylor, to acknowledge the uniqueness of her community. To acknowledge the uniqueness of a community is to endorse its right to safeguard its heritage. Here Taylor reveals his pro-Quebec agenda: 'it is axiomatic for Quebec governments that the survival and flourishing of French culture in Quebec is a good' (Taylor 1994: 58). The government in this case is not interested merely in making the French language accessible to those who wish to avail themselves of it. The object is to ensure 'cultural survival' – that is, they 'actively seek to *create* members of the community, for instance, in assuring that future generations continue to identify as French-speakers' (Taylor 1994: 58–9). This justifies current Quebec policy that requires all commercial signage to be in French, and that stipulates that francophone children and children of immigrants have to attend French-language schools – only children of anglophones can attend English-language schools. Taylor insists, however, that such a society can be essentially liberal, adhering to such important principles as 'rights to life, liberty, due process, free speech, free practice of religion, and so on' (Taylor 1994: 59).

Finally, Taylor examines the demands of those who argue for more strongly multicultural curricula – that is, for non-traditional (non-male, non-Eurocentric) academic works to be used as set material or reference works in university and high school courses (Taylor, 1994: 65). After Taylor's strong support for state-sponsored preservation of cultural identity, it comes as something of a surprise that he takes a rather cool view of the claims made by the curriculum multiculturalists. Although he reaffirms the importance of all cultures to their particular members, he stops short of acceding to demands that we must automatically accept all cultures as being of equal worth. The most we are entitled to assume is that most established cultures will have something positive to offer, but exactly what that is will have to be shown through critical inspection. 'On examination, either we will find something of great value in culture C, or we will not. But it makes no more sense to demand that we do so than it does to demand that we find the earth round or flat, the temperature of the air hot or cold' (Taylor 1994: 69). More generally, although 'other' cultures may have value, the state is not obligated to recognize this in its national identity. On the contrary, it is entitled to its historic traditions. His emphasis here is on survival of the dominant national culture and identity.

The strengths of Taylor's position surely include his acknowledgement of the importance of positive recognition to human well-being and his argument that people want recognition not just of their universal humanity but also of some of the more distinctive features of their identity, including their cultural heritage. But questions arise over the status of individual rights and liberties in his view, and over the extent to which people will be treated equally. For reasons such as these Brian Barry sees Taylor's position as 'continuous with a kind of ethnic nationalism that is profoundly at odds with liberalism' (Barry 2001: 65).

Concerns about individual liberty are raised by several aspects of Taylor's politics of recognition, as they were by his communitarianism. First, there is the danger that the cultural heritage in question might involve the imposition on a society's citizens of a very substantial conception of the good that they do not all accept. While the language-related demands of Quebec nationalists do not seem excessive in this respect, one can easily imagine other cases where 'cultural heritage' stands for the privileging, say, of a majority religion. Taylor would reply that this possibility is covered by his insistence on basic rights and liberties, including freedom of religion. But in the light of his emphasis on recognition of *group* identity this comes across as somewhat ad hoc, appealing to universal principles that are in tension with his more characteristic particularism. The worry about individual liberty is intensified when Taylor argues not only that national groups such as the French Québécois are entitled to use the state to preserve their cultural identity, but that they are entitled to do so in perpetuity. This demand seems at odds with the now-accepted view that cultures are fluid and evolving, and also with the basic liberal principle of personal autonomy, the idea that people should be free to revise their conception of the good through a process of critical reflection.

Indeed, Taylor's position is at odds not only with liberalism but also with his own communitarianism. While he regards the subsuming of francophone Québécois into the English-speaking culture of Canada as a serious injustice, he seems to believe that 'the French goal of culturally assimilating other minorities is perfectly laudable'

(Lamey 1999: 14). His basic case for Québécois self-determination is grounded in the human need for recognition of one's cultural or community identity. Since this is a human need, it is presumably claimable in respect of any significant community. Why, then, does Taylor not emphasize the claims of those communities that resist the secession of Quebec, including on the one hand the community of greater Canada, and on the other those minorities, such as indigenous peoples, within Quebec? Why should these collective identities be any less entitled to recognition than that of Quebec nationalists?

In this respect Taylor's work exemplifies the ambiguity of the idea of community mentioned earlier. To say simply that we ought to promote 'community' is to say very little. Depending on what community we are talking about, this approach can yield a wide range of political results. It might lead, as in Taylor, to support for a monocultural nationalism, if the claims of a single dominant culture are stressed. On the other hand, the logic of Taylor's own thinking suggests that it might equally lead to multiculturalism, where minority cultural identities are brought into the public realm. Communitarianism, then, having begun as a demand for social and cultural unity, has evolved into a case for social and cultural plurality. But the selectivity and arbitrariness of the plurality favoured by Taylor are evidence of the problems raised by the communitarian stream of multiculturalist thought.

Is Liberalism Imperialist? Tully

Another line of multiculturalist criticism alleges that liberalism is essentially imperialist. Advocates of this claim have sometimes attempted to justify it simply by correlating the emergence of European colonialism with the birth of liberalism in the late seventeenth century. Therefore, it is supposed, liberal thought must serve imperialist practice or imperialism grows naturally out of liberalism (Losurdo 2011). This argument is easily refuted, since although the classical liberal thinkers of the seventeenth to nineteenth centuries included some defenders of imperialism, like Mill and Tocqueville, they also included many anti-imperialists, such as Diderot, Bentham and Kant (Mehta 1999; Pitts 2005: Muthu 2003). Certainly no reputable contemporary theorist of liberalism defends imperialism or colonialism, and much of the contemporary case against these practices rests on liberal conceptions of liberty, equality and human rights.

However, a more sophisticated argument tying liberalism to imperialism is offered by the Canadian political theorist James Tully. In

Strange Multiplicity (1995), Tully argues that the legitimate demands of 'the politics of recognition' – claims to public recognition and special rights by various social groups: national, ethnic, linguistic, female, indigenous and so on – are currently being stifled by the dead hand of 'modern constitutionalism'. This modern approach to political thought is dominated by three schools: nationalism, liberalism and communitarianism. Despite their differences, they all share a tendency to impose an 'empire of uniformity' where there was once diversity, a uniformity that is basically male, European and imperialistic (Tully 1995: 34). In particular, Tully is concerned with the record of modern constitutionalism in suppressing the sovereignty of aboriginal peoples and minority nationalities. His examples are usually Canadian, dealing with the experiences of the native peoples of North America and the French-speaking province of Quebec, groups whose just claims to self-rule, according to Tully, have been denied.

Tully lists several features of modern constitutionalism that 'serve to exclude or assimilate cultural diversity' (Tully 1995: 62). First, the modern approach is 'monological' rather than 'dialogical' – that is, it is the result of an abstract process of reasoning that could occur within a single mind rather than an actual conversation among the affected parties. Second, the political community is conceived monolithically as a single, united body of people, whose various differences are not politically relevant. Modern governments are pictured as presiding over culturally homogeneous citizens who are subject to, and the authors of, identical laws and rights. Third, this unitary 'people' is taken to be absolutely sovereign, and therefore entitled to impose its will by force. Modern constitutions are thus 'imposed' by popular will rather than negotiated among parties with pre-existing sovereign claims of their own, as on the ancient model. Fourth, the modern approach is presented as historically more progressive or advanced than the ancient model. The ancient respect for custom has been undermined by the rational questioning of modernity. Finally, respect for custom and group identity is impugned by their association with conflict, 'irregularity' or irrationality and instability.

However, the broader language of contemporary constitutionalism also contains, in addition to the distinctively modern rigidities, certain resources that can rescue diversity. These are the principles of the 'ancient' constitution that emphasized the customary rights of groups and the practice of inter-group negotiation. A 'post-imperial' society will be characterized by the revival of these ancient ways, in particular by a focus on an intercultural dialogue. The result will be a 'diverse federalism' in which the self-rule of cultural and other groups will be restored (Tully 1995: 140).

All this diversity and dialogue is subject to certain guidelines, however. The ancient practice of inter-group negotiation reveals a widespread respect for 'three conventions'. First, 'recognition, to be just, must be mutual' (Tully 1995: 167). Each party to the dialogue must listen to the other parties' views in their own terms, accepting their position, including their self-description, as valid. Indigenous groups in dialogue with modern states, for example, should be accepted as they see themselves: as independent nations (Tully 1995: 117). Second, it follows that if a group presents itself as an equal and independent partner in the dialogue, then decisions affecting it can only be made justly with its consent (Tully 1995: 122). Third, there is a presumption of 'continuity': 'mutually recognised cultural identities of the parties continue through the constitutional negotiations and associations agreed to unless they explicitly consent to amend them' (Tully 1995: 124–5). For example, when the British took Quebec from the French in the eighteenth century, they initially respected continuity by permitting the continuation of French culture, language and laws in the province, only later repudiating that policy and moving towards uniformity on the modern model (Tully 1995: 145–6).

Tully sums up his vision of post-imperial diversity and dialogue in a central image, 'The Spirit of Haida Gwaii', a large sculpture of a black canoe crewed by a variety of mythical creatures. The sculpture represents the 'spirit or myth creatures' of the indigenous nation of Haida Gwaii in the Queen Charlotte Islands off the northwest coast of North America: bears, ravens, eagles, wolves, frogs and 'the mysterious, intercultural dogfish woman' (Tully 1995: 17). Tully uses the sculpture as a metaphor for a society that is both diverse and unified. On the one hand, the crew members are very different from one another. All 'are recognised and speak in their own language and customary ways' (Tully 1995: 24). On the other hand, they are all literally in the same boat, they are in dialogue with one another, and they are paddling in the same direction.

Towards the end of the book, Tully describes how the canoe brings together two public goods, 'the critical freedom to question in thought and challenge in practice one's inherited cultural ways, on one hand, and the aspiration to belong to a culture and place, and so to be at home in the world, on the other' (Tully 1995: 202). Indeed, these goods are harmonized, since (given the three conventions of mutual recognition, consent and continuity) to belong is to identify not only with one's own culture but with the diverse collectivity of the canoe as a whole, and that in turn gives people a degree of critical distance from their narrower identities. Contrary to modern constitutionalism, which sacrifices belonging to critical freedom, Tully argues that these goods 'support rather than oppose each other' (Tully 1995: 207).

How persuasive is Tully? First, consider his critique of modern constitutionalism, focusing on its liberal version. Here, his basic point is that liberal constitutionalism imposes on cultural groups 'the language of the master', which is 'masculine, European or imperial' (Tully 1995: 34). Setting aside the issue of masculinity, is liberalism essentially European or essentially imperialist?[3]

Tully actually produces little evidence of the distinctively European character of liberalism; this allegation is pursued more fully by Bhikhu Parekh, whose work will be discussed in the next section. Tully's main point in this connection is that a distinctively European outlook is presupposed by Locke's influential account of property acquisition in the state of nature. According to Tully, Locke assumed that only European forms of agriculture counted as proper 'cultivation' of natural resources. Where this appeared to be absent, as in aboriginal hunter-gatherer societies, the implication was that such people remained in a state of nature with neither property rights nor 'civil government'. Consequently, the local resources could be fairly appropriated by Europeans, who could also legitimately declare political sovereignty over the territory. But while Locke's view does indeed look like a licence for imperialism, it scarcely implicates liberalism as a whole, since it is not essential to liberalism. Indeed, no contemporary liberal would endorse such a view.

The same broad reply can be made to Tully's claim that liberal constitutionalism implies an imperialist outlook. Recall that this allegation rests on a picture of modern constitutions as insisting on identical laws and rights for all citizens regardless of circumstance, a conception of sovereignty as monolithic and absolute, a scheme of historical development in which respect for custom is associated with 'backward' stages of social evolution and a general denigration of custom as divisive and irrational – all justified by monological rather than dialogical reasoning. Liberals can again respond that none of these elements is required by liberalism. Of the items on the list, probably the strongest candidate as a liberal essential is monological reasoning, but even that is not really necessary, as shown by the strong links between liberalism and deliberative democracy, which I discuss in Chapter 6.

Even if monological thinking were essential to liberalism, is it necessarily imperialist? Kymlicka takes a monological approach in his account of rights, but in his hands this is used to reject rather than endorse the various dimensions of uniformity Tully complains of – Kymlicka quite clearly defends differentiated cultural rights, rejects absolute sovereignty and values indigenous and national cultures. Indeed, when Tully connects cultural recognition with individual self-respect and personal autonomy he sounds just like Kymlicka (Tully 1995: 190–1).

Nevertheless, on Tully's view Kymlicka still counts as an imperialist. Although Kymlicka is listed by Tully among those liberal thinkers who have defended cultural recognition to a degree, these are all said to accept the primacy of the 'modern' framework, 'no manipulation' of which can ever be entirely satisfactory (Tully 1995: 44). In Kymlicka's case, there seem to be two problems. First, group recognition is presented by liberals like Kymlicka not as a fundamental norm but as a qualification to a presumption in favour of identical treatment.[4] Tully sees this as a classic universalist bias, but there is a fundamental rationale for this approach that he does not acknowledge. The liberal presumption in favour of identical treatment is an expression not just of uniformity for its own sake but of the basic principle of equality of moral worth. If human beings are fundamentally equal in dignity, then they should be treated identically unless there is good reason to treat them otherwise. There may well be good reason to treat them differently if particular circumstances warrant it – as Kymlicka argues in the case of cultural disadvantage. The presumption is rebuttable, but it has a strong justification.

A second reason why Kymlicka remains an imperialist on Tully's view is that Kymlicka qualifies his cultural rights in favour of individual autonomy. In balancing individual freedom and cultural belonging, Kymlicka leans distinctly towards freedom. Tully, by contrast, insists that the claims of cultures are equal to those of individual freedom, and that ultimately the goods of belonging and freedom are in harmony. At this point we pass beyond Tully's critique of liberalism to his positive vision of 'post-imperial' diversity. Also at this point liberal alarm-bells will be ringing loudly. Does Tully's strong promotion of cultures not risk a serious collision with individual liberty?

The obvious liberal concern is that some of the cultures whose claims Tully advocates will harbour practices that violate basic individual rights. In an interesting example cited by Tully a person who was a member by birth of the Canadian Coast Salish nation, but who had little interest in its traditional practices, was kidnapped and forced 'to participate in a spirit dance' (Tully 1995: 172). He successfully sued for assault, battery and false imprisonment, and Tully endorses the court's decision, presenting it as evidence that in this and similar cases 'rights are taken seriously'. However, the rationale offered by the court, and apparently accepted by Tully, was not simply that 'rights are trumps', as Ronald Dworkin would say, but that in this case the practice complained of was not 'a central feature of the Salish way of life' – leaving open the implication that if it had been a central feature it would have been justified (Barry 2001: 257).

Tully later argued that this implication should not be drawn, and that even if the practice were found to be central, the rights of the individual still needed to be taken into account. Even then, however, Tully's view is that the rights must be weighed against the 'good public reasons' there may be for maintaining the traditional practice (Tully 2002: 107). Rights are still not trumps; rather, we should, ideally, try to reach an 'accommodation' between the rights and the tradition. Many liberals would want to press Tully on what would happen if no such accommodation were possible, and would express concern that if rights are not trumps when they are violated by cultural practices then their whole point is lost (Barry 2002: 208).

Tully does admit to 'a genuine concern' that, in the absence of constitutional constraints, indigenous self-rule may in effect cede power to 'a class of Aboriginal male elites' (Tully 1995: 193). But he responds that 'the patriarchal structures that the elites occupy were set up by colonial administrators'. Surely, though, many of these elites and authority structures are older than European colonialism. One is tempted here to suggest that Tully is apt to romanticize or sentimentalize indigenous cultures, picturing them as oases of natural harmony and well-being and ignoring the less attractive realities of premodern life. As Barry puts it, 'environmental damage, mutilation of children, cruelty to animals, sex discrimination and denial of religious freedom are all among the abuses that have been claimed to be defensible as long as they form part of some traditional custom or way' (Barry 2002: 209). To say this is not to agree with the old imperialists that such societies are wholly inferior or lower on a moral scale of development compared with modern societies; it is simply to allow that they are no more perfect than any human society, and that wholesale endorsement of their traditions is no more justifiable than wholesale rejection.

Tully's principal reply to the worry about individual rights is that the violation of rights is 'impossible' as long as the three conventions are in operation, because these protect not only groups but also 'the citizens within them' (Tully 1995: 191). There is some unclarity in this – what does it mean to apply the convention of 'continuity' to individuals? – but presumably the basic idea is that individual consent and mutual recognition within groups must be weighed in the scales along with the recognition and consent of groups as a whole. The problem is, again, that Tully gives no guidance on what should happen when these considerations come into conflict. On the face of it, the claims of the group are once more on a par with those of its individual members.

Indeed, Tully tends to downplay the very possibility of conflict between groups and their members. For example, he defines 'custom' as 'long use and practice' that 'reflects and manifests the deliberate judgement of reason, and so the consent, of a free people', and he rejects the modern association of custom with unexamined habit that is vulnerable to critical questioning (Tully 1995: 61, 88). This glosses over the extent to which custom *can* become habit, outliving its original rationale and inviting reform that will be contested. There is also the possibility (conceded by Tully above) that even the original rationale may serve the interests of some members of the group rather than others. In such cases what 'the group' or 'custom' stands for will be appropriated by some powerful sub-group like an elite or a majority, leaving dissenters oppressed or marginalized. Under those rather routine conditions it will not be true that the same conventions that protect the group as a whole also protect its members – at least, not all of them.[5]

A related objection to Tully's view is that it depends on an 'essentialist' understanding of culture (Barry 2001: 11, 255–7). If a group's customs imply the consent of its members, then that suggests that the group speaks with a single cultural voice. This view seems to fit most comfortably with the essentialist idea that a cultural group possesses a core identity that cannot be changed without destroying that identity. Tully vehemently denies that he holds such a view, pointing out that he repeatedly rejects the 'billiard-ball' image of culture as self-contained, externally bounded and internally homogeneous (Tully 2002: 104–5). But might traces of the billiard-ball remain in his thought nevertheless?

A case in point is the spirit dance case already mentioned, where the key issue was said to be whether or not the practice was 'central' to the culture. Another is the case of the Canadian aboriginal Musqueam nation, who were granted special consideration in a conservation dispute because their practice of fishing a particular stretch of water was held by a court to be 'constitutive of [their] cultural identity' (Tully 1995: 172). As Barry asks, 'unless we assume their culture is a monolith, why couldn't the Musqueam still be the Musqueam without fishing that stretch of water, just as societies all over the world have coped with change without thereby losing their distinct identities or their capacity to function as norm-governed collectivities?' (Barry 2002: 207).

Tully would perhaps reply that the Musqueam may indeed have to change, and that the necessary changes need not mean total loss of identity, but that they should have a say on the extent and shape of those changes. It remains a difficult question, though, what force should be attached, in such negotiations, to claims about existing 'cultural identity'. On the one hand, 'the way we do things' cannot be automatically decisive, since there are other considerations, such as individual liberty and environmental conservation. On the other hand, the way we do things may have a certain value too. Kymlicka gives one account of that value, as a context for choice. Even Barry concedes that tradition carries a certain instrumental value, because 'it keeps the cost of coordinating behaviour to a minimum: each person knows what to expect from others and what are the expectations of others' (Barry 2001: 259).

Tully would probably go further. Although he is never explicit about the ethical foundations of his view, he would probably see de facto cultural identities as valuable not only instrumentally but in themselves. He seems in general to accept cultural codes as morally authoritative – in contrast with universal principles, which he usually pictures as imperialist impositions. According to Tully, we must always respect the 'irreducible diversity' of the Haida Gwaii canoe by looking at it from the particular perspectives of its crew-members, refusing any comprehensive or transcendent view (Tully 1995: 204). This leads Barry to see Tully as a cultural relativist, and thus open to the standard objections to relativist open-endedness (see Chapter 1). Yet Tully also wants to endorse certain 'universal principles', namely the three conventions (Tully 2002: 109).

The question is, how successful is Tully at combining the universal components of his view with the relativist or particularist components? To put it another way, given the moral sovereignty he attributes to cultural groups, why should they accept the three conventions at all? Tully imagines the bear in the canoe – presumably a metaphor for liberal constitutionalism – asserting that the ways of the bear are superior to those of the other creatures or universally valid for all, and comments that the injustice of the bear's claims is 'glaringly obvious' (Tully 1995: 203). Tully's reason why the bear's claims are unjust is that they violate the conventions, beginning with mutual recognition – that is, recognition of other cultural groups as independent and self-governing. But why should the bear (or any other creature) accept this constraint, given the initial assumption of the moral sovereignty of one's own group? The perspective of the imperialist bear has to be respected along with the others, a point pressed by Barry in a section of *Culture and Equality* entitled 'Up the Creek in the Black Canoe' (Barry 2001: 258).

This difficulty undermines Tully's claim that critical freedom and cultural belonging are ultimately harmonious. What harmonizes these goods, according to Tully, is that when people identify with their own culture they identify with the place of that culture in the diverse society of which it is a part (Tully 1995: 207–8). In effect they identify with that diverse society as a whole, and such an identification in turn enables them to reflect critically on their own culture. But this argument quietly smuggles in the objective or canoe-wide perspective that Tully ruled out with his insistence on irreducible diversity. If one's own cultural perspective is sovereign and indefeasible, why should one accede to the moral claims of other perspectives? Of course, the bear has to acknowledge the presence of other creatures in the canoe, but why should he accept them as his moral equals – or as having any moral status at all?

There is, then, a persistent underlying tension (to say the least) in Tully's thought between its relative and universal elements. On the one hand Tully emphasizes the particularism of moral perspectives, stressing the ethical sovereignty of cultural groups. On the other hand he wants to constrain group perspectives with the three conventions. The upshot seems to be a dilemma: either cultures are ethically sovereign, in which case there is no reason why they must accept the universal conventions, or the universal conventions are valid and obligatory, in which case cultural perspectives are not sovereign. In the former case Tully's 'post-imperialist' diversity is no defence against imperialism and in fact permits its justification. In the latter case it is unclear how Tully's position is really that different from the liberal constitutionalism he claims to reject.

Is Liberalism Ethnocentric? Parekh

One of the most persistent objections to liberalism as a framework for multiculturalism is that liberal values are distinctively 'individualist' and 'Western', hence 'ethnocentric'. Liberal norms originated in Western Europe. Hence, it is sometimes argued, they express the norms characteristic of European cultures rather than other ways of life. Consequently, even if liberalism were acquitted of imperialism – that is, of forcing its values on non-liberal cultures – might it still be convicted of ethnocentrism? Liberals may want to accommodate rather than dominate other ways of life, but perhaps they cannot do so because their principles are not sufficiently universal to embrace the full range of legitimate human interests, ends and conceptions of the good. Rather, we must look beyond liberalism for a truly multicultural political framework.

The crudest form of this view can be quickly dismissed. This is the claim that liberal norms are unsuitable for non-Western societies simply because historically they were first formulated in the West. The problem here is the mistaken belief that it is enough to impugn the validity of an idea merely by pointing to where it came from. Human rights are not invalid simply because they were formulated first (if that is true) in the West. A good idea is good wherever it comes from. Paper was invented in China but that does not mean it is suitable only for the Chinese. But might the objection from ethnocentrism be restated more persuasively? Perhaps it can be argued that liberalism is ethnocentric as a matter not merely of historical origins but of deep cultural affiliation.

One of the more balanced versions of this critique is found in the work of Bhikhu Parekh, a British political theorist of Indian descent who has become something of a spokesman for the 'Asian' community in the United Kingdom, entering the House of Lords in 2000. In such writings as *Rethinking Multiculturalism* (2nd edition 2006) and the more recent *A New Politics of Identity* (2008), Parekh defends a number of specifically liberal 'principles and institutions' and allows that his theory as a whole 'has a strong liberal orientation' (Parekh 2006: 14). But he also argues that liberalism, although culturally accommodating to a degree, is too culturally specific to embrace all the legitimate requirements of multiculturalism. We do need universal principles to regulate multicultural societies and relationships, but these should be more genuinely universal than the principles of liberalism. We should look for them at 'a higher level of philosophical abstraction', in a 'dialogue between cultures' within which liberal ideas must be represented, but only on the same level as ideas from alternative cultural backgrounds.

According to Parekh, liberal values are specific and appropriate to certain cultures rather than others. When liberalism is universalized 'it imposes on other countries systems of government unsuited to their talents and skills, destroys the coherence and integrity of their ways of life, and reduces them to mimics, unable and unwilling to be true either to their traditions or to the imported norms' (Parekh 1992: 169). Some societies are just not cut out, culturally, for liberalism. These non-liberal societies turn out to fit a familiar 'non-Western' pattern – Parekh's examples include Saudi Arabia, Kuwait, 'Middle Eastern and African polities', Bangladesh and 'traditional Muslim society' (Parekh 1992: 169–70). Liberal values are not appropriate to non-Western societies, it seems.

Specifically which liberal values should be identified as ethnocentric in this sense? Parekh proposes various candidates: concern for 'the isolated individual', 'aggressive self-assertion' and 'scientific reason', an instrumental and rational approach to the value of a culture, secularism and insufficient respect for religion and the defence of freedom of speech that permits disrespectful comments on religious sensibilities (Parekh 1992: 173; 2006: 98; 2008: 111–12). Gender equality is also 'resisted by some' non-liberal societies (Parekh 2008: 110). Capitalism, however, Parekh seems to regard as crossing cultural lines, since 'many' non-liberal societies 'welcome' it (Parekh 1992: 172).

To simplify matters, however, let us focus on the value most frequently cited by Parekh as an example of liberal ethnocentrism – namely, personal autonomy. Thus, Mill 'exaggerated the importance of such values as autonomy', which he supposed (wrongly) to be a distinctively European achievement, in contrast with the stationary, tradition-bound outlook of 'the East' (Parekh 1994: 12). In so doing he 'ruled out a wide variety of ways of life, such as the traditional, the community-centred and the religious', all of which have their own value (Parekh 2006: 44). Among contemporary liberals, Joseph Raz 'associates autonomy with the Western way of life', whereas 'groups such as immigrants, indigenous peoples and religious communities . . . do not set much store [by autonomy]' (Parekh 1994: 12; 2006: 93). Kymlicka sees his guiding 'idea of living life from the inside' – being prepared always to question and revise one's life commitments – as universal, but in reality it 'is essentially Protestant', involving an 'interiorization of morality' that is missing from other cultures (Parekh 2006: 106).

These passages immediately suggest a question about Parekh's position. Are liberals ethnocentric because they claim that personal autonomy is peculiar to the West when it is really universal (the mistake supposedly made by Mill and Raz), or because they claim that personal autonomy is a value of universal application when it is really peculiar to the West (Kymlicka's alleged mistake)? Parekh seems to have a bet each way, although he tends more often to the second allegation. His usual objection is that even the best-intentioned, most diversity-friendly liberal theories rest on a commitment to individual autonomy that carries with it an ethical outlook that is distinctive of certain modern European cultures. That outlook excludes and denigrates the legitimate values of other – non-liberal or non-Western – cultures. From the perspective of these latter, liberal autonomy is an alien imposition.

The basic liberal reply to this charge is that individual autonomy is not 'alien' to any society, since it is present in all societies at least to some degree (Kymlicka 1995a: 94). Parekh actually makes this point himself – 'autonomy is a matter of degree, and . . . no human community can dispense with it altogether' – when he criticizes Raz and Mill for claiming autonomy as a uniquely European achievement (Parekh 1994: 12). He gives the example of 'the Hindu', who can 'choose his gods', borrow from other religions and 'make up his own religion without ceasing to be a Hindu'. But Parekh adds the qualification, 'this is not at all to say that all ways of life are equally autonomous, only that none is wholly devoid of that quality' (Parekh 1994: 12). So presumably his argument is that some cultures are inherently more apt than others to *emphasize* individual autonomy or value it highly.

It is true that autonomy is at present more developed and more highly valued in some cultures rather than others, but that does not show that it is out of place or that it cannot or should not be encouraged in those cultures where it has not yet flourished more fully. Those societies Parekh describes as liberal were not always as hospitable to autonomy as they are now, and even now they could go further in that direction: their current support for autonomy is the product of a process of development, a process that may be continuing. How do we know that a similar process of development is not possible and desirable for so-called 'non-liberal' societies? Parekh seems to accept this point when he is criticizing Mill and Raz, but to forget it when he is insisting against Kymlicka that liberal arguments for autonomy are parochial.

Perhaps Parekh may respond that the 'autonomy' that he concedes to be present in all ways of life is not the same thing as full-blown autonomy in the liberal sense. So, for example, when he speaks of the religious autonomy of Hindus he means their freedom to make choices within a Hindu framework that is itself unquestioned, rather than a stronger capacity to question the whole Hindu way of life.[6] More generally, it might be argued that while critical thinking is universal, critical reflection on one's own conception of the good – the core of liberal autonomy – is not (Parekh 2006: 177).

To this, liberals could reply that wherever there is critical thinking, there we already have at least the seeds of critical reflection from which the roots of autonomy may emerge. It is true that traditions of critical thinking are often circumscribed by unquestioned assumptions, such as the acceptance of certain texts as sacred. In such cases, critical thought tends to be limited to argument over rival interpretations of the text. But where questions can be raised about the meaning of texts, questions can and will eventually be raised about the authority of the text itself. Critical thinking leads naturally to critical reflection, although this may take some time.[7] In this connection, Parekh observes that 'Muslims do have a problem with a critical and historical study of the Qur'an, and it is likely to take decades before they become used to it' (Parekh 2008: 112). Here he is emphasizing current Muslim resistance to more radical forms of critical reflection, but at the same time holding out the prospect of change, and of change emerging from a process with roots in current practices.

Another objection to this liberal line of defence may be that when liberals emphasize the pro-autonomy (or critical reflection) aspects of world cultures, they are being unduly selective. Even if we concede that there are such strands in all cultures, we should recognize that there are also strands of heteronomy, faith and unreflective allegiance. The pro-autonomy strand does not necessarily represent the true face of the culture. The truth is that all cultures contain both aspects – indeed, that on balance most are arguably more hostile to critical reflection than accepting of it (Fabre and Miller 2003: 13).

But the point of the liberal argument here is not to claim that all human cultures are 'truly' or 'really' or 'essentially' committed to critical reflection and autonomy. On the contrary, the point is to deny that cultures have any such essence one way or the other. Liberals' immediate purpose in this connection is just to keep open the possibility that any culture may evolve or develop in the direction of individual autonomy, that such an evolution or development is not 'alien' to some cultures. It is the opponents of autonomy as a universal ideal, like Parekh, who tend to justify their view by appeal, often implicit, to a background understanding of certain cultures as having essential identities or fixed characters that exclude the possibility or desirability of autonomy. After all, it is not much to the point for critics of liberalism simply to show that, as a matter of fact, autonomy is not highly valued in a given culture at present. That is common ground. The whole purpose of the liberal case is to argue that autonomy *ought* to be more widely or consistently respected than it is.

The anti-liberal reply, typified by Parekh, is not just that autonomy is not highly valued in some cultures at present, but that liberal claims that it ought to be more highly valued are inappropriate, that there is something about such claims that is out of place or inauthentic in the relevant cultural context. Societies that try to satisfy such claims fail to be, in Parekh's phrase, 'true to their traditions'. It is hard to see how such a critique can avoid depending on essentialist assumptions – for example, that essentially 'liberal' cultures can be distinguished from 'non-liberal' cultures, or that 'Western' cultures are inherently distinct from 'non-Western'. It is only given assumptions such as these that Parekh can assert that individual autonomy is an alien imposition in the context of 'non-liberal' or 'non-Western' cultures.

In fact Parekh oscillates between rejecting these essentialist assumptions when he believes he has detected them in the thinking of others, and relying on them when he is relativizing liberalism. For example, he chastises liberals like Mill and Raz for 'absolutising' liberalism – that is, for making liberalism the central point of reference in a way that crudely divides the world into societies that are either liberal or non-liberal (Parekh 2006: 110). Yet Parekh himself often generalizes about 'non-liberal' societies, especially when he wants to argue that the value of autonomy is alien to them. Moreover, he tends to equate non-liberal with non-Western, as we have seen. In order to sequester the claims of liberalism he ends up relying on the same old East–West division that he condemns when he claims to find it in Mill and Raz.[8]

Finally, Parekh's whole tendency to declare 'non-liberal' or 'non-Western' societies off-limits to autonomy rests on an essentialist view of culture in general that, again, he rightly rejects elsewhere. 'A culture has no essence', he writes. 'It includes different strands of thought, and reformers are right to highlight those that have been marginalized, suppressed or misconstrued by the dominant interpretation of their tradition' (Parekh 2006: 175). In that case reformers are entitled to protest when dominant cultural views have marginalized, suppressed or misconstrued the claims of individual autonomy and critical thinking.

Parekh's rejection of cultural essentialism is especially strong in his discussion of modern globalization (Parekh 2008: ch. 9), and again this has significant implications for the validity of personal autonomy as a universal ideal. Globalization has not only economic, technological and political dimensions, but also a moral aspect under which certain values and assumptions are increasingly shared on a global scale. Personal autonomy is arguably one such value. Joseph Raz makes this case when he argues that under the fluid and changeable conditions of modern industrial life, the value of personal autonomy, which enables people to be flexible and adjust to change, becomes inescapable (Raz 1986: 369–70, 394). Having rightly emphasized the dynamism of culture, especially modern culture, Parekh is hardly in a position to insist that certain values, such as autonomy, should be seen as inherently Western and inappropriate for non-Western cultures.

Once we get beyond the idea that there are essentially liberal and non-liberal, Western and non-Western cultures, the way is clear to embrace the view that liberal values such as personal autonomy can be found, at least in embryo, in many cultures, including those whose currently dominant values are non-liberal or 'non-Western', and that in all such cultures there is a legitimate potential for autonomy to be promoted further. Of course, the converse also holds: that non-liberal tendencies and potentialities are also to be found in liberal and Western societies. From this more cosmopolitan perspective, the debate over the place of individual autonomy appears less as a contest between inherently liberal or Western (pro-autonomy) societies and inherently non-liberal or non-Western (anti-autonomy) societies and more as a struggle between the proponents and opponents of autonomy wherever they are found. On this view the contemporary liberal commendation of individual autonomy may be controversial but it is not ethnocentric. I shall return to the alleged boundaries between 'the West and the rest' in Chapter 8.

Summary

The claim that liberalism can provide an adequate framework for multiculturalism has come under sustained attack from a range of critics. Taylor and other communitarians see liberalism as neglectful of community, both as a source and as an object of value. Tully is among those who see an intimate link between liberalism and imperialist practices under which alien values and institutions are forced upon societies, in particular indigenous societies. Parekh alleges that, even at its most accommodating, liberalism remains irreducibly ethnocentric, since it rests on values, in particular personal autonomy, that are peculiar to Western cultures. However, liberals can reply strongly to these charges. 'Community' is a highly ambiguous ethical ideal; imperialism is a regrettable feature of modern (and premodern) history, but there is no good reason to see imperialism as a necessary component of liberalism; and the key liberal ideal of personal autonomy is not ethnocentric because it is found, at least in embryo, in many cultures besides Western ones and it is a legitimate aspiration for any society. Liberals would accuse their critics of sliding into forms of relativism that leave basic individual liberties poorly secured, of picking and choosing arbitrarily which communities to privilege and of tacitly relying on discredited essentialist notions of culture that the critics claim to reject.

6

Democrats

As we saw in the last chapter, multiculturalist critics of liberalism often argue that liberal democracies do not allow minority groups a sufficient say in deciding both their own fate and that of the society at large. However, a concern for democracy is not confined to antiliberal multiculturalists. Liberal multiculturalists, too, have reason to value democratic processes. The place and character of democracy in a multicultural society will be the focus of this chapter.

Multicultural democracy can take various forms. I begin by discussing Iris Marion Young's advocacy of group representation before returning to the work of Parekh to consider his account of intercultural dialogue. However, these views have themselves been criticized from a democratic perspective. The critics have charged that Young and Parekh tend to regard democracy and dialogue as, fairly straightforwardly, conduits for expressing the hitherto suppressed voices of minority cultures and other groups. For Seyla Benhabib, however, democracy should not be a mere instrument for preserving existing cultures; rather, it should provide a critical process through which cultural identities can be contested and revised, both from without and within. Benhabib advocates the application in a multicultural context of 'deliberative' democracy, a public dialogue of ordinary citizens and groups as well as political leaders. The standard deliberative model has in turn been challenged as impracticable and unfair, especially given multicultural differences. In this connection I conclude with another look at Young, who in her later work embraces deliberative democracy, but in a form designed to accommodate those differences more thoroughly.

Group Representation: Young

In her extremely influential *Justice and the Politics of Difference* (1990) and later in *Inclusion and Democracy* (2000), Iris Marion Young argues that, rather than the individual rights and liberties that liberals defend, it is democratic participation that should be the centre of a just society. Only a more vigorous form of democracy, in which traditionally oppressed groups are given a stronger voice in deciding the terms of justice, will answer fully to the legitimate demands of contemporary multiculturalism.

Young's broad political background is that of the 'new social movements' of the 1960s and 1970s: feminism, Black liberation, indigenous rights organizations and gay and lesbian groups (Young 1990: 3). These movements, she argues, have drawn attention to the fact that injustice in modern societies is not only about unfair distribution of material resources – the 'distributive paradigm' accepted by most contemporary theorists of justice, such as Rawls. Rather, there are several dimensions or 'faces' of injustice that are irreducibly distinct both from distribution and from each other: exploitation, marginalization, powerlessness, cultural imperialism and violence (Young 1990: ch. 2).

'Cultural imperialism', for example, exists when the dominant norms of a society reflect the outlook of a culturally dominant group, whose view of other groups (often derogatory) is taken to define their identities, leaving their own perspectives 'invisible'. According to Young this is the fate in the United States of women, African-Americans and the other groups represented by the new social movements (Young 1990: 58–9). It is no answer to this kind of injustice to insist on a fair distribution of material resources, since that could take place while cultural imperialism persists.

Beyond the distributive paradigm, justice must therefore concern itself with issues of recognition and participation in collective decision making. Although Young is suspicious of all universal claims in morality, she does subscribe to a broad framework for what counts as 'the good life' for all human beings. This has two basic components, mirroring what Young sees as the two main sources of injustice: first, in contrast with 'oppression' (in its various forms), one should be capable of 'developing and exercising one's capacities and expressing one's experience'; second, in contrast with 'domination', one should be capable of 'participating in determining one's action and the conditions of one's action' (Young 1990: 37). So, justice requires an approach to politics that goes beyond fair shares and that emphasizes democratic participation.

Further, it will do so at the level of groups, not just of individuals. Young contends that liberal individualism – the liberal focus on individual well-being – has led to the ignoring of group-based claims that are real and legitimate. For Young, social groups are neither mere collections of individuals nor unchanging essences. Rather, they are collectivities held together by the mutual 'affinity' of their members, which gives them a shared identity (Young 1990: 42–8). All groups have a 'culture' in this sense, and 'cultural minority' is defined by Young to include 'any group subject to cultural imperialism', a definition that she applies not only to 'ethnic or national' groups, but also to women, the elderly, the disabled, gays and lesbians and the working class (Young 1990: 175). Young's spectrum of group-right claimants is therefore much wider than Kymlicka's, for example, but it does include the ethnic and national groups that concern him. The members of all these groups suffer from collective injustices that cannot be reduced to terms of individual mistreatment and cannot be corrected by uniform individual rights. For instance, women may have the formal right to stand for political office, yet often be poorly placed to exercise that right because of child-care expectations.

According to Young, such injustices are crucially a function of the various ways in which contemporary liberal democracies deny or disvalue legitimate differences among people. This suppression of difference is abetted by the dominant contemporary political theories. Communitarianism, for instance, emphasizes 'the Rousseauist dream' of a wholly unified public in which identities are 'fused' in pursuit of a single particular conception of the common good (Young 1990: 229–32). Similarly, contemporary liberalism and republicanism appeal to the bogus notion of a 'civic public' in which people transcend their particular interests and conceptions of the good when it comes to decision making in the public realm (Young 1990: 97). Moreover, the liberal ideal of impartiality masks the reality that putatively 'neutral' principles and policies always express the preferences and worldview of some privileged group – neutrality is really cultural imperialism in disguise (Young 1990: 115).

If, in reply, liberals point to the manifest individual and cultural plurality of actual liberal societies, Young's rejoinder is that this is merely privatized difference. Liberalism tolerates differences as long as people keep these to themselves; it does not extend public acknowledgement to difference. So, for example, 'gay pride asserts that sexual identity is a matter of culture and politics, and not merely "behavior" to be tolerated or forbidden' (Young 1990: 161). Such differences should be re-evaluated in a positive light, and given the backing of public recognition and support.

In policy terms, the thrust of Young's view is away from 'difference-blind' approaches that aspire to impartiality and neutrality. These ideals are impossible, dangerous and must be abandoned. Rather, key group differences should be publicly acknowledged and endorsed in a new ideal of 'democratic cultural pluralism' (Young 1990: 163). More specifically, this involves group-specific rights, such as rights of affirmative action and, above all, group representation – for example, rules setting quotas for the representation of particular groups in political and other institutions, and 'group veto power regulating specific policies that affect a group directly, such as reproductive rights policy for women, or land use policy for Indian reservations' (Young 1990: 184).[1]

Young's justification of special group representation begins with a general argument for democracy: people are most likely to be treated justly, their basic claims to self-development and self-determination advanced, if they have some say in the decisions that affect them. Yet in contemporary liberal democracies certain groups tend to be under-represented in the various institutions and forums where influential decisions are made. Such groups are typically those that have been historically oppressed or marginalized in various ways – 'working-class people', women, gays and lesbians and ethnic, racial and cultural minorities (Young 2000: 141). Consequently, special rights of group representation will be granted only to oppressed groups like these because dominant group interests are well served already (Young 1990: 187).

In general, such rights will aim 'to promote greater inclusion of members of under-represented social groups' (Young 2000: 141). These measures may involve, for example, 'quotas in electoral lists, proportional representation, reserved seats, [and] the drawing of boundaries for electoral jurisdictions'. These particular devices concern the legislature, but the general principle of special representation extends to other government and quasi-governmental bodies together with the non-governmental organizations of 'civil society'. Reform of this kind is needed, in Young's view, in order to overcome historical exclusion of particular groups from political influence, to expose the partiality of existing norms and institutions, and to take advantage of the 'situated knowledge' possessed by hitherto marginalized groups that could add to a society's overall stock of 'social knowledge' (Young 2000: 144).

Young's position has been much criticized. First, some critics object that the primary level of representation should be individual rather than group-based. Here Young responds that group orientations are unavoidable and salutary in contemporary politics, since people 'are better represented when they organize together to discuss their agreements and differences with each other and with officials' (Young 2000: 143). This is a reasonable extension, one might argue, of the lessons learnt by organized labour.

A more difficult set of issues is introduced by the question: *which* groups should be represented? According to one of Young's earlier formulations, what defines a 'social group' is the fact that certain people identify themselves as belonging to it as a matter of 'affinity'. But if every collectivity that identifies itself in this way must be represented, the results would be chaotic. Why not special representation for book clubs or craft circles? Young's answer is to insist that only oppressed groups should have special representation rights. But which groups count as 'oppressed'? It might be suggested that any group is oppressed whose interests and opinions are unpopular or rejected by the majority. But that would include neo-Nazis or the Ku Klux Klan.

Here Young draws a distinction between 'social perspectives', which should be represented if they are disadvantaged, and 'interests and opinions', which should not receive any special support. Social perspectives are 'basic in a way that many interests and opinions are not' (Young 2000: 146). While social perspectives are unchosen, 'structural' features of people's experience 'that position many people in similar ways whether they like it or not', interests and opinions tend to be 'voluntarily formed and organized'. More importantly still, according to Young, 'some asserted interests or opinions may be bad or illegitimate, whereas a social perspective is not in itself illegitimate'. For example, white supremacist opinions are illegitimate (because they deny basic equality) but the social perspective of white people is not.

Can interests and opinions be separated from social perspectives as neatly as Young supposes? Many interests and opinions are arguably just as unchosen as the broader perspectives from which they emerge. White supremacist opinions are not the necessary result of a white perspective (if there is such a thing), but certain kinds of white upbringing may make such views harder to avoid or shake off.[2] Young might respond (in the manner of liberals) that it is always possible for people to question and revise their interests and opinions, but the example of white supremacism suggests that in some cases this will involve getting some critical distance from the more 'structural' perspective too.

Young's distinction between interests and perspectives also has an ad hoc feel about it. One wonders whether she might look more favourably on special support for interests and opinions if they were on the side of the angels – and indeed, she does allow such a possibility for groups 'with legitimate interests but few resources' (Young 2000: 147). This suggests that what really matters is not whether we are dealing with an interest or a perspective, but whether an interest or perspective is ethically unobjectionable and unfairly disadvantaged in some way. But if that is the test for special representation, then few groups would fail to qualify. Even middle-class white males may be able to work up a case if they can point to at least one component of their identity in virtue of which their self-development and determination are less than they might be. This possibility recalls the point, forcefully made by the cosmopolitans, that any one person has multiple identities and that these cut across one another (see Chapter 4). Young acknowledges this but does not seem to consider its implications for her own view (Young 1990: 171). Kymlicka does consider the implication, suggesting that those who count as oppressed on Young's definition amount to about 80 per cent of the population of the United States (Kymlicka 1995a: 145).

Supposing that some plausible class of oppressed groups can be identified as deserving of special representation, who will speak for these groups? Must the representative be a member of the relevant group or could he or she be an outsider? One line of objection to Young's approach takes her to be advocating a 'descriptive' or 'mirror' theory of representation, according to which 'to represent' is narrowly interpreted to mean 'to stand for', like a copy, rather than the more active sense of representation required for advancing the political interests of a group (Young 2000: 142).[3] Women must be represented by women, Hispanics must be represented by Hispanics. Young replies that this is a narrow reading of her position, which looks for better representation not of particular group attributes (e.g. gender or cultural identity) but of the group's social perspective. For this purpose it is not essential that the representative possess the 'descriptive attributes' typical of group members, although for someone to be able to represent the perspective without the attributes would be 'not very common' (Young 2000: 148).

But that response raises another set of problems. Given that it is the group's social perspective that is to be represented, how is this to be identified? For one thing, can it be identified without invoking an 'essentialist' account of the group, attributing to it a core set of values and norms that express a permanent character, and thus ignoring the dynamic and internally contested nature of all groups? Young argues that while negative, imperialist images of groups are always essentialist, the positive re-evaluations asserted by the groups themselves can take account of their own constructed nature. But she also concedes that 'to be sure, it is difficult to articulate positive elements of group affinity without essentializing them, and these movements do not always succeed in doing so' (Young 1990: 172). This problem is likely to be exacerbated by her insistence that the special rights she champions must be conceived not as temporary routes to integration but as permanent markers of abiding difference.

Further, even if a group's perspective can be identified without essentialism, who is to decide what that perspective is? Groups can be just as oppressive of their own members as larger societies can be of minority groups in their midst. This is especially so in the case of 'traditional' ethnic and religious groups dominated by elite leaders, usually male and/or elderly, who see themselves as guardians of a fixed way of life involving a strict division and hierarchy of roles, usually gendered. We have seen this problem of intra-group domination and conflict raised many times, and it is rightly a major liberal concern.

Once again, Young formally acknowledges the difficulty, but does little to address it. She notes the objection that group representation may 'obscure differences within the group', and concedes that social perspectives are not so unified that they exclude the likelihood of divergent views within them (Young 2000: 143, 148). In reply she raises the idea of 'pluralizing' group representation: a group could be represented by 'a small committee' rather than just one person (Young 2000: 148). But this would do little to solve the problem of the 'traditional' group dominated by an elite, since the committee would likely be just another forum for those with influence. More reliable protection is likely to be provided by respect for individual rights, but Young's hostility to liberal universality and her insistence on respect for cultural difference make the fate of individual rights in her democracy uncertain.

Perhaps this problem weighs less with Young because the groups she usually has in mind are exemplified by the new social movements rather than by indigenous or religious groups – the example she gives of representation by committee concerns representation of 'the perspective of women' (Young 2000: 148). But, as mentioned before, her theory is explicitly intended to encompass ethnic and cultural groups, such as Native American groups. And even in the case of the new social movements, she allows that 'separation and self-organization risk creating pressures toward homogenization of the groups themselves, creating new privileges and exclusions' (Young 1990: 167–8). Still, Young's salient message is that group autonomy is to be pursued in the name of democracy and justice. How emancipatory is that course likely to be without the kind of liberal constraints that Young condemns as false neutrality and cultural imperialism?

A final set of issues concerns the practical application of special group representation. Reviewing the main candidates for institutions that might turn the principle into practice, Young concedes that all have problems. Reserved seats (exemplified by the Maori seats in the New Zealand parliament) tend to freeze group identity and intergroup relations, marginalize the represented group and make it complacent about stating its case to the wider public. Young concludes that reserved seats 'should be a last resort and temporary option' (Young 2000: 150). Similar difficulties attach to group quotas within party lists and to the redrawing of electoral boundaries. On the whole, Young insists that all these measures are just, but allows that they all have serious costs. She herself seems to doubt that the costs are always worth paying.[4]

Overall, the strength of Young's view lies in the intuitive attraction of democracy: the idea that, for many reasons, people should be given a role in making the rules that govern them. But the particular version of democracy that Young champions, group representation, is fraught with difficulty.

Intercultural Dialogue: Parekh

Another approach to multicultural democracy is presented by Parekh. As we have already seen, Parekh rejects liberalism as an adequate framework for multiculturalism, seeking the materials for that framework at 'a higher level of philosophical abstraction' (Parekh 2006: 14). He recommends a search for 'dialogical consensus', which can only be achieved when majority and minority cultural groups resolve their conflicts through public conversation and debate (Parekh 2006: 266). For Parekh, dialogue should be 'contextual' rather than abstract, starting from a society's 'public' or 'operative' values, by which he means those shared values that are most central to the society's public institutions, laws and civic culture.

However, this is only a starting point, not a rigid set of limits. As a dialogue develops, the parties may appeal to universal values. The conversation is 'bifocal', involving critical reflection not only on the minority practices in question but also on the majority norms with which they conflict (Parekh 2006: 271). Further, the debate is unlikely to be a simple matter of polarization between the majority and the minority, but will probably involve disagreements among sub-groups within these larger parties. As a result, intercultural dialogue is potentially transformative – for both the minority and the wider society.

Parekh goes on to analyse the structure of a typical intercultural dialogue. He begins by assuming that the wider society's operative values are those of a liberal democracy, and that these are confronted by a minority practice such as female circumcision or polygamy. The subsequent debate will proceed in three phases.

First, the minority will defend itself against majority criticism by reference to the authority of its culture, or perhaps of a sacred text. This alone is unlikely to persuade the majority, says Parekh, since 'no culture is self-authenticating' – no culture is in the right just because it asserts that it is (Parekh 2006: 272). The debate will then move to a second phase in which the minority argues that the relevant practice is 'interlocked' with other elements of its culture, so that it must be regarded as central or essential or inextricable from what is central or essential. This may persuade the majority, but its obvious weakness is that – as we have seen many times – the whole idea of a culture as having an essence or core is highly questionable. Even if the notion of indispensability or inextricability can be separated from that of essence, it is usually difficult to prove that any particular practice is indispensable to, or inextricable from, a culture.

Consequently, the dialogue is likely to enter a third phase, in which the minority defends its practice by reference to values allegedly shared with it by the majority, the values of either the majority's cultural core or the majority's public political culture. Again, this defence may succeed or it may not, its principal weakness being that the majority is likely to interpret its core or operative values in its own way.

In the event that, at this third stage, consensus is still not forthcoming, Parekh concedes that 'a difficult situation arises' (Parekh 2006: 272). At this point it may be that the best thing to do is, if possible, postpone further discussion of the issue in the hope that people's views may change at some later date. If a decision has to be made, then Parekh concludes that the operative values of the majority culture should prevail. These are 'woven into its institutions and practices' and cannot be changed, against the will of the majority, without excessive disruption (Parekh 2006: 273). A society cannot be expected to accommodate practices it sincerely disagrees with 'at the cost of its own' practices and norms, and where the minority is an immigrant group they should accept that 'they are unfamiliar with the wider society's way of life, [and] they should defer to its judgement in contentious matters'.

In general and in many points of detail, Parekh's account of intercultural dialogue is a model of fairness and balance. He pays due attention to all relevant points of view and reaches conclusions on specific questions that many people will find satisfying, or at least the best that can be hoped for in situations that are often, as he says, extremely difficult.

One may wonder, however, how Parekh's dialogical theory fits with his attitude to liberalism. Recall from Chapter 5 that he regards liberalism as too culturally specific to serve as a truly universal framework for a multicultural society. This, indeed, is the point of the emphasis on dialogue: since liberalism is too narrow, we must look to dialogue to frame multicultural relations. But might it be that the dialogue he describes is as satisfactory as it is only because it trades on implicit assumptions and norms that are distinctively liberal?

This possibility is illustrated by Parekh's construction of an intercultural dialogue on polygamy – in particular, the Muslim practice of polygyny, where a man can have multiple wives. Parekh's principal, recurring objection to this practice is that it 'violates the principle of the equality of the sexes' (Parekh 2006: 284). He immediately adds that this is 'not just a Western or liberal but a rationally defensible universal moral value'. But the principle of sexual equality is widely rejected in currently non-liberal societies and was uniformly absent from pre-liberal societies, including those of the 'West'. Sexual equality seems to be an ideal that has emerged out of a distinctively liberal (and modern) sensibility, whether one wishes to see this as Western or not. To conclude that such a principle should override the sexist practices and norms of certain traditional forms of Islam is surely to side ultimately with the liberal outlook. So much, one may think, for treating liberalism as just one culturally conditioned political view among others.

Moreover, one might suspect that liberal values are smuggled into Parekh's account of dialogue at a deeper level. He assumes that the dialogue he describes will include as participants all those affected by the outcome, including groups such as women and internal dissenters. But why should dialogue include such groups unless it is framed by something like the distinctive liberal commitments to sexual equality, freedom of speech and ultimately universal equality of moral worth? If liberalism is not a framework but just one view among others, on a par with traditional cultures in which women and dissenters have no right to speak, then the inclusion of these groups could be legitimately challenged at the start.

Parekh's account represents a distinct advance on some other theories of intercultural dialogue. His view does not suffer from the excessive emphasis on difference and incommensurability that hamstrings communication in Tully's theory. Compared with Appiah's stress on narrative, it returns us to the realm of reason-giving and consequently to the possibility of a more determinate consensus. But it also relies, in the end, on a framework of liberal values and principles that Parekh claimed to reject when he was criticizing liberalism. For a family of theories in which such a liberal framework is explicitly acknowledged and endorsed, we should consider deliberative democracy.

Deliberative Democracy: Benhabib

It may be objected to both Young and Parekh that their use of democracy and dialogue is too uncritical, directed too much to the preservation of existing cultures rather than to the questioning and reformation of those cultures. Support for this view can be found in Seyla Benhabib's *The Claims of Culture* (2002). For Benhabib, multiculturalism and democracy are not always allies; they may be at odds. Certain 'strong' forms of multiculturalism endorse 'an all-too-quick reification of given groups' identities' that risks 'freezing existing group differences' in a way that often privileges the power of elites and stifles other voices (Benhabib 2002: viii–ix). But Benhabib also believes that multiculturalism and democracy can work in tandem if multiculturalists accept cultures as fluid and contestable constructions and democratic processes as critical rather than merely defensive. The form of democracy best suited to this role is 'deliberative'.

Benhabib begins with a vigorous rejection of 'strong' or 'mosaic' multiculturalism, which emphasizes the distinctiveness of cultures: 'I mean the view that human groups and cultures are clearly delineated and identifiable entities that coexist, while maintaining firm boundaries, as would pieces of a mosaic' (Benhabib 2002: 8). One implication of this mosaic view is that each culture possesses its own independent ethical perspective, which is consequently impervious to criticism from any other point of view. Strong multiculturalism is essentially cultural relativism.

As an example of strong multiculturalism in action, Benhabib cites a Californian criminal case in which a Cambodian immigrant from the Hmong ethnic group presented a 'cultural defence' to a charge of kidnapping and rape. In his culture, he argued, these were the customary ways of choosing a bride. This defence seems to have been partially accepted as mitigating the sentence handed down after conviction. For Benhabib, the Hmong case is an instance of a widespread, and mistaken, multiculturalist insistence that cultures must be respected regardless of their content.

According to Benhabib, strong multiculturalism rests on the familiar but mistaken Herderian understanding of cultures as each possessing a unique 'personality', sharply distinguished from – indeed, incommensurable with – that of other cultures but internally 'unified and homogeneous' (Benhabib 2002: 2). Since each culture sets the terms of well-being for those who live within it, the survival and flourishing of cultures become imperative: 'above all, we are told, it is good to preserve and propagate such cultures and cultural differences' (Benhabib 2002: 4). The individual can live well only by developing the distinctive identity offered by her own cultural tradition.

For Benhabib, all this is bad politics, bad sociology and bad philosophy. It is bad politics because it locks people into traditions and identities that may be quite unjust and harmful, such as the patriarchal traditions of which Okin complained (Chapter 3). It is bad sociology because cultures are not internally univocal but subject to dissent and contestation by their members as well as by outsiders. People do not form their identities by realizing some pre-existing cultural essence. Rather, identities emerge through continuing dialogue among many different individuals and groups bearing different and often conflicting descriptions of, and prescriptions for, themselves and others. This identity-forming dialogue is carried on across cultures and within them. The boundaries between cultures are not as sharp, nor are their internal elements as harmonious, as strong multiculturalism supposes.

Strong multiculturalism is also bad philosophy because it is logically incoherent (Benhabib 2002: 28–9, 30). If cultures were really as radically distinct as the thesis supposes, each constituting its own discrete mental world, we would not even be able to have that thought because we would not recognize other such worlds as having enough in common with our own to count as 'cultures' at all.

When it comes to identifying the strong multiculturalists with whom Benhabib takes issue, one might have thought that Young, Tully and Parekh would figure prominently on her list, but in fact she singles out Taylor and Kymlicka. Both, in her view, place too much emphasis on the preservation of existing cultures because of their background commitment to cultural uniqueness and essentialism. This is thoroughly unfair to Kymlicka, although it may have some purchase on Taylor (see Chapters 2 and 5).

Nor, however, is Benhabib entirely happy with some of the more universalist alternatives on offer. For example, Barry's liberal egalitarianism is flawed, according to Benhabib, because it fails to acknowledge distinctively cultural forms of disadvantage that cannot be addressed in terms of legal or economic equality.[5] Similarly, Rawls's reworking of the traditional liberal privatization strategy does not go far enough in acknowledging multicultural realities. Rawls is both too timid and too optimistic. On the one hand he confines the topic of public debate to 'constitutional essentials' and allows discussion of these matters only through a constrained 'public reason' that generally excludes reference to controversial conceptions of the good. On the other hand he expects this process to produce an 'overlapping consensus' on those same constitutional essentials. Benhabib is sceptical of the prospects for such a consensus being reached under conditions of contemporary multicultural diversity (Benhabib 2002: 108, 111). In particular she sees this as unlikely in advance of the kind of public discussion, involving appeal to controversial religious and cultural beliefs, of the kind that Rawls wants kept out of public discourse.

This is where Benhabib's own proposal comes in. In contrast to Rawls's privatization of culture and filtering of 'public reason', she emphasizes the value of public dialogue that tackles controversial issues openly. In short, her response to multiculturalism is her own version of 'deliberative democracy'.[6] Controversial issues of public policy should be decided through a process of open discussion in which all the affected parties have a voice and are allowed and expected to justify their positions by giving reasons that can be understood by the other parties. Deliberation requires actual public debate, and so contrasts with conventional liberal reliance on fixed constitutional principles, and also with relativist reifications of cultural boundaries. This makes possible the critical revision not only of a society's basic political principles if that is necessary to respond to minority perspectives, but also of minority identities in keeping with the fluid and contested nature of groups.

Deliberation also contrasts with more familiar forms of democracy in that it requires an attempt to persuade opponents by means of reasoned argument rather than the mere assertion of interests and prejudices backed by power-plays and horse-trading. Deliberative democracy is therefore a universalist position in that it appeals to the possibility and authority of disinterested reason. In Benhabib's case this reflects her commitment to the 'discourse ethics' of Jürgen Habermas, in which 'norms and normative institutional arrangements can be deemed valid only if all who would be affected by their consequences can be participants in a practical discourse through which the norms are adopted' (Benhabib 2002: 11).[7] Universal principles of respect and reciprocity (all participants have the same rights to speak and raise questions) are presupposed by the notion of unforced and unbiased discussion.

For Benhabib, deliberative democracy is a natural solution to the problems of multicultural coexistence. In a multicultural deliberative system the members of cultural, religious and other groups will negotiate their place in the larger society by sharing in a free and fair dialogue. Through such a dialogue the contours not only of public policy but also of minority-group identity are open to discussion and revision. The hallmark of this arrangement will be its flexibility, in contrast with the rigidity of both relativist and universalist alternatives.

As an example of what deliberation might achieve, Benhabib discusses the French 'scarf affair'. This began in 1989 when three Muslim girls were suspended from their high school for continuing to wear their headscarves in defiance of a ruling by their headmaster. The headmaster believed that his ruling was necessary in order to maintain the French republican principle of *laïcité*, which involves a strict separation of state from religion: a public high school is part of the public sphere from which prominent religious symbols are to be excluded. The headmaster thus took the headscarves to be Muslim religious requirements, and that interpretation was accepted both by many of those who condemned the headscarf on feminist grounds and by many who defended the girls' actions on the basis of freedom of religion.

The problem with these approaches, according to Benhabib, is that little attention was paid to what the girls themselves meant by their actions. Rather than helpless victims of religious repression, perhaps they were making an autonomous political and personal statement of their own. In any case, 'it would have been both more democratic and fairer had the school authorities not simply dictated the meaning of their act to these girls, and had the girls been given a public say in the interpretation of their own actions' (Benhabib 2002: 118). This reflects one of the basic ideals of deliberative democracy: allow, even require, those affected by a public policy to be given a respectful hearing in public.

Deliberative democracy is not without its problems. The whole notion hovers uneasily between two tendencies. On the one hand the 'democratic' emphasis suggests an affinity with the old republican ideal of political participation. But participation, especially mass participation, has a spotty political record and dubious prospects from a liberal point of view, since popular political movements have often trampled on the rights of individuals and minorities. Public dialogue therefore seems to be no guarantee of just and desirable political outcomes.

On the other hand, as its supporters will no doubt reply, deliberative democracy stands not for unqualified popular participation but for *deliberation*, that is, public decision making by reasoned argument. Reasoned argument may indeed help minority groups. But this deliberative aspect of the ideal is in obvious tension with its democratic dimension, since reasoned argument is seldom the currency of public political engagement even among group representatives and elites. For deliberative democracy to work, public debate would have to be disciplined in ways that would be new and perhaps alien to many contributors.

This problem is only amplified by the addition of a multicultural dimension in which some parties to the conversation are traditionally disinclined to accept its most basic assumptions, such as equality of respect (for women, for example). Here the question arises, is Benhabib's deliberative approach any more likely than Rawls's to achieve consensus in the face of deep cultural differences? Benhabib herself acknowledges this objection in the words of Joseph Valadez: 'differences in worldview or disagreements in needs and interests between cultural groups can be so deep that the disadvantages of cultural minorities to induce social co-operation to attain their political objectives can remain very significant' (Valadez quoted by Benhabib 2002: 133).

In reply, Benhabib begins by rejecting this worry so far as it depends on the assumption that cultural perspectives are so different as to be incommensurable. Her philosophical objection to that assumption, that it is logically incoherent, has already been noted. In addition, she argues, it is simply not true empirically that intercultural disagreement is usually among perspectives that are quite so different. Further, it is only through dialogue that we can assess how much disagreement there is. 'Most democratic dialogue is not about incommensurables, but about divergent and convergent beliefs, and very often we do not know how deep these divergences are, or how great their overlap may be, until we have engaged in conversation' (Benhabib 2002: 136).

Of course, short of radical incommensurability there remains the likelihood of considerable divergence of belief in a multicultural society, hence the likelihood of considerable difficulty, even given the fairest and most open of conversations, in achieving consensus. Here Benhabib's basic point is that partial agreements may still be possible

– for example, agreements on conclusions but for different reasons (much like Rawls's overlapping consensus), or compromises (Benhabib 2002: 142–5). Moreover, even if there is no consensus, dialogue may still be useful in providing a learning process on both sides. In the scarf case 'the larger French society needs to learn not to stigmatize and stereotype as "backward and oppressed creatures" all those who wear what appears at first glance to be a religiously mandated piece of clothing; the girls themselves and their supporters, in the Muslim community and elsewhere, must learn to give a justification of their actions with "good reasons in the public sphere"' (Benhabib 2002: 118).

Another line along which Benhabib's view can be questioned concerns institutions.[8] What practical arrangements will ensure that multicultural (and other) dialogue is actually 'deliberative' rather than merely reflective of group interests and prejudices? Benhabib does not offer much detail on this point, insisting that her position is 'not a blueprint for institutions', and mentioning the need for 'democratic experimentation with institutional design and redesign' (Benhabib 2002: 107, 184). Among the concrete measures she does suggest are 'certain land, language and representation rights for indigenous populations', and the containment of rising fundamentalisms by 'the splitting of the private spheres of family and religious observance from politics and the economy' (Benhabib 2002: 185). These suggestions are reasonable but scarcely new. Indeed they are identical with policies advanced by writers whom Benhabib criticizes, respectively Kymlicka and Rawls. Nor do they seem to have much to do with deliberative democracy.

Benhabib's most distinctive proposal in this connection is her notion of a 'dual-track' approach. This refers on the one hand to 'established institutions, like the legislature and the judiciary in liberal-democratic societies; on the other hand [to] the political activities and struggles of social movements, associations, and groups in civil society' (Benhabib 2002: 106). Benhabib contrasts her position with that of Rawls, who requires a constrained public reason in the realm of 'established institutions', allowing the authentic voices of particular cultural and other groups to speak only in non-government settings. Benhabib wants intercultural dialogue to flourish in both of these arenas.

However, is Benhabib's position really very different from Rawls's, or indeed from existing liberal-democratic practice? Her intercultural dialogue is itself hedged by the norms of discourse ethics – standard liberal requirements of egalitarian reciprocity, voluntary self-ascription (participants are in general entitled to choose how they will be identified), and freedom of exit and association. In the end, her position comes down to a plea for greater and more sensitive public dialogue among groups and individuals within civil society. It is not obvious how this would make much difference to the way the Hmong rape case was decided, or the French scarf case. Once the various voices have been heard, what then? A decision will still have to be made, and on Benhabib's own account it will be made by the existing institutions: the courts and the legislatures.

A final line of objection might go further still. Up to this point I have considered suggestions that Benhabib's deliberative democracy does not help much in a multicultural context or add much to the resources that liberal democracies have available currently. But might it be that in the multicultural field deliberation is positively harmful? For example, might it be biased in favour of some cultures against others? This issue is pursued by Iris Young.

Deliberative Democracy Expanded: Young

In her later work Young endorses deliberative democracy, but in a version that aims at greater 'inclusion' than some others (Young 2000: 5–6).[9] In particular she worries that orthodox forms of deliberative democracy place too much stress on the role of formal argument, a tendency that excludes or marginalizes those groups for whom structured argument from premise to conclusion is not their strong suit. Rather, Young argues, democratic interaction should be recognized as including other forms of political communication too.

Young begins this phase of her thought by contrasting deliberation with 'aggregative' democracy, the dominant contemporary model in which public decisions are made simply by adding up votes without requiring any public reason-giving or interaction on the part of the voters. The drawbacks of aggregative democracy include the rawness of the preferences aggregated – that is, the ignorance and prejudice often embodied in such preferences – and the system's lack of any test for 'normative and evaluative objectivity' (Young 2000: 21). By contrast, deliberative democracy, with its constitutive principles of reason-giving, reasonableness and publicity, is more faithful to the basic democratic ideals of political equality and inclusion, and more likely to lead to 'wise and just' outcomes because of its strongly interactive character, hence its greater potential for transforming people's views.

However, although she endorses the general deliberative framework, Young regards certain versions of deliberative theory as too narrow and exclusive. These tend to be the more mainstream forms of the theory, associated with Habermas and Rawls, that emphasize reasoned argument as the primary form of deliberation. Benhabib belongs in this camp too. The basic problem with that emphasis, according to Young, is that argument needs shared premises to get it off the ground, and these are lacking under conditions of social and cultural difference. In this connection she cites Lyotard's notion of the 'différend', where a dominant discourse of justice does not recognize the kind of injustice suffered by some people, and in effect silences them (Young 2000: 37). In addition, the privileging of argument tends to bring with it the privileging of the kind of articulateness characteristic of highly educated people, and the kind of formal and dispassionate reasoning specific to certain cultures rather than others.[10]

Further, Young objects to the tendency of the mainstream deliberative theories to privilege other ideals in addition to argument (Young 2000: 40–51). First, there is the notion of a unified common good, conceived either as a precondition for deliberation or a goal at which deliberation should aim. Here Young invokes her long-held view that any notion of a unified public with a single common good is likely to express, in reality, the outlook of some particular dominant subgroup (Young 2000: 40–4). Second, mainstream deliberation tends to privilege 'face-to-face' discussion, when the reality of mass society makes representation a necessity, along with a 'decentred' conception of deliberation in which political power is not exercised in any single and decisive arena but disseminated throughout a society and always subject to review (Young 2000: 44–7). Third, deliberation is often equated with 'orderliness', thus 'excluding modes of political communication deemed disorderly or disruptive' – for example, 'rowdy street demonstrations' (Young 2000: 47).

In all these respects, Young believes, leading theories of deliberation have the effect of excluding certain kinds of people from the democratic process. The exclusion may be 'external', where groups are kept out of public discussion altogether, or more subtly internal, where they are formally admitted but effectively ignored or marginalized or denigrated once there (Young 2000: 53–7). Young is especially concerned with this second, internal form of exclusion, and proposes that our understanding of legitimate political communication be framed more expansively.

Defenders of orthodox, reason-based deliberation would reply to Young along lines indicated by Benhabib. To begin with, Young's appeal to Lyotard implies that group perspectives can be understood as incommensurable, but that notion is condemned by Benhabib as unrealistic and incoherent, as we have seen. Young's further claim that the use of reasoned argument automatically disadvantages underprivileged groups is dismissed by Benhabib as 'a species of exoticism' (Benhabib 2002: 139). Why suppose that such groups are incapable of constructing rational arguments?[11] Nor does Benhabib assume that deliberation must take place in a unified public sphere in pursuit of a single common good. On her view, no such common good precedes dialogue, and even post-dialogue consensus is not guaranteed. Finally, Benhabib is not wedded to the idea that deliberation must always be face-to-face or that dialogue must always be 'orderly' – although she does insist that it be orderly enough to include all affected parties in a respectful way. Young would surely not reject that.

On the whole, reason-based deliberation stands up well to the critical aspect of Young's view. But might the constructive phase of her view still provide the more orthodox position with a useful supplement?

Young states a case for three alternative modes of political communication in particular. First, 'greeting' is the public acknowledgement of the parties to a discussion, exemplified by the elaborate greeting of Maori tradition and by the protocols of international diplomacy (Young 2000: 57–62). Such practices affirm the presence and standing of different groups in a given arena, and thus communicate norms of respect and willingness to listen.

Second, the role of 'rhetoric', or *how* things are put across, should be acknowledged (Young 2000: 63–70). While orthodox deliberative theory emphasizes dispassionate reasoning, a more natural mode of communication for many groups is to speak passionately or figuratively, or to convey their message without speech – for example, through gestures. Communication should not be dismissed simply because it is rhetorical rather than more narrowly rational. Rhetoric may be important, for example, in identifying and addressing a particular audience.

Third, there is an important role for narrative or storytelling – again, a more natural form of communication than structured argument for some groups (Young 2000: 70–7).[12] Narrative can advance public discussion in various ways: as a bridge between groups when shared assumptions are lacking, as a way of raising people's consciousness of their shared experience and identity, as a means of overcoming prejudice – personal testimony can be a highly effective weapon against generalization and stereotype – as a route to understanding a group's deep values and assumptions, and as a device for eliciting the 'situated knowledge' of particular groups, thus contributing to a cumulative 'social knowledge'.

Overall, these three modes of communication are not intended to displace reason-giving and argument in deliberation, but rather to supplement it (Young 2000: 77). In this way, democracy will remain broadly deliberative, but in a manner that is more inclusive of different groups, with their varying communicative idioms, than the orthodox deliberative theories, with their stress on argument.

One obvious objection to Young's position is that her non-argumentative modes of political communication are open to abuse and manipulation. Greeting may be pro forma or insincere, rhetoric may be calculated to appeal to prejudice and stir up irrational and destructive feelings, and narratives may be misleading or delusional or fabricated. In particular, disorderly demonstration may degenerate into violence or coercion.

Young concedes all this but responds that argument is open to abuse too. The remedy for manipulative greeting, rhetoric and narrative is the same as 'for false or invalid argument', namely 'criticism': applying 'standards of evaluation to them as well as to argument' (Young 2000: 79). Such standards include the characteristic deliberative principles of justifiability, respectfulness and publicity. Similarly, street demonstrations and the like can be disorderly and still satisfy the requirement of reasonableness, which involves, among other things, non-violence.

Does this mean that Young regards argument as no more central to democracy than the other kinds of communication she discusses? She sometimes gives the impression that whether people make their point through argument or rhetoric does not matter, as long as they observe the norms of reasonableness and publicity. But her position is ambiguous. On the one hand she asserts that 'an inclusive theory and practice of communicative democracy should not privilege specific ways of making claims and arguments' (Young 2000: 80). So, presumably, storytelling is just as good as argument in principle. There may be varying levels of excellence in the way people perform in each of these spheres – some people are better at argument, others at narrative – but the spheres themselves are equally valid and equally appropriate for democratic debate. On the other hand, she more than once insists that her stress on narrative and the other modes is intended 'to add to rather than replace theorizing that emphasizes the role of argument', suggesting that argument is central after all and that the other forms are adjuncts (Young 2000: 57, 79).

Whatever Young's own view, there is good reason to insist that it is argument that should be primary from a democratic perspective. The other forms of communication she discusses, while significant and valuable, should be regarded as secondary. First, disorderliness does carry a risk of descent into violence. Indeed, it is arguable that even formally non-violent forms of disruptive protest can be coercive, as in the case of the shouting down of unpopular speakers.

Second, if rhetoric, narrative and disruption are allowed to override argument, that may well worsen the position of precisely those disadvantaged groups whose interests Young is most concerned to advance. It is those groups that, historically, have most often been the victims of inflammatory rhetoric, false and manipulative narratives and intimidating public gatherings. The German Jews provide the classic example, but there are many others.

More generally, Young's account lacks any adequate sense that argument and the other forms of communication can be in tension with one another. She assumes that the latter will 'add to' the former, never that they will obstruct or inhibit argument. In part this is because she wants to get away from the opposite assumption that argument and the other modes are always opposed. But the truth is probably somewhere in between: greeting, rhetoric, narrative and disruption can support argument, but they can also undermine it. Disruption is especially troubling in this regard. Young suggests that disruptive protest is acceptable as long as those doing the disrupting are representing disadvantaged groups. But even if that can be justified along affirmative action lines, it returns us to the fraught question of which groups count as 'disadvantaged' and who are entitled to speak for them.

Third, while it is true that argument can be abused too, it does not follow that it is just as open to abuse as greeting, rhetoric, narrative and disruptive protest – that all these modes are ethically symmetrical. Argument is self-correcting and fundamental in a way that Young's other modes of political communication are not. Bad arguments are corrected by better arguments. But the abuse of rhetoric, for example, is not corrected simply by better rhetoric, since 'better' here just means more effective, not truer or more just. It takes the methods of argument – analysis and questioning – to test rhetoric thoroughly. The same goes for greeting and narrative. The abuse of these forms of communication can be reliably checked, in the end, only by argument. Argument, on the other hand, polices itself.

The upshot is that, while Young is right to point to a significant role in democracy for modes of communication other than formal argument, she goes too far when she suggests that these operate on the same ethical level as argument. The most basic feature of the deliberative model, which Young says she accepts in general, is the idea that democratic decisions should be justified by reasons. Reason-giving, analysis and questioning are fundamental to this whole approach. To the extent that Young denies this, she is no longer working within a deliberative framework. More importantly, she is to that extent inviting a form of politics that is not only chaotic but likely to disadvantage further the very groups she claims to champion.

Summary

Democratic approaches to multiculturalism start with the attractive idea that justice for minority cultural groups requires giving them a say in the institutions and processes by which they are governed. This broad demand may be advanced in several ways, all of which have strengths and weaknesses. Young's group representation acknowledges that conventional interest-group politics is not a level playing-field, but her definition of 'oppressed' groups is unclear and it remains uncertain how such groups can be represented in a way that generates more benefits than costs. Parekh's intercultural dialogue is really a systematic account of existing best practice in liberal democracies, which is both to his credit and also at odds with his claim to be transcending liberalism. Similarly, Benhabib, while appearing to be ambitious in her demand for greater 'deliberation', in the end proposes little in the way of institutional change. Young's plea for alternative modes of political engagement fails to supplant reasoned argument as the dominant form of democratic participation. On the whole, democratic multiculturalism tends to be rich in aspiration and rhetoric but poor in credible concrete proposals for reform.

7

Value Pluralists

A major issue was left hanging at the end of Chapter 1. What happens when, as the capability theorists suppose, universal values are conflicting and incommensurable – that is, lacking a common currency or single ranking formula? This is the territory of value pluralism, an idea especially associated with Isaiah Berlin. One might suppose that the pluralist outlook would tend naturally towards support for multiculturalism. Different combinations of incommensurable goods would seem to constitute a multiplicity of genuinely valuable ways of life. Hence, one would expect that value pluralism and multiculturalism would be mutually sympathetic points of view, the major point of overlap being an emphasis on the value of cultural diversity.

Pluralists do indeed agree on the value of cultural diversity, at least within limits, but beyond that common ground there is little agreement on anything else. Opinion divides over two issues in particular. First, does pluralist support for cultural diversity point towards multiculturalism proper – that is, to the positive valuation and political promotion of multiple cultures within a society – or only towards the toleration of multiple cultures? Second, whatever the pluralist answer to that first question may be, should pluralist politics be bounded by liberal principles or should liberalism itself be regarded as just one bundle of values among others with no authority over the rest?

I commence by setting out Berlin's basic concept of value pluralism and his account of its political implications, which are broadly liberal and supportive of a tolerant majoritarian nationalism rather than multiculturalism. The second section deals with two pluralists, John

Gray and Bhikhu Parekh, who both reject liberalism as a universal position but who diverge in their treatment of cultures. While Parekh defends multiculturalism as a general political formula, Gray advocates a diversity of political forms among which multiculturalism itself is only one possibility. Finally, the liberal reading of pluralism is revived by William Galston and Joseph Raz, although in different ways, Galston arguing for a scheme based on group toleration while Raz favours multiculturalism qualified by the state promotion of personal autonomy.

Value Pluralism, Liberalism and Cultural Diversity: Berlin

Berlin's idea of value pluralism reacts against the notion of moral monism, the view that all ethical questions have a single correct answer that can be read off from a single formula applicable in all cases (Berlin 1990; 2000a: 11–14; 2002: 212–17). Such a system will be dominated by one value, or a small set of values, which overrides or serves as a common currency for all others. Examples of an overriding good include Plato's Form of the Good and Aristotle's ideal of the life of contemplation; Bentham's utilitarianism is the classic account of a common currency for all values. In these varying forms, Berlin believes, monism has been the dominant approach to morality throughout the history of Western thought.

Moral monism is a dangerous idea, Berlin argues, because it encourages utopianism, hence the justification of authoritarian, even totalitarian politics when utopia proves elusive. If there is one right answer to all moral questions, then there is a single correct way of life and a single perfect model for society. If perfection is at stake then no price can be too high to pay for it. This is the logic of modern totalitarianism, Berlin argues.

Monism is also false, according to Berlin, because it does not do justice to the depth and persistence of conflict in human moral experience. Rather, 'the world that we encounter in ordinary experience is one in which we are faced with choices between ends equally ultimate, and claims equally absolute, the realization of some of which must inevitably involve the sacrifice of others' (Berlin 2002: 213–14). There is not always one right answer; rather, there may sometimes be a range of legitimate answers depending on where the emphasis falls along a spectrum of competing goods.

This moral reality is captured by the idea of value pluralism.[1] For Berlin and other value pluralists, basic human goods are objective and universal but also irreducibly plural and incommensurable. If goods are irreducibly plural, then they may clash. More liberty may require less equality, reconciliation may have to be bought at the price of justice. Moreover, if goods are incommensurable, then each is its own measure or speaks with its own unique voice. Consequently, when such goods conflict, there is no single way of ranking them or trading them off that is correct in all cases. Depending on the circumstances, there may be many reasonable ways of responding to conflicts among them – hence the pluralist emphasis on moral experience as characterized by frequent disagreement and dilemma.

Consequently there is no possibility in a pluralist world of a 'final solution' to all moral and political problems, no chance of moral or political perfection (Berlin 2002: 212). Along with monist utopianism falls the standard justification of totalitarian dictatorship, the idea that one goal overrides all others and justifies any sacrifice. The political form that fits best with the pluralist outlook, Berlin believes, is that of a moderate liberalism that will maintain spaces of individual liberty within which people will be free to choose among competing incommensurables for themselves.

Is Berlinian pluralism a kind of relativism? One might suppose so, since pluralism proposes that are many legitimate ways of ranking goods, from which it might seem to follow that whole cultures are incommensurable, hence equally authoritative. This would suggest, in turn, support for a radical form of multiculturalism, unrestricted by any single political framework. Berlin does sometimes come close to expressing such a view, especially in his earlier interpretation of Herder (Momigliano 1976). For Herder, Berlin writes with apparent approval, each culture or 'nation' has its own unique outlook, incommensurable with that of any other nation (Berlin 2000b: 234–5).

However, Berlin's more considered position is that value pluralism is distinct from cultural relativism and superior to it as an account of morality. Relativists, Berlin writes, misconceive cultures as 'impenetrable bubbles' or 'windowless boxes', wholly separate worlds among which there is no human commonality and so no real understanding and communication (Berlin 1990: 11, 85). According to Berlin, that is not the view of proto-pluralists like Herder and Vico, who rightly believe that we can understand other cultures by a process of imaginative empathy (Berlin 2000b: 49, 197, 211, 236). What makes this understanding possible is the universality of basic human ends – liberty, equality, justice, and courage, for example – that is denied by strong cultural relativists.

It is worth adding a point of distinction between pluralism and cultural relativism that Berlin does not spell out, but which has been noted by other pluralists – namely, that pluralists are better placed than relativists to explain moral conflict. Cultural relativists tend to see moral disagreement in terms of the divergence of cultural perspectives, each unique and infallible – the model of cultures as internally univocal and externally bounded that is now so widely discredited (see Chapter 1). For pluralists, on the other hand, there is more room to see moral conflict as not merely intercultural but also intra-cultural and intra-personal. Conflict arises not only among cultures but also among goods within cultures, consequently among people who disagree about the proper ranking of these goods, and even within individuals who feel torn in different directions. Moreover, similar patterns of conflict tend to be repeated, in different local forms, across cultural lines – for example, conflicts between family obligations and wider duties recur in many cultures and periods. Pluralists argue that their view is truer to our experience of both goods and conflicts among those goods that transcend cultural boundaries (Williams 1979: 225; Lukes 2003: 104).

Still, the pluralist emphasis on hard moral choices might seem to have one feature in common with strong relativism: it might appear to undermine not only utopianism and totalitarianism but also the liberalism supported by Berlin. Indeed, any reasoned universalist political position will involve judgements that privilege certain values or packages of values over others. If those values are incommensurable, what reason do we have to choose one package rather than another? In particular (contra Berlin), why should we choose a liberal package rather than a socialist or conservative one?

There are at least three different responses to this problem in Berlin's work. First, he sometimes seems to believe that incommensurable values are wholly incomparable with one another, and that consequently choices among them must be ultimately non-rational, or not guided by any reason that is decisive over others (Berlin 1979: 69–70, 74–5). If this is his view then his commitment to liberal solutions in preference to the alternatives looks arbitrary. Indeed, on this strong reading of incommensurability, no political position is rationally justifiable since any such position rests ultimately on a non-rational plumping for one set of values rather than another.

However, Berlin eventually rejected the strong interpretation of incommensurability. In a later article he insists that reasoned choice among incommensurable goods is possible, if not in the abstract then at least in particular cases (Berlin and Williams 1994). He gives no examples, but one can see how this is true of a choice between justice and reconciliation, say. Although in most cases a judicial system ought to pursue justice above all, there may be circumstances in which there is good reason for strict justice to give way, at least in part, to a policy of reconciliation.[2]

Consequently, Berlin's second view of choice under pluralism allows room for rational choice. Incommensurability does not rule out the possibility of reasoned choice within a particular context. A classic explanation of how this is possible is Aristotle's account of practical reasoning, which sees ethical decision making not as the application of abstract rules but rather as a matter of specific judgements tailored to concrete situations (*phronesis*). Berlin does not make this Aristotelian connection himself but it has been noticed by other pluralists (Nussbaum 1992; 2001; Richardson 1997).

But although this contextual view amounts to an improvement on the crude subjectivism of Berlin's first position, it still comes close to the cultural relativism he is supposed to reject. What sort of context should we look to for guidance? One obvious candidate is cultural context, and indeed Berlin sometimes speaks in just those terms, referring to the possibility of resolving hard choices by appeal to 'the general pattern of life in which we believe', or 'the forms of life of the society to which one belongs' (Berlin 2002: 47; 1990: 18). In these passages cultural convention seems to be authoritative.

However, there is a third response to the problem of pluralist choice in Berlin, one that appeals beyond particular contexts to principles of universal scope. These principles he finds implicit in the concept of pluralism itself. His main argument along these lines turns on the idea and value of choice. If pluralism is true, 'the necessity of choosing between absolute claims is then an inescapable characteristic of the human condition. This gives its value to freedom' (Berlin 2002: 214). The value-pluralist outlook emphasizes moral plurality and conflict. On this view choice moves to centre-stage in moral experience as unavoidable. If we must choose, Berlin argues, we must value freedom of choice, hence by implication a liberal order based on negative liberty.

This argument is flawed, at least in the form in which Berlin presents it, because it passes too rapidly from the necessity of choice to the value of choice, hence freedom of choice (Crowder 1994: 297–9; 2002: 81–2). To say that something is unavoidable is not to say that it is desirable. Berlin himself observes that many choices among incommensurables are painful, even tragic. Why then should we value such choices or the freedom with which to make them? A better solution might be to avoid these choices as far as possible, and one way of doing so may be to surrender such decisions to a dictator or enlightened despot. The necessity of moral choice, without more, is compatible with authoritarian as well as with liberal politics.

Nevertheless, Berlin's argument from choice is important because it hints at the possibility that the idea of pluralism itself can generate principles to frame and guide our choices among conflicting incommensurables. Such principles will cut across the claims of specific cultures, and qualify or condition the kind of multiculturalism that is acceptable from a pluralist point of view. I pursue this possibility in Chapter 9.

Berlin is an enthusiast for cultural diversity, but is he a multiculturalist? In general, he believes that human cultures are valuable and that cultural diversity is desirable. In particular, he emphasizes the role and value of 'national' cultures, for two main reasons. First, a sense of belonging, of feeling at home in your surroundings among people who understand you, is a basic good for all human beings (Berlin 2002: 200–3). Of the many forms that belonging might take, national identity is especially powerful and resilient. This claim is borne out by the survival of nationalism as a political force despite cosmopolitan predictions of its imminent demise, and by Berlin's personal identification with the Jewish experience of diaspora Zionism.[3]

Second, a case for cultural diversity is implicit in Berlin's account of pluralism. If no single way of ranking and combining values is universally correct, then many such rankings and combinations must be permissible, at least within some wide range of possibilities. Since cultures represent, in effect, particular value rankings, this is to say that many human cultures are morally valid. In this respect, Berlin is especially influenced by his reading of Vico and Herder, as we have seen.

However, Berlin's delight in cultural diversity does not amount to multiculturalism proper, because he does not support the political recognition of minority cultures within a given state. When he was asked for his views on multiculturalism in American university curricula, he replied:

> Yes, I know. Black studies, Puerto Rican studies, and the rest. I suppose this too is a bent-twig revolt of minorities which feel at a disadvantage in the context of American polyethnicity. But I believe that the common culture which all societies deeply need can only be disrupted by more than a moderate degree of self-assertion on the part of ethnic or other minorities conscious of a common identity. (Gardels 1991: 21)

Clearly, Berlin is no multiculturalist. Globally, he is a kind of liberal nationalist, favouring a world in which the dominant culture within a given territory is protected and expressed by its own nation-state. Domestically, his view is close to Barry's, supporting an egalitarian welfare state underpinned by a single majority culture within which minority groups are expected to integrate (although not necessarily assimilate) subject to safeguards for standard civil liberties.

Is Berlin's position justified? It contains some major tensions. First, if he is willing to extend political protection to national cultures that express the outlook of the majority within a state, why is he not willing to do the same for minority national cultures? This is, of course, Kymlicka's central concern. Social unity is a legitimate counterweight, as Berlin rightly points out, but the apparent viability of various forms of self-determination and devolution shows that it is not conclusive.

Second, if national cultures are valuable because they satisfy the human need for belonging, then presumably the same must be said for other cultures, such as those of immigrants. If so, might there not be a case for recognizing such groups with something like the polyethnic rights advocated by Kymlicka?[4] Since these rights are much weaker than national rights, the concern for social unity would be reduced still further. Berlin is not a multiculturalist, but perhaps he should be.

Pluralist Critics of Liberalism: Gray and Parekh

Berlin believes that pluralism and liberalism are linked somehow. That supposed link has been challenged by critics such as John Gray and Bhikhu Parekh. But although these writers agree that for pluralists liberalism is not the answer, they disagree about what to put in its place. Especially interesting for my purposes is the contrast between Parekh's pluralist defence of non-liberal multiculturalism and Gray's anti-liberal diversity.

For Gray, Berlin is correct in his basic formulation of pluralism but does not fully grasp its radical political implications (1995a: 1). Gray agrees with Berlin that pluralism implies a commitment to cultural diversity – that is, to the validity of many 'worthwhile forms of life' (Gray 1995a: 152). But he denies that liberalism or liberal cultures have any special place in that diversity. At the most Gray allows an 'agonistic' liberalism that makes no claims to universality. Rather, the best world, from a pluralist point of view, will be one containing many different political forms, some liberal and some not. That is a kind of diversity, but is it multiculturalism?

In much of his work Gray takes up a broadly conservative position emphasizing the role of tradition in resolving conflicts among incommensurables. Echoing Berlin's reference to choice guided by 'the general pattern of life in which we believe', he writes that 'the context of cultural tradition in which conflicts of value occur will itself suggest reasons for resolving such conflicts in some ways rather than others' (Gray 1995a: 155).

However, conservative traditionalism is at other times repudiated by Gray in favour of a more pragmatic notion of 'modus vivendi'. The trouble with following traditions, he reflects, is that they tend to conflict with one another. 'It is often the rival intimations of the different traditions to which we belong that engender our ethical dilemmas' (Gray 2000: 53). Which tradition, then, should we follow? His answer is that we should negotiate between them in a case-by-case way aiming at mutual accommodation or compromise. 'We do not need common values in order to live together in peace', he writes. 'We need common institutions in which many forms of life can coexist' (Gray 2000: 6).

Gray is consistent in one matter – namely, his hostility to liberalism, at any rate mainstream liberal theory.[5] Orthodox liberal thinkers – for example, Locke, Kant, Mill, Rawls and Dworkin – differ in many ways, but one crucial feature that they have in common is their universalism. They propose the liberal package of values, whatever content they ascribe to this, as optimal for all human societies and all human beings, overriding alternative accounts of the human good. They justify this by appeal to an abstract notion of 'rational choice' that Gray traces to Hobbes, who believes that certain value rankings are rational independent of particular circumstances or context (Gray 1995a; 145–6; 1995b: 66–7).

This universalism, Gray continues, is precisely what is denied by value pluralism. 'Whereas value-pluralism admits of reasonings about conflicting values in particular cases it disallows any universal principles in arbitrating their conflicts' (Gray 1995a: 156). On the pluralist view, there may be good reason to rank incommensurables in a particular situation, but there can be no such ranking that applies in all cases. Yet such a ranking is proposed by liberals, who variously advance some conception of liberty, equality, utility or justice, or some combination of these, as their overriding value. Consequently, Gray writes, the 'rationalist and universalist tradition of liberal philosophy runs aground, along with the rest of the Enlightenment project, on the reef of value pluralism' (Gray 1995b: 67).

There does remain, for Gray, the possibility of an alternative, more modest, 'agonistic' form of liberalism. This will renounce universalist claims and merely present itself as one political form among others, with no more than local authority derived from local traditions where these happen to be liberal. If universal justifications are not available, 'then the ground of liberalism must instead be found in a particular cultural tradition or form of life. This cultural tradition is that of the liberal societies themselves, in which self-creation through choice-making is a valued activity, and restraint of the negative freedom to engage in this activity is resented and stands in need of justification' (Gray 1995a: 161). And again, where traditions conflict and we have to look for a modus vivendi, this need not be liberal. 'For pluralists, a liberal regime may sometimes be the best framework for *modus vivendi*. At other times a non-liberal regime may do as well, or better' (Gray 2000: 20).

Is Gray's interpretation of pluralism a vision of multiculturalism? The answer is no, except so far as multiculturalism happens to be favoured by local traditions or a particular modus vivendi. Multiculturalism cannot be a universal prescription on Gray's view because he repudiates any universal political theory. The closest Gray comes to multiculturalism is at the global level, where he links the pluralist outlook with the valuing of a diversity of cultures, represented by a diversity of political regimes: 'the human world will be still richer in value if it contains not only liberal societies but also illiberal regimes that shelter worthwhile forms of life that would otherwise perish' (Gray 1995a: 153). But that is a defence of a certain kind of diversity, or toleration, rather than of multiculturalism proper. The latter, as we have seen, requires the active promotion of cultural diversity as a political goal within a single polity, and Gray says nothing about that.

Indeed, a general defence of domestic multiculturalism, or even of domestic cultural diversity, is contradicted by Gray's position. Among the variety of political regimes he is prepared to defend on pluralist grounds are explicitly 'authoritarian or illiberal' systems (Gray 1995a: 151). Such systems would presumably be entitled, if such was their cultural background, to assimilate or suppress cultural diversity within their sphere of influence. This view would seem to justify the cultural practices of the Soviet Union, for example, a regime which Gray roundly, and rightly, condemns elsewhere (Gray 1995b: ch. 4). If Gray is attracted to cultural and political diversity at a global level, he is also, as a consequence, indifferent to diversity at a domestic level.

Gray's argument might be challenged on many grounds, but I shall mention only one point here.[6] His argument contains a major assumption: that the pluralist case for valuing many cultures equates with a case for valuing many political regimes. But some political regimes are more hospitable to cultural diversity than others. Which is more culturally diverse, a world that contains Fascist regimes or (other things being equal) one that does not? Arguably, the world without

Fascism is more culturally diverse, because Fascism is by nature externally expansionist, hostile to societies beyond its borders, and internally totalitarian, repressive of cultural and other differences at home. Fascist regimes would, it is true, add something to cultural diversity, but they would take away a good deal more. I shall return to the notion of diversity shortly.[7]

Turning now to Parekh, recall that he is a defender of multiculturalism who rejects liberalism as a framework on the ground of its alleged ethnocentricity (Chapter 5). Rather, multiculturalism needs to be framed by a 'higher level' of principle, and this is to be found in intercultural dialogue (Chapter 6). I also took note of counter-arguments to the effect that liberalism is not ethnocentric, and that Parekh's conception of democratic dialogue turns out to depend on distinctively liberal values after all.

Parekh is also a value pluralist in the tradition of Berlin (Parekh 2006: 374 note 1). His work includes an interesting attempt to defend a non-liberal multiculturalism on the basis of, or at least consistently with, value pluralism.

Like Berlin, Parekh begins by contrasting pluralism with both moral monism and moral relativism. Monists (or 'naturalists') believe that there is one true or rational way of understanding human nature and the human good, dismissing as erroneous any cultural perspective that departs from this: 'only one way of life is fully human, true, or the best' (Parekh, 2006: 10, 16). At the opposite extreme, cultural relativists regard all cultural perspectives as equally legitimate and authoritative (Parekh 2006: 10–11, ch. 2).[8] The truth, Parekh argues, lies between these extremes, in a view that accepts both universal and cultural components to human experience.

This middle view is equivalent to the account I have given of Berlinian pluralism. Both culturalists and monists fail to do justice to the internal complexity of cultures. To begin with, culturalists misunderstand cultures by interpreting them as self-authorizing, distinct and unitary organisms, thereby ignoring both their commonalities with other cultures and their internal diversity (Parekh 2006: 11). By contrast, these latter dimensions of culture are well captured by the pluralist picture of universal patterns of moral conflict – between, say, liberty and equality, or loyalty and impartiality – that occur both across and within cultures.

However, it is Parekh's critique of monism that brings out his Berlinian antecedents more vividly. The monist faith in a single best form of life is incoherent because 'it rests on the naïve assumption that valuable human capacities, desires, virtues and dispositions form a harmonious whole and can be combined without loss' (Parekh

2006: 48). The truth is that these various capacities and virtues – 'justice and mercy, respect and pity, equality and excellence', for example, – realize goods or values that may come into conflict, so that to emphasize one is to diminish another. Moreover, the relevant values are so distinct that it is difficult to weigh them against one another, making it difficult to arrive at an overall ranking of the respective ways of life in which they are embedded.

The upshot of pluralism, for Parekh, is that it supports a case for multiculturalism. Since the basic human capacities and values can be combined in different ways, there must be a multiplicity of legitimate ways of life, or cultures. Further, since all cultures contain practices of real value, all must, to that extent, deserve respect, not merely toleration. Moreover, under modern conditions of globalization, cultures cannot be kept separate, but must often be accommodated within the same political society (Parekh 2006: 8). Finally, such respectful accommodation implies not merely 'benign neglect', to use Kymlicka's phrase, but public recognition. In Parekh's case the key form taken by public recognition is promotion of intercultural dialogue. All these elements add up to a case for multiculturalism constructed on a value-pluralist foundation.

As we have seen, Parekh denies that multiculturalism can be adequately accommodated by liberalism. His pluralist reason for that conclusion is that liberalism is too close to moral monism (Parekh 2006: chs. 1 and 3). Liberals are not as strongly monistic as earlier thinkers, such as the Greeks or medieval Christians, and they clearly try to make room for a degree of diversity, especially in the fields of religious belief and personal development. Nevertheless, Parekh argues, all liberals insist on the universality of certain claims about human nature and the human good, in particular the dignity of the individual and the desirability of individual autonomy. These attitudes are not universally accepted; rather, they are characteristic of a certain range of cultures, namely the individualistic cultures of the modern West in contrast with non-individualistic and non-Western cultures. Consequently, liberalism asserts in effect that one kind of culture is superior to another. That flies in the face of the pluralist reality that human values and virtues are too various to be wholly contained by any single way of life. Many different ways of life are equally valid.

We have already seen (in Chapter 5) a partial reply to this charge: the values characteristic of liberalism, in particular personal autonomy, are not the exclusive property of any one particular culture or narrow range of 'Western' cultures. But consistently with this it might still be argued that the liberal package of values is none the less a selective subset of the full range of human goods, and one that is no more valuable and legitimate than the alternatives. Liberalism may not be ethnocentric, but is it still too monistic?

Parekh's argument here depends on the assumption that the 'pluralism' we are talking about is a plurality of cultures or ways of life. On this assumption cultures are incommensurable and so they cannot be ranked against one another. Liberalism therefore is just one political culture among others and cannot be judged superior to its rivals. Pluralism tells us to promote a diversity of cultures, whether liberal or not.

This assumption confuses value pluralism with cultural pluralism and, indirectly, with cultural relativism. First, a diversity of cultures is not the same as a diversity of values, since some cultures are more open to a diversity of values than others. A world in which all cultures are liberal, allowing and encouraging individuals and groups to seek many different ends, is arguably more diverse, in terms of values or goods, than one in which there is a greater variety of cultures but some of these are authoritarian or internally monistic.[9]

Second, value pluralism is the idea that values or goods are incommensurable, not whole cultures. If whole cultures were incommensurable they could not be compared or criticized or perhaps even understood from the outside, since there would be no common ground on which such comparison or criticism or understanding could be based. This would equate to a strong form of cultural relativism, which was distinguished from relativism earlier in this chapter during the discussion of Berlin. On the value-pluralist view, by contrast with relativism, there are universal values, such as Nussbaum's human capabilities. It follows that cultures will almost certainly share at least some of those universals, and to that extent will be commensurable.[10] For value pluralists, then, cultures can usually be critically compared along particular universal dimensions. If that is so, then liberal cultures can be critically compared with the alternatives in a way that brings out their advantages and disadvantages.

Parekh acknowledges this point by implication when he is not trying to relativize liberalism. At these times he is clear that cultures are not wholly incommensurable (Parekh 2006: 172–3). This fits with his view that, 'although all cultures have worth and deserve basic respect, they are not equally worthy and do not merit equal respect' (Parekh 2006: 177). Every culture enables its members to realize some human values, but these may be achieved at the cost of other values that we can see more fully enjoyed in other cultures. Some cultures are more egalitarian than others, while some may do better than their rivals on the score of individual liberty. Further, we may conclude of a culture that, compared to the alternatives, 'the overall quality of life it offers its members leaves much to be desired' (Parekh 2006: 177).[11] This approach is clearly distinct from cultural relativism, according to which cultures cannot be judged from the outside, but it is in line with a Berlinian pluralism of values, in which incommensurability is a relation among goods rather than whole ways of life.

Of course, even if we understand pluralism as being primarily about the deep plurality of values rather than cultures, it will still be true that many ways of life are legitimate and deserve respect. As noted already, if pluralism is true then no single ranking of goods will be correct for all cases and many different rankings will be permissible, depending on the circumstances. Hence, value pluralism implies the legitimacy of a wide range of cultures. Pluralism in this sense is a natural ally of multiculturalism, as Parekh argues.

The question is, within what limits? More specifically, can the full range of goods and ways of life that must be accepted as legitimate from a pluralist perspective be adequately accommodated within the political framework of liberalism? Parekh says no: liberalism is just one possible package of goods among others. The liberal emphasis on liberty, equality and toleration makes this an exceptionally wide, embracing package, but it cannot embrace the full range of genuine goods and genuinely valuable ways of life.

However, to insist that liberalism (or any political doctrine) cannot be a legitimate framework for multiculturalism unless it accommodates every existing way of life is too demanding a test. For one thing, we have already seen that Parekh himself denies that all cultures deserve equal respect. Indeed, he agrees that some existing cultures are gravely defective from a moral perspective, and even broadly legitimate cultures often harbour particular practices that are 'grossly outrageous' and 'obviously need to be changed' (Parekh, 1992: 171). Such cultures and practices need not be accommodated by a legitimate multiculturalism.

Further, even if liberalism cannot accommodate all acceptable cultures and practices, that objection is not fatal. The accommodation it does provide may be the best we can do. Whatever the full range of actual and potential goods and ways of life in the abstract, in practical terms any political community needs some framework of basic values and principles. The most a pluralist can ask is that the framework respect the plurality of legitimate goods and cultures to the greatest extent possible. Liberals are in a strong position to argue that their framework passes this more reasonable test.

Indeed, Parekh effectively concedes this in several places. For example, he allows that liberalism is 'the most hospitable of all political doctrines to cultural diversity' (Parekh 2006: 11). Again, during a critical analysis of religious literalism he notes that literalists are always members of a wider political community and that they ought to consider the interests and rights of other members too.

> This means that they all need to agree on a form of association that respects their equal rights and is acceptable to them all. A liberal democracy meets this requirement. It is just because it treats all its members equally. It does not impose particular religious beliefs on them, and thus respects their integrity. And it is the only form of association capable of commanding general acceptance. (Parekh 2008: 139)

This actually goes further than liberals need to, since they need only show that liberal democracy does better in this respect than the alternatives. To see the pro-liberal line of argument developed, I turn to the liberal pluralists, Galston and Raz.

Liberal Pluralists: Galston and Raz

We saw earlier in this chapter that Berlin proposes various links between pluralism and liberalism, but also that none is convincing. Can such links be restated more persuasively and, if so, what are their implications for multiculturalism?

One writer who takes up this challenge is William Galston, an American political theorist. In *Liberal Pluralism* (2002) and *The Practice of Liberal Pluralism* (2005), Galston associates value pluralism with the celebration of cultural diversity. Like Berlin, but unlike Gray and Parekh, he sees this as best promoted under liberalism – specifically, a toleration-based form that he calls 'Reformation' liberalism, contrasted with the 'Enlightenment' liberalism that emphasizes the value of personal autonomy.

Once again the starting point is a link between pluralism and the validity of many cultures. Pluralists, Galston writes, hold that 'some goods are basic in the sense that they form part of any choiceworthy conception of a human life', but beyond those basic universals 'there is a wide range of legitimate diversity – of individual conceptions of good lives, and also of public cultures and public purposes' (Galston 2002: 6). If pluralism is true then many different cultures have value.

Further, liberalism teaches us that we should treat as 'a robust but rebuttable presumption' the idea that people are entitled to 'expressive liberty' – that is, individuals and groups should not be prevented from 'leading their lives as they see fit, within a broad range of legitimate variation, in accordance with their own understanding of what gives life meaning and value' (Galston 2002: 3). Expressive liberty protects not only liberal ways of life but also 'the ability of individuals and groups to live in ways that others would regard as unfree' (Galston 2002: 29).

When pluralism and expressive liberty are combined, Galston argues, the result is an imperative to tolerate a wide range of cultures, including non-liberal ones. The pluralist society should 'pursue a policy of *maximum feasible accommodation*' of different conceptions of the good and ways of life (Galston 2002: 20).

Such a society will be a liberal society. Liberalism has a strong claim to being acknowledged as the political form most accommodating of cultural diversity because its distinctive commitment to individual rights and liberties enables individuals and groups within the same society to follow disparate paths. This is not to claim that a liberal society is limitlessly accommodating or wholly neutral among conceptions of the good life. Liberal pluralists should concede that even the most liberal of orders is based implicitly on a value ranking that privileges some goods and places limits on others. But some such ranking is unavoidable in any political system. The liberal ranking, however, is uniquely capacious: it leaves more room for a variety of goods and conceptions of the good to be pursued than any known alternative. While non-liberal societies typically impose unnecessary limits on the 'natural diversity' of human flourishing, 'to the maximum extent possible in human affairs, liberal societies avoid this stunting of human lives' (Galston 2002: 60). Contrary to Gray and Parekh, Galston holds that the kind of diversity commended by value pluralism provides an argument in favour of liberalism rather than against it.

This will be a particular kind of liberal state, however, since it must be one that tolerates even non-liberal ways of life in its midst. That is because the range of cultures legitimated by pluralism is wider than those endorsed by liberalism. In this connection Galston draws a distinction between 'Reformation' and 'Enlightenment' forms of liberalism (Galston 2002: ch. 2). Reformation liberalism is based on toleration and sees the liberal state as a political container for many different conceptions of the good, including some non-liberal ones. Enlightenment liberalism takes personal autonomy as its guiding ideal and supports a state willing actively to promote characteristically liberal conceptions of the good. For Galston, Enlightenment liberalism is too sectarian, since the ideal of autonomy is rejected by so many cultural groups to be found in modern societies (Galston 2002: 24–6). Rather, a full measure of expressive liberty and maximum feasible accommodation is possible only under toleration-based Reformation liberalism.

Galston's view raises several critical questions. First, by employing the language of 'toleration', Galston stops short of endorsing multiculturalism proper. By and large he favours a Berlinian stress on negative liberty, and consequently on groups' being left alone to go their own way, rather than any positive programme of state recognition or assistance.[12] Yet, as in the case of Berlin, it may be asked whether the pluralist outlook does not push us towards recognition. On the pluralist view, multiple cultures have real value. That suggests that they should be respected rather than merely tolerated. This is not yet a complete case for multiculturalism, since that would require a link from respect to public recognition – something like Kymlicka's 'benign neglect' argument. But already, in the logic of the pluralist outlook, we would seem to have a strong reason for going beyond toleration.

Second, there is the matter of expressive liberty. What justifies the emphasis on expressive liberty, especially when value pluralism tells us, as Galston concedes, that 'it is not the only good' (Galston 2002: 29)? Further, if we are going to accept a central liberal commitment like this, why should it be expressive liberty and not the stronger notion of personal autonomy? Expressive liberty is essentially the right to live according to conscience. But conscience can be mistaken and people also have an interest in living in accordance with the truth. No one wants to live according to ideals that are in reality false or deluded. So, why should we not supplement pluralism with an emphasis on personal autonomy, the capacity to follow a plan of life that we have subjected to critical reflection?

Galston's answer is, of course, that personal autonomy is too sectarian an ideal, since it is rejected by many cultures. But liberals might reply, as earlier in response to Parekh, that what happens to be rejected or endorsed by existing cultures cannot be the last word since so many existing cultural beliefs and practices are questionable. It is quite true that for some groups what gives meaning to life is adherence to traditions that are deeply hostile to fundamental liberal values such as personal autonomy. If Galston's expressive liberty accommodates traditions like these, then his position seems to leave individuals and internal minorities vulnerable to oppressive treatment. In that case, many if not most liberals would say, so much the worse for Galston's expressive liberty.

Galston sees this problem and lists a series of qualifications to the kind of expressive liberty that is acceptable for a liberal state. These amount to protections for individuals and minorities within groups, including recognition of civil liberties, toleration of the expressive liberty of other groups and of the group's own members, and a right of exit for the group's members (Galston 2002: 102, 122–3). Thus far, Galston's position is less like Kukathas's almost untrammelled authority for groups and more like Barry's constrained group freedom. These requirements remain consistent with the Reformation stress on toleration rather than individual autonomy.

However, might it be that Galston's view collapses into an autonomy-based Enlightenment liberalism after all? When he discusses the right of exit, he rightly insists that this must be 'more than formal' (Galston 2002: 104). Such a right must involve more than mere absence of coercive interference with a person's decision to leave the group. It must also involve access to information that would enable the person to make an informed decision, including information about alternatives to the group's way of life. Most important of all, a genuine right of exit requires the prevention of attempts to inculcate 'servility' in the thinking of children (Galston 2002: 105).

This last requirement, in particular, implies acceptance of the value of independent thought. To think and judge in a non-servile way is to think for oneself rather than to defer uncritically to the authority of others. What is this if not a conception of personal autonomy? Galston claims to reject personal autonomy as a political ideal for contemporary liberalism, yet his own account of the right of exit from non-liberal groups amounts to a commitment to personal autonomy after all – and rightly so (Crowder 2007b). But then it is Enlightenment rather than Reformation liberalism that he should be defending.

The autonomy-based approach is pursued explicitly by another seminal value pluralist, Joseph Raz. In works such as *The Morality of Freedom* (1986) and 'Multiculturalism: A Liberal Perspective' (1995), Raz constructs a case for liberal multiculturalism from two different directions: from a basis in value pluralism, and from a liberal commitment to individual freedom conceived as personal autonomy.

In the first of these arguments Raz begins in a familiar way by observing that there are many genuine values and that these, ranked or arranged in different ways, are expressed in many correspondingly valid practices and ways of life. All of these ways of life are valuable, and each is valuable in its own way, representing a unique package of goods that is irreducible to any other terms – 'value pluralism takes the plurality of valuable activities and lives to be ultimate and ineliminable' (Raz 1995: 179). Moreover, 'none of them can be judged superior to the others' (Raz 1995: 183). This 'equal standing of all the stable and viable communities' within a society must be recognized politically (Raz 1995: 174).

This line of argument should be qualified. The opening assertion that different combinations of values yield multiple valid ways of life is unobjectionable. But the subsequent claim that all such ways of life have 'equal standing' should be accepted only with strong qualification for the reasons given before. Ways of life may be different but they cannot be wholly incommensurable on the pluralist view because they overlap on the basic human universals. Consequently, they can be critically compared at those points of overlap: one culture may do better than another at providing its members with liberty or equality or community, for example. It is only the difficulty of converting all these particular judgements into an overall ranking of cultures that rescues the notion of 'equal standing', although even this should perhaps be regarded as a rebuttable presumption.[13]

In any case, Raz's sequence of reasoning based on pluralism is strongly qualified by his other line of argument, which appeals to a liberal conception of individual freedom and its value. Here his position is much like Kymlicka's. From a liberal point of view, the prospects for a person's well-being turn crucially on his or her prospects of enjoying individual liberty, understood as personal autonomy: 'liberalism upholds the value for people of being in charge of their life, charting its course by their own successive choices' (Raz 1995: 175). Genuine autonomy is not mere licence, or the mere availability of options, but rather the capacity someone has to choose among her options for reasons that make sense to her. For that to be possible, she needs to be able to understand the meaning and significance of her choices, which in turn requires that she be able to locate them in a context of interlocking social practices – that is, a culture.

Membership of a flourishing culture is thus an essential component of individual well-being, since it provides a necessary context within which people can identify and make sense of their choices. It follows that if one's culture is slighted or harmed, one is harmed oneself. Consequently, the basic liberal concern for individual well-being, especially as this involves personal freedom, requires that one's culture be respected and sustained as a matter of public policy. 'This case', Raz concludes, 'is a liberal case, for it emphasizes the role of cultures as a precondition for, and a factor which gives shape and content to, individual freedom' (Raz 1995: 178).

By the same token, however, this freedom-based argument implies a set of limits to multiculturalism that are similar to those set by Kymlicka. On this view cultures are valuable and worthy of public support only so far as they provide a supportive context for individual freedom. 'Such cultures may be supported only to the degree that it is possible to neutralize their oppressive aspects, or compensate for them (for example, by providing convenient exit from the oppressive community to members of the discriminated-against group)' (Raz 1995: 184). Indeed, this line of thought would seem to authorize 'imposing liberal protection of individual freedom on those cultures' (Raz 1995: 183), which suggests not only a realistic right of exit but also state-mandated reforms of a group or its practices.

There would seem, then, to be a major tension within Raz's view between its pluralist limb, with its conclusion in favour of 'equal standing' for all viable cultures, and its liberal freedom-based limb, with its built-in critique of those cultures that constrict people's autonomy. Raz appears to resolve this conflict by giving priority to the freedom-based side of his case. His conclusion is that all cultures should be treated with the respect due to what is valuable in them, that all cultures have something of value to offer their members, but that some are distinctly more oppressive than others in their effect on personal freedom. The latter sort of culture should be respected to the degree appropriate, but at the same time the liberal-multiculturalist state is entitled to intervene in such a culture to protect individual liberty.[14]

This is a sensible conclusion, but one may still ask how Raz justifies it, especially in view of his commitment to value pluralism. If many different ways of life are valuable because they embody many valid packages of values, why should we privilege that distinctively liberal package that centres upon personal autonomy?

Raz sees a link between pluralism and autonomy, but he deploys this to justify the truth of pluralism rather than the primacy of autonomy (Raz 1986: ch. 14). The direction of the argument is from autonomy to pluralism rather than the other way round: the value of autonomy, which is assumed here, demonstrates the truth of pluralism. For autonomy to be possible for someone, he must have multiple options to choose from. If autonomy is valuable, then the multiple options must be genuinely valuable. But although this may give us a reason to accept the truth of value pluralism, it does not give us a reason to value autonomy.

Raz does provide a justification for his privileging of personal autonomy, but this does not appeal to pluralism and indeed leaves the pluralist objection open. The argument is that a capacity for personal autonomy is essential for a successful life under the circumstances of modern industrial civilization. Those circumstances 'call for an ability to cope with changing technological, economic and social conditions, for an ability to adjust, to acquire new skills, to move from one subculture to another, to come to terms with new scientific and moral views' (Raz 1986: 369–70).

This argument justifies attention to personal autonomy by appealing to historical context rather than value pluralism. It also remains open to the pluralist objection because someone may still ask whether the focus on autonomy is the only possible response to modern industrial conditions, and, if there are alternative responses, why autonomy should be preferred. Gray points out that the promotion of personal autonomy does not seem to be a high political priority in some East Asian countries, like Singapore, which are nevertheless very successful economically under the prevailing conditions (Gray 1995b: 83).

To sum up: Raz takes an important step in bringing together value pluralism, multiculturalism and personal autonomy, but he fails to combine these in a coherent argument. When he speaks as a pluralist the result is an emphasis on the 'equal standing' of all cultures, which seems to be much the same view as that taken by Gray, and which consequently undermines the claims of liberalism. When he speaks as an autonomy-based liberal he places major qualifications on that view, but does not show how these are consistent with his pluralism.

Summary

The value-pluralist outlook has given rise to several different interpretations of its implications for both multiculturalism and liberalism. All of the thinkers discussed hold that if pluralism is true then there must be a substantial range of legitimate cultures, hence that cultural diversity is in general to be defended. But whether that yields a case for multiculturalism proper or only for toleration, and whether pluralism requires or opposes liberalism are matters over which opinions differ sharply. Gray and Parekh see pluralism as ruling out liberal universalism, but their view is marred by a failure to distinguish clearly enough between value plurality and the plurality of political regimes or cultures. Galston and Raz uphold liberal pluralism but interpret this differently, Galston emphasizing toleration and Raz autonomy. Galston's position relies heavily on people being free to exit from oppressive groups, and that is difficult without autonomy.

Raz, on the other hand, does see a link between pluralism and autonomy but gets this the wrong way round, leaving his stress on autonomy open to question. It remains to gather up these threads – pluralism, multiculturalism and individual autonomy – and draw them together. I take up that task in Chapter 9. Before I do that, however, I want to consider the issues raised by 'global' cultures.

8

Global Cultures

Certain cultures are especially important wherever multiculturalism is in prospect simply because of their worldwide influence. These are the global cultures or world civilizations that can be found in many societies across the world, in some cases as the majority group within a given society, in others as a minority. I shall be especially concerned with Islam and Confucianism, because these are so ubiquitous and because their basic principles appear to be in tension with liberal democracy. My question is, must they be in conflict with liberalism or might there be a possibility of reconciliation? If the former, then the prospects for multiculturalism, at any rate in its liberal form, are seriously limited.

I begin with Samuel Huntington, who argues that liberal democracy, which he understands as the political culture of 'the West', is indeed in irreconcilable conflict with other world civilizations, including those of Islam and China. In his influential and highly controversial 'clash of civilizations' thesis, Huntington sees contemporary world politics in terms of competitive relations among distinct civilizations. In particular, he is concerned with the fate of Western civilization, which he sees as threatened by the rise of aggressive external rivals and by internal multiculturalists who are trying to dilute the shared culture that has been the West's strength in the past.

The two 'challenger' civilizations that worry Huntington most are Islam and China. In the remainder of the chapter I consider these in turn. Many writers have argued that Islam is fundamentally at odds with liberal democracy. I examine this claim as it is presented by Roger Scruton, and then look at the responses suggested by the work of Edward Said and Abdullah Ahmed An-Na'im. In the case of China I investigate the argument of Daniel A. Bell that Confucianism and Western liberal democracy both have things to learn from each other.

The West Imperilled? Huntington

In Samuel Huntington's *The Clash of Civilizations* (1996), the world is undeniably multicultural in a descriptive sense at a global level, but multiculturalism as a normative project at a domestic level threatens the cultural survival of any state that pursues it. Western states are currently beset by the twin dangers of a moral universalism that draws them into conflict with other societies internationally and a domestic multiculturalism that fragments their cultural identity at home.

Huntington's basic prescription is encapsulated in the book's final sentence: 'In the emerging era, clashes of civilizations are the greatest threat to world peace, and an international order based on civilizations is the surest safeguard against world war' (Huntington 1996: 321). In the aftermath of the Cold War the central theme of global politics is not ideology but culture, and the most important cultural relationships are those among rival civilizations, or large cultural groupings with global influence or significance. The major civilizations are irreducibly different from one another and, partly as a consequence, tend to come into conflict. The West is just one such civilization among others, dominant in the recent past but now declining in power. If it wishes to preserve itself it should refrain from trying to promote its ideals internationally and concentrate on reaffirming its unique civilizational identity at home.

This 'paradigm' for understanding current global politics is positioned by Huntington against several alternatives. We must, for a start, accept that we no longer inhabit a political landscape divided by ideology among the 'three worlds' of the Cold War period – capitalist West, communist East and the Third World where the first two fought their proxy wars. On the other hand, Huntington also rejects the various 'one world' pictures, or theories according to which the world's societies are all tending to converge on a single 'world civilization'. The most famous recent version of this view is the 'end of history' thesis proposed by Francis Fukuyama (1992), who argues that the end of the Cold War has signalled the end of history conceived as a long process of ideological struggle over how human societies ought to be organized. According to Fukuyama, that struggle has now been finally decided in favour of liberal democracy and capitalism, the social and political system developed by Western societies such as the United States and Britain. That system has now been accepted as the ideal universally.

For Huntington, however, Fukuyama's claim is merely post-Cold War Western hubris, which was exposed as delusional by the outbreak of violent Balkan nationalism in the 1990s (Huntington 1996: 31–2). Since then the unreality of the one-world thesis has been reinforced less dramatically but more pervasively by the reassertion of local cultural and religious identities all around the world. There is modernization (or globalization), of course, but that is not the same as Westernization. While there is a global demand for Western technology, consumer goods and entertainment, all of that is compatible with rejection of core Western beliefs, values and institutions. 'Non-Western societies can modernize and have modernized without abandoning their own cultures and adopting wholesale Western values, institutions, and practices' (Huntington 1996: 78). China and other East Asian societies are perhaps the strongest examples, with their extremely rapid modernization coupled with continued resistance to Western liberal and democratic values.

So, contemporary politics can be understood neither in terms of three worlds nor of one world. Rather, current conditions are shaped by a multiplicity of 'cultural identities, which at the broadest level are civilization identities', and 'for the first time in history global politics is both multipolar and multicivilizational' (Huntington 1996: 20). Ours is a world focused on multiple civilizations.[1] According to Huntington there are probably (with some room for argument) eight 'major contemporary civilizations': Sinic (China and other societies moulded by Chinese culture), Japanese, Hindu, Islamic, Orthodox (especially Russia), Western, Latin American and (possibly) African (Huntington 1996: 45–7).

An obviously salient defining feature of the civilizations on this list (although not the only defining feature) is religion (Huntington 1996: 47). A central aspect of the global 'indigenization' of culture, or re-assertion of local culture especially in response to modernization and Westernization, is what Huntington labels 'la revanche de Dieu' (God's revenge), the upsurge around the world of the religious belief that modernist thinkers, both liberal and Marxist, assumed would wither away (Huntington 1996: 95–101). Nationalism falls into the same category.[2]

Relations among the major civilizations have passed through several historical stages. An early period in which civilizations met only in occasional 'encounters' was succeeded by a period of global domination by the West (from 1500 to the late twentieth century).

This in turn has been followed by a revolt against the West, ushering in 'an era in which multiple civilizations will interact, compete, coexist, and accommodate each other' (Huntington 1996: 95).

Intercivilizational relations always contain the danger of conflict. That is because civilizations provide people with identities, and 'identity at any level – personal, tribal, racial, civilizational – can only be defined in relation to an "other", a different person, tribe, race, or civilization' (Huntington 1996: 129). The other provokes in us feelings of fear and lack of trust, and superiority or inferiority. The divide between 'the civilizational "us" and the extracivilizational "them" is a constant in human history' (Huntington 1996: 129). Such confrontations are especially dangerous at the level of civilizations, since these are capable of mobilizing such large quantities of power.

In addition to religion, another prominent source of conflict is what Huntington refers to as the 'universalist pretensions' of the West (Huntington 1996: 20). Westerners have long believed that their values and institutions – 'democracy, free markets, limited government, human rights, individualism, the rule of law' – are universally valid and ought to be adopted by all societies (Huntington 1996: 184). Yet non-Western societies continue to cling to their own cultures, and 'what is universalism to the West is imperialism to the rest'.

Western universalism is objectionable in part because the West has so frequently failed to live up to the ideals it preaches for others (Huntington 1996: 184). But mere hypocrisy does not invalidate the ideals themselves. Another objection advanced by Huntington is that (much like Parekh's argument examined in Chapter 5) the values and institutions promoted by the West are 'peculiar to the West' (Huntington 1996: 311). They have developed out of the West's specific historical experience, which includes the Christian and Classical legacies, the European languages, the division between religious and temporal authority, the notion of the rule of law, social pluralism, political representation and ethical and cultural individualism (Huntington 1996: 69–71). These components of the Western heritage 'distinguish it from other civilizations' (Huntington 1996: 69). Although Huntington never quite says so, the implication seems to be that these values and practices are therefore not appropriate for non-Western societies.

At any rate, non-Western societies have in fact been largely resistant to Western norms, especially in the current period of 'revolt against the West' and indigenization. During its period of dominance the West had some success in imposing its ideas on others through the exercise of its global power, including its military capability. Huntington makes a general connection between culture and power:

cultures tend to be influential in proportion to the power of the states or groups that promote them, and conversely to decline in influence when there is less power to back them up (Huntington 1996: 91).

Western power is now in decline, according to Huntington, and so non-Western societies are much less inclined to be impressed by Western culture. The decline of the West is especially marked in relation to the main challenger civilizations, China and Islam (Huntington 1996: ch. 5). Chinese civilization is rapidly overtaking the West in the economic field, while Islam is expanding its influence in part through the power wielded by Muslim countries that export oil but also through sheer population growth, which in the Muslim world is faster than anywhere else. Consequently the West is increasingly less able to impose its culture on its rivals by force, and they are less likely to accept it. In these new circumstances the West's continuing universalist ambitions are provocative.

Huntington also sees the West as undergoing a moral decline, and this is where he addresses multiculturalism directly. That the world as a whole is multicultural is simply an empirical reality that must be faced. But the idea that multiple cultures should be encouraged and supported domestically is civilizational suicide. The problem is especially pressing in the United States. Huntington approvingly quotes Arthur Schlesinger's observation that multiculturalists are '"very often ethnocentric separatists who see little in the Western heritage other than Western crimes". Their "mood is one of divesting Americans of the sinful European inheritance and seeking redemptive infusions from non-Western cultures"' (Huntington 1996: 305). For Huntington, multiculturalists 'wish to create a country of many civilizations, which is to say a country not belonging to any civilization and lacking a cultural core. History shows that no country so constituted can long endure as a coherent society. A multicivilizational United States will not be the United States; it will be the United Nations' (Huntington 1996: 306).

Huntington's prescription for the West, if it wishes to survive as a civilization, is threefold. First, it must recognize the reality of a multicivilizational world. Second, it must give up its universalism, which is really just an attempt to impose uniquely Western norms where they do not belong, a project that requires a projection of power of which the West is no longer capable. Third, the West must turn away from domestic multiculturalism, which fragments Western civilizational identity, and reaffirm that identity as valuable because unique (Huntington 1996: 311).

Overall, then, Huntington's view of multiculturalism has two distinct aspects. On the one hand he insists on the reality of multiple cultures as a true description of the world at a global level; on the other hand he condemns multiculturalism as a policy goal domestically. These two aspects of his position are linked: assuming that cultures at the global level are in competition, those that wish to prosper must assert their identity domestically and admit no Trojan horses.

This view of multiculturalism cuts across all those I have discussed previously. Liberal multiculturalists like Kymlicka will, of course, be unhappy with the rejection of multiculturalism domestically. Liberal critics of multiculturalism like Barry will agree with Huntington domestically but join with other liberals in having reservations about Huntington's global view. All liberals can accept some degree of cultural difference as a feature of the world that is both true currently and likely to remain so in the foreseeable future. But they will bridle at the depth of difference that Huntington regards as current, permanent and (apparently) legitimate, since this excludes all but 'a "thin" minimal morality' involving the most basic rules against such universally condemned crimes as murder (Huntington 1996: 318). For Huntington, the more substantial human rights demanded by liberals, including freedom of speech and religion, are distinctively Western cultural products with no universal legitimacy.

Anti-liberal or 'difference' multiculturalists like Young, Tully and Parekh will be more sympathetic to Huntington's global multiculturalism, but they will not approve of his domestic monoculturalism. If Western values, for example, are not universally valid, then why should they be privileged at home any more than abroad? I shall return to this question shortly.

Even at the global level, though, the difference multiculturalists are not entirely on the same page as Huntington, since it is one thing to emphasize difference but another to stress conflict. While the difference theorists tend to commend intercultural dialogue, Huntington leaves little room for cross-civilizational conversation until the very end of his book. On the final page he does endorse Lester Pearson's declaration that 'different civilizations will have to learn to live side by side in peaceful interchange, learning from each other, studying each other's history and ideas and art and culture, mutually enriching each others' lives' (Huntington 1996: 321). But this comes across as something of an afterthought and is out of keeping with the book's persistent message of intercultural competition, tension and conflict. What kind of dialogue can there be if differences are so deep? This is a question not only for Huntington but also for the difference multiculturalists.

Huntington's thesis has attracted a huge critical literature. One frequent charge is that of 'cultural reductionism' (Parekh 2008: 156). By placing so much stress on the role of culture, Huntington ignores or underestimates the importance of other factors in shaping politics and identity, such as economics, state interests and universal values. For example, if we adopt Huntington's culturalist lens, it becomes difficult to explain cross-cultural alliances, such as that mobilized against Saddam Hussein in the First Gulf War (1991), and the relative success of multiculturalist states such as Canada, Australia and New Zealand. As Parekh puts it, 'cultural identity matters to people, but so do other things such as decent existence, justice, self-respect and the respect of others' (Parekh 2008: 156). This point will resonate especially strongly with value pluralists.

Second, Huntington's focus on 'civilizations' has been the target of a welter of criticism, including attacks on his definition of civilization and consequently on his classification of particular civilizations. Huntington defines civilization primarily along religious lines, but that is open to objection from a number of directions. Perhaps the most general point to make in this connection is Sen's insistence that people's identities always have multiple dimensions, so that 'while religious categories have received much airing in recent years, they cannot be presumed to obliterate other distinctions, and even less can they be seen as the only relevant system of classifying people across the globe' (Sen 2006: 10–11). To take just one example, 'the West' is not readily identifiable with a religion, since the main contender, Christianity, is an object of indifference or even revulsion to many Westerners.

Further, Huntington can plausibly be accused of falling into the classic culturalist trap of presenting his civilizations as bounded monoliths (Parekh 2008: 159). The values that Huntington identifies as distinctively Western – toleration, personal liberty and democracy – have long been respected, in varying degrees, in many different societies, not just those of the West. For example, Sen traces the ideal of religious toleration to the policies of the Indian Emperor Ashoka in the third century BC, and the roots of democracy in 'the tradition of public discussion can be found across the world' (Sen 2006: 50, 53). Nor are civilizations or cultures internally homogeneous. Even on Huntington's own account the cultural identity of the West springs from different sources, including Christianity, Classical paganism and modern secularism, and he might have added that these have left legacies that often come into conflict with one another. Similarly, Parekh writes that 'the Indian, Islamic and Sinic civilizations have rationalist, liberal, radical, religious and anti-modern strands of thought, just as Western civilization has, and these are in constant tension' (Parekh 2006: 162). Indeed, Parekh concludes, 'civilizations do not clash, only their opposite strands or interpretations do. And the clash is as much within civilizations as between them' (Parekh 2006: 162).

Even assuming that we can distinguish different civilizations and concede some degree of conflict at that level, the extent and depth of the conflict is another issue. Huntington's general view is that conflict is the dominant, even natural, form of relationship among civilizations; that the clash of civilizations is a current fact, a historical norm and inevitable in the future, capable only of being managed or contained rather than overcome. There seems little prospect in this picture of any kind of convergence through dialogue – despite the gesture in that direction at the end of the book.

Again, this bleak picture rests on a set of dubious assumptions about the nature of cultures and civilizations, in this case as not only bounded and univocal but also unchanging. Although this is never made explicit, Huntington's view is essentialist. When he lists the values of his civilizations it is unclear whether he is merely stating current facts or pointing to something permanent. We are told that the West separates politics from religion and that Islam does not (Huntington 1996: 70, 210–11). Are these contingent facts or essences? The words themselves could be understood either way, but in the context of Huntington's overall view there is not much doubt that his meaning extends beyond empirical description.

For Huntington, each culture or civilization is what it is and cannot allow the influence of others without surrendering its authenticity. If Islam and China were to move towards greater personal liberties they would be 'Westernizing'. They would not just be adopting a different set of values, they would be submitting to ideals that are deeply alien to them. It is fruitless for the West to preach the virtues of liberty and democracy to the non-West because these are 'uniquely' Western ideals. Western values are bound to be rejected by non-Western societies unless the West imposes them by force.

Conversely, the United States cannot admit the influence of non-Western civilizations, through multiculturalism, without ceasing to be the United States. The identity of the West was established in premodern times, and to subject it to any kind of multiculturalism can only destroy it. In Huntington's world cultures are like marbles, either complete and whole, bouncing off one another but never penetrated, or else shattered by their rivals. There is little sense of the mutual influence and overlap, the general fluidity that characterizes the real world of intercultural relations.

It follows that Huntington's policy prescriptions for the West are also open to objection. His rejection of Western universalism is unjustified and contradictory. It is unjustified because if so-called 'Western' values are also present in 'non-Western' cultures and civilizations, then to advocate them as universals is not necessarily impertinent. Nor must universalism be as dangerous as Huntington supposes, since to argue for the universality of a set of ideals is not the same thing as 'imposing' them on others coercively. Huntington's dismissal of Western universalism is also contradictory. He urges the West to reaffirm its values, but does not seem to notice that these are unavoidably universal – how else can we understand 'human rights'?

Huntington's opposition to domestic multiculturalist policy is also questionable. He sees this as sapping the moral strength of the West. That may be true of the anti-liberal or difference kind of multiculturalism (e.g. Young, Tully, Parekh) that treats basic liberal values as merely Western products with no universal validity. (Oddly, that appears to be Huntington's own view when he is talking at the global level, a point I shall return to in a moment.) But multiculturalism within liberal-democratic limits, the multiculturalism of Kymlicka and Raz, arguably contributes to the West's moral strength, since it builds on the liberal tradition of the accommodation within a single society of different beliefs and ways of life. It is not just the economic prosperity of Western societies that makes them attractive to migrants from all over the world, but also their capacity to allow the coexistence of so many different groups.

There is a curious disjunction between Huntington's acceptance of cultural diversity at the global level and his rejection of cultural diversity domestically. If global diversity is simply a fact that must be accepted, why is the best Western response the denial of diversity at home? Huntington's answer is that he sees the global civilizations as competing aggressively with one another in a zero-sum game – the promotion of one civilization must mean the decline of another. So, to allow the influence of non-Western civilizations to enter Western societies must be to weaken Western civilization. I have already questioned this view as neglecting the role of shared values and dialogue. But even if we accept Huntington's view as true to some extent, there is another problem with it.

Supposing that the promotion of non-Western norms does threaten the ideals of the West to some extent, why should Westerners (or anyone) care about that? Huntington usually speaks the language of prudence: the West must reassert its values if it wants to survive culturally. But why *should* we want the West to survive culturally? In other words, why is the Western heritage valuable?

Here, Huntington is, of course, unwilling to use the language of universality: at the global level Western civilization is just one among others. So, on the score of its value he says only that 'Western civilization is valuable not because it is universal but because it is unique' (Huntington 1996: 311). But uniqueness alone does not make a culture valuable: Nazi society was uniquely appalling. To explain why Westerners should bother to reassert their basic ideals, Huntington needs to explain not just how those ideas are (allegedly) distinct from others but why they have value. And that means he needs to explain why they have value not just for those who happen to value them now but for anyone – why, that is, someone *ought* to value those ideals. Otherwise he cannot motivate those, from whatever culture, who are hostile or indifferent to the goods of liberal democracy. In other words, Huntington needs to make a universalist case. The moral clarity that he wants domestically will not be possible without the universalism that he denies globally.

The West and Islam: Scruton, Said and An-Na'im

Huntington's clash of civilizations thesis emphasizes the potential for conflict between the West and two 'challenger civilizations' in particular, the Islamic and the Chinese. In each instance cultural differences are said to be profound, essential and therefore permanent. In the case of Islam the most fundamental difference, according to Huntington, is that Islam rejects the division between state and religion that is the bedrock of the personal rights and liberties characteristic of the West (Huntington 1996: 70, 210–11).

The view that Islam is essentially anti-liberal is developed by Roger Scruton in *The West and the Rest* (2002).[3] Writing in the shadow of the Al-Qaida terrorist attacks against the United States on 11 September 2001, Scruton declares that Huntington's thesis 'has more credibility today than it had in 1993, when it was put forward' (Scruton 2002: vii). The Western and Islamic worlds are essentially opposed in cultural terms. In this global confrontation the West cannot allow itself to be weakened by multiculturalism (Scruton 2002: 62–4). Rather, it must rediscover and reaffirm its own deepest values, which in Scruton's conservative view are those of national and religious identity as well as those of the Enlightenment. However, to try to export such ideals to Muslim societies is not only futile but dangerous, since 'to transfer those values to places that have been deeply inoculated against them by culture and custom is to invite the very confrontations that we seek to avoid' (Scruton 2002: vii). This is Huntington's position almost to the letter. Once again, the West and the rest are ships passing in the night, and the best we can hope for is to avoid a collision.

Scruton also follows Huntington in identifying as the key point of difference between the West and Islam the division between state and religion that is accepted by the West but rejected by Islam. But Scruton goes on to tell us much more about this than Huntington does. According to Scruton, the general view of Islam is that there is only one source of legitimate law, and that is the law of God as revealed to the Prophet Muhammad. The man-made laws of secular political leaders are mere 'expedients' that can always be set aside in the name of holy law (Scruton 2002: 108). This contrasts with the Western tradition of regarding secular and religious laws as occupying separate spheres, each with its own legitimacy. Of course, Christians see the law of God as the higher law, and ideally this will be reflected in the law of the state. But they also believe that the ideal is not realistically attainable on earth, and for mundane purposes people are obligated to 'render therefore to Caesar the things that are Caesar's; and unto God the things that are God's' (Matthew 22: 21). For Christians, the law of God is the ideal, but secular law has its own independent authority too.

The rejection of any such independent authority for secular law in Islam, according to Scruton, leads to what he calls:

> a *confiscation of the political*. Those matters which, in Western societies, are resolved by negotiation, compromise, and the laborious work of offices and committees are the object of immovable and eternal decrees, either laid down explicitly in the holy book, or discerned there by some religious figurehead. (Scruton 2002: 91)

The only relationship of authority that really matters in Islam is that between the individual and his God, and the only leaders who really count are those best able to pass on the divine commands, namely the Prophet and his successors. Beyond that, there is virtually no attention to political institutions or processes.

> There seems to be no room in Islamic thinking for the idea – vital to the history of Western constitutional government – of an office that works for the benefit of the community, regardless of the virtues and vices of the one who fills it. (Scruton 2002: 94).

In addition to monopolizing the field of moral obligation, Islamic religious law is, in Scruton's view, so comprehensive that it allows scarcely any 'zone of freedom' of the kind permitted by Western legal systems. 'Laws governing marriage, property, usury, and commerce occur side-by-side with rules of domestic ritual, good manners, and personal hygiene' (Scruton 2002: 92). Nothing is private.

Further, while Scruton allows that Islam is a powerful and in some ways beneficial system of belief, he also sees it as potentially dangerous. On the one hand the certainties and absolutes of Islam offer, especially for Muslim immigrants to the West, 'an unrivalled ability to compensate for what is lacking in modern experience' (Scruton 2002: 104). This includes in particular a deeper sense of membership than can be accounted for by the standard liberal notion of a social contract, which Scruton sees as depending on 'pre-political' identities that go unacknowledged in liberal theory (Scruton 2002: 11–12, 60). Western societies have, at least since the French Revolution, implicitly supplied those identities by encouraging in people a sense of citizenship within a territorial and secular nation – that is, Western societies have made up for the shortcomings of liberalism by promoting nationalism.

In Muslim societies, however, national identifications have been weak, playing second-fiddle to family and tribal loyalties on the one hand, and the overarching religious obligation to Islam on the other. In other words, there is little to temper or restrain Muslims' commitment to the project of Islam, which is inherently universalist.

Moreover, that project contains deep veins of resentment and latent aggression. For Scruton, Islam is suffused with an atmosphere of nostalgia that makes it hard for Muslims to reconcile themselves to the modern world. While this is especially true of the Shi'ite minority, who remain loyal to the defeated Hussein Ibn 'Ali, 'the third Imam', it is also true of Islam in general, which carries a strong message of exile and longing for the restoration of a lost purity (Scruton 2002: 101–2, 120–1). Unqualified by the Christian emphasis on forgiveness, the Islamic project is uncompromising. Faced with the increasing spread of Western values through globalization, Muslims feel themselves to be on the defensive, resisting a tide of corruption that cannot be ignored. At an extreme, these feelings express themselves in the terrorism of Al-Qaida, but they are present, at a lower intensity, throughout the Muslim world.

Overall, the picture of Islam that Scruton presents is of a global culture that is deeply and permanently opposed to Western norms of personal liberty, equality, human rights and the rule of law, basically a totalitarian culture that brooks no departures from a rigid and unchallengeable set of religious norms. Currently its adherents are angry, defensive and potentially aggressive towards the West, but even if that were not so there would be no substantial meeting point, only deep, permanent and essential difference.

How far should we accept the view presented by Huntington and Scruton? One line of criticism might be drawn from Edward Said's *Orientalism* (1978). Said defines the eponymous tendency as one in which Western culture asserts and promotes its own identity 'by setting itself off against the Orient as a sort of surrogate and even underground self' (Said 1978: 3). Basically, 'the Orient' is an identity, or family of identities, constructed by Western scholarship and politics, in which 'the Oriental' is presented as contrasting with that which is essentially Western, in a way that values the Western as superior and the oriental as inferior. Developed in a context of colonial exploitation, orientalism is an expression and instrument of intellectual, economic and political power.

According to the orientalist literature, typical oriental features include splendour, cruelty, sensuality, untruthfulness, gullibility, a lack of energy and initiative, a tendency to flatter, cunning and unkindness to animals (Said 1978: 4, 38). Crucially, 'the Oriental generally acts, speaks, and thinks in a manner opposite to the European': while the European is rational, virtuous, mature and normal, the Oriental is irrational, depraved, childlike and 'different' (Sir Evelyn Baring quoted by Said 1978: 39, 40). Above all, in the political context, the oriental is addicted to despotism, hence incapable of self-government and in need of the guidance of others (Said 1978: 32–3). The link between orientalist thinking and imperialism is obvious.

Although the orient, understood in this way, may include any culture or civilization regarded as 'Eastern' from a European point of view, Said focuses his study on the orient of the 'Near East' – that is, of 'the Arabs and Islam' (Said 1978: 17). Does the treatment of Islam by Huntington and Scruton fall within the category of orientalism identified by Said, with its dubious stereotypes and colonialist connotations? Huntington and Scruton certainly present Muslim societies as different from Western societies, both empirically and essentially. That is the basis for their shared judgement that Western values such as human rights are 'alien' to societies shaped by Islam. But to count as an orientalist position there must in addition be the crucial charge of Western superiority and oriental inferiority. How far is that part of their view?

The answer is perhaps surprising. Neither Huntington nor Scruton makes any bones about being on the side of the West, or at any rate about offering Western societies sage advice. But on the face of it the advice they offer is merely prudential – 'this is what you must do if you want to survive' – rather than clearly tied to any larger claim of moral superiority. I have already made this point in relation to Huntington. Indeed, I suggested that it is a weakness of his outlook, since he consequently offers no motivation for those who may be prepared to question their allegiance to Western values.

Scruton is more ambiguous, since he places so much emphasis on alleged features of Islam that must seem unattractive to Western sensibilities. But then again he also has this to say about Muslims:

> why blame them for rejecting [Western technology, institutions and conceptions of political freedom] when they, in their turn, involve a rejection of the idea on which Islam is founded – the idea of God's immutable will, revealed once and for all to his Prophet, in the form of an unbreachable and unchangeable code of law? (Scruton 2002: x)

As a conservative thinker, Scruton has more than a little sympathy with the moral clarity provided by Islam, for the role of religion in underwriting that clarity and for the sense of communal belonging generated by membership in the *umma* (the community of believers) in the face of globalization and modernity.

So, it is not entirely clear that Huntington and Scruton are the orientalists one might suppose them to be. Further, Said's notion of orientalism has problems of its own. For one thing, its usefulness as a critical tool is hampered by Said's ambivalent, postmodernist attitude to truth (Dalacoura 2003: 40). Sometimes he seems to assume that there is an objective truth about 'the orient' that is obscured or distorted by orientalism, but more often he appeals to the authority of Michel Foucault to insist that all 'truth' is ultimately (and sometimes immediately) an expression of power (Dalacoura 2003: 3, 23–4, 45). However, if we accept the latter view, then why should we regard the oriental identities constructed by the British, French and Americans as any less valid than the self-identifications of Muslims, since all these are equally expressions of power?[4]

A more straightforward way of questioning Huntington and Scruton is to ask whether the picture they present of Islam is in fact correct.[5] In a later article Said points out that 'Islam' is not a single, bounded monolith; rather, it is internally complex, subject to many different interpretations, and externally linked to other religions by way of exchanges and overlaps of various kinds (Said 2001). For example, Scruton's allegation of Islam's fundamentally aggressive, nostalgic and resentful nature may be true of some Muslims (as it is of some Christians) but it is not true of others. Indeed, Said quotes Eqbal Ahmad as arguing that the 'religious right' of the Muslim world 'distorts' Islam.

The same kind of point may be made with respect to the claim that Islam can accommodate no division between religion and the state, hence no secular government or freedom of religion. The fact is that only in a minority of societies where Islam is the dominant religion is the state explicitly dedicated to the enforcement of the religious law of Islam, *sharia* – Iran and Saudi Arabia are examples. In the great majority of Muslim societies, including Turkey, Egypt, Indonesia, Algeria, Malaysia and Pakistan, the state is secular. It is true that in these societies Islam is usually regarded as having a special place in the social system, and in some cases *sharia* is enforced in state or local jurisdictions. It is also true that some of these societies have questionable records on human rights – although there are many reasons for this apart from their religious cultures. Still, a separation of political from religious authority appears to be possible in practice in Muslim societies.

This is a significant response to Huntington and Scruton, but not conclusive. Scruton replies that the secular states of the Muslim world are alien impositions, superficial and fragile contrivances which are always liable to be swept aside by a reassertion of the more fundamental Islamic cultural base (Scruton 2002: 32–5). Even those writers who support a rapprochement between Muslim cultures and Western notions of constitutional government and human rights are often dismissive of outright secularism as a realistic model for the former (An-Na'im 1990; Dalacoura 2003). In the face of the 'Islamic resurgence', they say, the best hope for a convergence between Western liberal principles and Islam lies in the reform of Islam itself.

How far is that possible? Supposing that *sharia* is the law of the land, must its principles be at loggerheads with liberal commitments such as freedom of religion, equal citizenship or gender equality? An interesting argument to the contrary is presented by Abdullahi Ahmed An-Na'im, a jurist from the Sudan, in his book *Toward an Islamic Reformation* (1990).[6]

An-Na'im begins by conceding that *sharia* in its current form, orthodox or 'historical' *sharia*, is irretrievably in conflict with the principles mentioned and with 'constitutionalism' in general – that is, with rights-based limitations on government authority. Judged by those standards, historical *sharia* fails to accord adequate respect to non-Muslims and women (An-Na'im 1990: 87–90). Non-Muslims within an Islamic state are regarded at best as *dhimma*, a 'protected' status but one that excludes them from participating in the politics of the state. Women are subjected to various forms of unfair discrimination in the areas of public expression, voting, public office, marriage divorce and inheritance.

More fundamentally still, according to An-Na'im, constitutionalism is not possible within the framework of historical *sharia* because of its fixation on the model of political authority bequeathed by the Prophet (An-Na'im 1990: 77–84). As God's agent on earth, Muhammed ruled with absolute authority, and that authority has been passed to his successors, or *caliphs*. Although the *caliphs* are supposed to 'consult' the people, there is no explicit mechanism for how and when this should happen, and its results are not binding on the ruler. Nor is there any explicit arrangement for how a *caliph* is chosen. On the most democratic interpretation, the whole *umma* (people) may be regarded as sovereign (after God), but again the *umma* excludes non-Muslims and women. An-Na'im concludes that the historical *sharia* is indeed fundamentally illiberal and undemocratic.

However, An-Na'im also believes that Islam can be radically reformed. All the problems of historical *sharia* stem from those verses of the Qur'an that date from the period in which the Prophet and his followers had to flee from Mecca to Medina in order to avoid persecution (An-Na'im 1990: 52, 99). That experience produced verses of a more defensive, authoritarian character compared with those revealed earlier, at Mecca, where the new sect had been initially unmolested. The Meccan verses emphasize 'the inherent dignity of all human beings, regardless of gender, religious belief, race, and so forth', and endorse 'equality between men and women and complete freedom of choice in matters of religion and faith' (An-Na'im 1990: 52).

While the later Medinese verses laid down principles appropriate for the harsh and unstable conditions of seventh-century Arabia, An-Na'im argues, it is the Meccan verses that fit better with current conditions. For example, while it made sense under dangerous seventh-century conditions to place women under the guardianship of men, that no longer applies in modern societies where the rule of law prevails and where women are 'more capable of being economically independent' (An-Na'im 1990: 100). Since the Meccan verses can be read as according equal rights to both women and non-Muslims, an emphasis on that part of the Qur'an, justified by changed historical circumstances, draws Islam away from political authoritarianism and towards modern constitutionalism. 'The Qur'an does not mention constitutionalism, but human rational thinking and experience have shown that constitutionalism is necessary for realizing the just and good society prescribed by the Qur'an' (An-Na'im 1990: 100).

Although illuminating, this argument is not without its problems. In particular, the idea of ethical principles being more or less appropriate or fitting for different historical conditions is vague and open to numerous interpretations. The nature of the conditions themselves can be disputed, still more so the proper response to those conditions. What is to stop someone from arguing that twenty-first-century conditions are no less insecure and unstable than seventh-century conditions, requiring stern measures to defend the faith from outsiders and to protect vulnerable members within the group? Indeed, this is, of course, precisely one line of argument used by the more conservative and reactionary Muslim thinkers and by radical Islamists, as noted by Scruton.

An-Na'im's thesis is therefore not entirely convincing, but a more general point survives. Islam is a rich religious tradition that is capable of many different interpretations, some more authoritarian, some more liberal and democratic. To the extent that liberal and democratic interpretations of Islam are possible, some degree of convergence between Islam and 'Western' moral and political ideals is also possible.[7]

Asian Values: Bell

The 'Asian values' debate begins with the claim that 'Asian' or 'East Asian' societies have their own distinctive cultures.[8] In these terms, it is said, the political values of the West – including standard Anglo-American understandings of human rights and democracy – are alien and inappropriate. Distinctively Asian values stress the authority of the state rather than individual rights against the state, identification with the family or group rather than individualism and economic development rather than civil liberties.

Since such claims have often been made by authoritarian political leaders such as Lee Kuan Yew of Singapore and Mohammed Mahatir of Malaysia, the suspicion has been widespread that these ideas are merely convenient rationales for 'less-than-democratic' rule. Lee's People's Action Party, for example, has routinely silenced political opposition by invoking Singapore's defamation laws, justifying the practice by saying that it is in line with characteristically Asian restraints on freedom of speech (Lingle 1996; Rodan 2004).

Might it be, however, that there is more to the notion of Asian values than this kind of cynical practice would suggest? One of the best defences of Asian values is provided by Daniel A. Bell, a political theorist of Canadian origins who has lived and worked in East Asian countries – first Singapore, more recently China – since the early 1990s. In a substantial body of writing, notably including *East Meets West* (2000), *Beyond Liberal Democracy* (2006) and *China's New Confucianism* (2010), Bell tries to steer a course between, on the one hand, a purely strategic and reactionary form of Asian values, and on the other what he sees as a narrow, dogmatic and 'West-centric' view, in particular one that unreflectively treats American assumptions as universal, ignoring the different culture and historical experiences of the societies of East Asia.

Rather, Bell argues, we should attend to various dimensions of difference between East Asia and the West, including differences of economic and political history and current circumstances. He places especial stress on what he sees as the most distinctive East Asian cultural heritage, which he identifies as Confucianism. To a lesser extent he also refers to the 'Legalist' tradition of thinkers such as Han Fei Tze (Bell 2006: 330). From Confucianism East Asians inherit values such as filial piety and respect for scholarly learning; from the Legalists they take an acceptance of state sovereignty over all areas of life, albeit moderated in practice by a Confucian reliance on non-coercive measures (Bell 2000: 132, 255).

To do justice to East Asia, then, it is not enough merely to preach a set of Western norms based on the experience of Europe and North America. Only when we have acquired an adequate level of 'local knowledge' of East Asian culture and circumstances shall we be in a position to appreciate the important and legitimate differences between Eastern and Western approaches to human rights, democracy and economics (Bell 2000: 42, 48–9).

One set of differences concerns priorities. On the standard Western view civil and political human rights take precedence over socio-economic rights, but in East Asia this ranking is reversed. Further, it might be said that the goal of economic development overrides individual rights and democracy more generally (Bell 2000: 35). These priorities reflect the current circumstances of most East Asian states as developing societies. On the other hand, economic development in East Asia is not entirely about prosperity, as it tends to be in the West, but rather about securing the good life conceived in Confucian terms as involving not only material well-being but also flourishing affective relationships, especially within the family (Bell 2006: 278–80). Hence, East Asian capitalism is described by Bell as distinctively qualified by obligations to care for needy family members, which also take precedence over public duties, echoing the traditional Confucian value of filial piety (Bell 2006: 243–50).

Even where Western norms ought to be upheld, Bell argues that in East Asia their justification should address the conditions and cultural values that are characteristic of that context. Thus, if one is trying to construct a case for human rights or democracy in East Asia it is little use appealing to parochial American values, or to liberal autonomy, or even to the abstract articles of the UN Declaration on Human Rights, since these do not necessarily 'resonate' locally or speak to local circumstances (Bell 2000: 56, 63–8, 192–4). Rather, the case should be informed by local knowledge. For example, appeals to individual rights should take into account the concern for collective development already mentioned, and democracy is best recommended not as an intrinsic good but as instrumental in giving ordinary people a patriotic stake in their political system and contributing to nation building (Bell 2000: 239).

Legitimate divergence between East and West extends not only to differences of priority among shared values and different ways of justifying political principles held in common but also to different political conclusions altogether. In this connection I have already mentioned legal obligations to care for needy family members, but Bell's most striking examples concern restrictions on democracy. Even when this is defined 'minimally' as the provision of free and fair elections, Bell argues that East Asian societies may have legitimate reasons for qualifying democracy's operation (Bell 2000: 108). In particular, the populism and majoritarianism of democracy may, in the East Asian context, have deleterious consequences for national security, prosperity, civil liberties and the rights of minority groups (Bell 2000: ch. 3). In the case of Singapore, for example, defenders of the less-than-democratic status quo point to the island's prior history of ethnic tensions, to a perceived lack of education and sophistication among the ordinary citizenry and to an economic vulnerability that would lead to disastrous consequences if there were a populist raid on the country's financial reserves. Some of these considerations are adduced in the case of mainland China too.

In the case of China Bell goes further, appealing to Confucian tradition in order to propose a compromise between democracy and elitism. The proposal takes the form of a bicameral legislature in which a democratically elected lower house is dominated by an upper 'House of Scholars' consisting of an intellectual elite capable of restraining populist impulses (Bell 2000: 307). In accordance with Confucian principles, members of the House of Scholars will be selected by a process based principally on competitive examinations, which will identify outstanding generalists whose 'bird's-eye' or 'helicopter' view enables them to integrate the advice of specialists in the service of the common good (Bell 2000: 314–15). Such a proposal constitutes a desirable 'middle way between Confucianism and Western democracy, a 'democracy with Chinese characteristics'' (Bell 2000: 334).[9]

Indeed, Bell suggests that Confucian culture may yield insights that are pertinent not only for East Asia but also for the West. His broader view is not that the twain shall never meet, but rather that the two civilizations should enter into dialogue and that this should not be entirely a matter of the West guiding the East in the language of the West. It should instead be a genuinely two-way conversation in which each party is prepared to learn from the other (Bell 2000: 85).

Overall, Bell strives for a reasonable balance between a concern for the fundamentals of liberal democracy and attention to the particular local circumstances, history and culture of East Asia. The result is a qualified defence of liberal democratic values in that context, a defence that is culturally sensitive yet still recognizable and sympathetic to many Western liberals. Some of the more radical points of divergence from Western norms are, of course, controversial, but even there Bell presents interesting arguments worth considering carefully.

One point worth noting is that although Bell's ethical approach is particularistic to a strong degree, since he usually argues from within existing conditions and cultural norms, he is not a cultural relativist (Bell 2006: 328–9). He makes it clear that existing cultural practices are not necessarily justified, and warns that 'taking culture too seriously' is just as much a mistake as not taking it seriously enough (Bell 2000: 9). Not everything in existing or past forms of Confucianism must be taken as ethically authoritative.

If anything, Bell's ethical position is closer to Berlinian value pluralism, involving the recognition of generically universal goods that can reasonably be interpreted and ranked differently in different political, economic and cultural circumstances. 'I'm a pluralist. I want to allow for the possibility that there are different legitimate ways of prioritising values and organising societies' (Bell 2000: 329). This fits with his view of intercultural dialogue as a two-way street. Consistent relativists have little to say to one another apart from reporting their own perspectives and allowing that others are different, since each party is completely correct by his own lights. The pluralist view gives people more to talk about because it acknowledges cross-cultural norms in terms of which all cultures can be seen to have strengths and weaknesses. Each culture will tend to emphasize one set of values at the cost of neglecting or downplaying others. That opens up the possibility of comparing the balance struck by one's own culture with that of others, and consequently of learning from them.

Still, some of Bell's assumptions, arguments and conclusions can be questioned. To begin with, one may ask whether there really is a common 'East Asian' culture or civilization, since the term encompasses a number of very different countries, ranging from highly developed, liberal-democratic Japan to developing states like Muslim Indonesia and nominally communist China.[10] Moreover, most of these countries are internally multicultural (Langlois 2001: 27–9).

Bell replies that despite the differences, 'several societies in East Asia are bound by common political traditions', in particular 'Confucian and Legalist legacies' (Bell 2006: 330).[11] But that raises the further question of whether Confucianism is as dominant in the region as Bell claims. It has been argued that in China, for example, Confucianism, while not wholly displaced, has been largely overshadowed since the early twentieth century by modernizing influences, including not only Communism but also the 'New Culture Movement' that began with the foundation of the republic before the First World War (Mitter 2004).

Even supposing that Bell is right about the dominance of Confucianism in East Asia, it might also be objected that he is being unjustifiably selective in 'picking and choosing' certain Confucian norms rather than others – for example, filial piety but not the outright patriarchy that the Master and his followers sometimes upheld (Bell 2000: 51–2; Bell 2006: 331). Here, Bell's best response is that any argument about values has to try to separate 'desirable and undesirable aspects of traditions' (Bell 2000: 52). In order to do that one has to use the usual resources of argument, including the philosopher's main weapon, the demand for consistency. Of course this is no easy task, but at least it should not be ruled out by a relativist insistence on the authority of tradition.

What about Bell's more specific arguments and conclusions? Democrats will be concerned at the degree and kinds of elitism that Bell is prepared to contemplate, and indeed at the depth to which elitism appears to be inherent in the Confucian outlook. This might be defended to some extent by pointing, realistically, to the educational inequalities typical of developing countries, and to the familiar liberal worry about 'the tyranny of the majority'. Even a canonical liberal such as Mill is on record as proposing that these difficulties be resolved by a system of plural voting (Mill 1861 [1958]: ch. 8). But the strong suspicion is hard to shake that Confucian elitism goes deeper than anything allowed by liberals. I shall return to this in a moment.

The standard liberal solution to the tyranny of the majority is, of course, the institution of individual rights, and here too there may be worries that Bell's Confucianism does not offer adequate protection. His list of 'legitimate' departures from Western norms is disquieting, since it allows significant reductions of personal privacy (e.g. in the field of search and seizure), the criminalization of adultery and 'constraints on free speech, perhaps in the form of libel laws to protect cultures from various forms of defamation and hate speech' (Bell 2000: 90–2). Speech is nowhere absolutely free, and liberals themselves are divided over the merits of hate speech restrictions. Moreover, Bell stresses the tendency of Confucian tradition to prefer 'persuasion and transformative education over coercion as means to achieve social and political order' (Bell 2000: 303 note 51). But the notion that one can 'defame' a culture is arguably repugnant to a deep liberal commitment to free critical discussion, and it also seems to conflict with Bell's own recognition that culture should not have the last word.

Liberals will be happier with Bell's idea that in the East Asian context arguments for human rights should be sought from within the Confucian tradition. A good cause can have many friends. However, while Bell is convincing on the strategic merits of such a course, he does not identify many distinctive Confucian values and principles that would actually help in this regard. He concedes, perhaps too quickly, that the value of individual autonomy has little resonance in the tradition (Bell 2000: 191–4). What Confucian thought does offer, he argues, are instances of support for toleration, for restraints on the arbitrary power of rulers and for *ren*, or compassion for fellow human beings (Bell 2000: 53; Bell 2006: 63). But while, from a liberal perspective, these values are heading in the right direction, they hardly amount to decisive arguments for full-blown human rights. They can all be interpreted as consistent with authoritarian regimes that permit few rights to individuals.

The deepest problem with Confucianism for liberals is that the tradition does not clearly endorse the most fundamental liberal commitment of all – namely, equality of moral worth, Kant's respect for persons. Mill proposed plural votes for the educated, but only as long as the mass of the new democratic electorate remained uneducated – a temporary situation he believed could and should be remedied. The Confucian position seems more akin to that of Plato, for whom inequalities of intellectual and (therefore) moral capacity are inherent in the natures of individual human beings. This must be a deep concern not only for democrats but also for liberals, whose regime of equal rights presupposes a deeper moral equality. The notion of *ren* does not altogether meet this concern, since compassion for one's fellow beings is compatible with deep inequality.

A more promising resource for liberals may be the Confucian valuing of scholarly inquiry, which hints at support for critical thought. Although Confucianism appears to be a rather conservative doctrine in general, with its emphasis on tradition, ritual and respect for experience, Bell points out that it sometimes favours critical abilities too. A capacity for 'independent thought', for example, is one of the virtues that he recommends as a criterion for appointment to his House of Scholars (Bell 2000: 309). Since independent, critical thinking is at the heart of the liberal ideal of personal autonomy, perhaps that ideal resonates more strongly with Confucianism than one might suppose.[12]

Finally, liberal and other multiculturalists may be disappointed that Bell is not more enthusiastic about rights for minority groups. This is certainly a live issue in East Asia, with several indigenous cultures seeking greater political recognition – for example, the Tibetans and Uighurs in China – and migrant workers all over the region pursuing stronger social, economic and citizenship rights. Yet, on the whole, Bell is not strongly moved by these claims. In one chapter he cites the case of minorities as a reason to be wary of democratic reform in East Asia, since this might open the floodgates of populist discrimination against such groups (Bell 2006: ch. 7). The East Asian or Confucian solution to this problem is to let authority rest with a wise, paternalist leadership who can be relied upon to protect the vulnerable. This is not reassuring, since there are many examples of elites exploiting populism rather than restraining it. On the other hand, Bell seems happy to concede 'substantial self-administration' to minority ethnic groups within China, and also to guarantee such groups representation in the House of Scholars (Bell 2000: 327–8). So perhaps minority group rights are not off the table entirely.[13]

Summary

In relation to the global cultures, the prospects for multiculturalism, especially within a liberal-democratic framework, look decidedly mixed. Huntington articulates the concerns of many people in his clash of civilizations thesis, with its grim picture of eternally warring macro-cultures and its warning that the West is on a downhill path if it continues in its pursuit of ethical universalism and domestic multiculturalism. But there is reason to believe that much of this picture is exaggerated or confused. Only if cultural identities are conceived as static need we assume that current conflicts are inescapable, or that the promotion of human rights is unjustified and dangerous, or that any domestic accommodation of cultural diversity is asking for trouble. Huntington's picture seems to depend on an essentialist model of culture, ironically shared with some of the stronger multiculturalists whom he opposes, that has now been discredited. Indeed, it is questionable how far it makes sense to speak of any distinct entity called 'the West', or Islamic or Confucian civilization, at all. However, even if cultures are capable of change, it has to be admitted that there are significant gaps between liberal-democratic principles on the one hand and currently dominant forms of Islam and Confucianism on the other. Thinkers like An-Na'im and Bell show us possibilities for convergence, but these remain possibilities only and their realization probably lies a long way off.

9

A Liberal–Pluralist Approach

In this final chapter I gather together the main threads of the book and sketch my own approach to multiculturalism. This can be no more than an outline, since a full defence of this view would require another book.[1] My position draws on the whole of the previous discussion, but in particular on Chapter 7. There I suggested that attempts to work out the political implications of value pluralism can be divided into two main schools: liberal and anti-liberal. The liberal camp splits further into a Reformation or toleration-based form, and an Enlightenment version emphasizing the value of personal autonomy.

My argument will be that the kind of politics supported by pluralism is subject to liberal-democratic principles rather than a radical or unrestricted position in which liberal values represent only one legitimate cultural perspective on a moral par with others. More specifically, those liberal-democratic principles include a strong public commitment to the ideal of personal autonomy.

It is a further question whether the liberal pluralism I recommend will require 'multiculturalism proper' as I define it – namely, the public recognition of multiple cultures within a single polity. Pluralists should want more than just the toleration of different cultures, hard though that alone is to achieve. They will see different ways of life as possessing genuine value rather than simply entitled to non-interference. However, it will still have to be asked whether the positive valuation of a society's constituent cultures must take the form of public recognition or whether that can be left to private judgement.

My answer is that this matter will have to be determined in the specific context.

Finally, I briefly discuss the appropriate liberal-pluralist view of some of the other issues raised in the book – namely, the debates between nationalists and cosmopolitans, democrats and their critics and rival accounts of the relation between the 'global' cultures and liberal democracy.

Value Pluralism, Cultural Pluralism and Liberalism

My ethical starting point is a moderate universalism that emphasizes value pluralism. As we saw in Chapter 1, there is good reason to believe that neither traditional universalism nor its cultural relativist opposite provides a satisfactory view of human morality. Historically, the leading accounts of natural law and natural rights to be found in influential European thinkers such as Hobbes and Locke tended to universalize norms that were really ethnocentric, or specific to their own historical circumstances or local ways of life. On the other hand, the cultural relativism that developed out of the Counter-Enlightenment and modern social anthropology, while rightly more sensitive to legitimate moral variations among different cultures, took the notion of legitimate variation to an extreme, emptying the idea of *human* morality of all content and endorsing as legitimate any and all practices that happened to have cultural backing. It is not enough simply to define as morally right whatever a culture says is right. That would justify slavery, racism and sexism; it would justify the unjustifiable.

However, I also noted that ethical universalism can be restated in a moderate and pluralist form that balances a sense of universality with a proper regard for legitimate difference. Although there may be other ways of expressing this, the model I discussed was the human capability theory of Nussbaum and Sen. In the more elaborate form advanced by Nussbaum, this argues that human well-being requires that people enjoy certain basic capacities to do and be what they want. These capacities are universal in the sense that they are an essential part of the good life for all human beings, no matter what society or culture they may belong to. But the capacities also embrace legitimate difference in various ways, such as their 'multiple realizability' – that is, the same generic capability can be realized in different ways in different historical and cultural contexts.

A new set of questions arises, however, when one realizes that different capabilities, or different universal values however conceived, may come into conflict. Which of these rival values, or which combination of them, should we prioritize? The question is deepened when we understand the various elements of the human good as intrinsic values, each possessing a unique force that cannot be reduced to the terms of any other good. Liberty is a wholly different good from equality, for example. If there is no hierarchy among the basic goods, and no common currency to which they can be reduced, how do we choose among them when they conflict?

This is the realm of value pluralism, the view of morality advanced by Berlin and others (Chapter 7). The human good is objective and universal, but its elements are not only multiply realizable but also irreducibly plural, sometimes incommensurable and often conflicting.

What are the implications of value pluralism for multiculturalism? They have been widely misunderstood. In particular, there has been a tendency to move too rapidly from value pluralism to a strong cultural pluralism according to which not only basic human values but also cultures are conceived as plural and incommensurable. Indeed, the tendency has been to regard value pluralism and cultural pluralism as virtually synonymous. This view is especially pronounced in Gray and Parekh, but often present in Berlin himself and even in Galston, despite the universalist affiliations of the latter two.

The effect of this culturalist tendency among the pluralist writers has been to present pluralism as equally supportive of all cultures, whatever their character. But that view is mistaken. Value pluralism is not identical with unrestricted cultural pluralism because the incommensurability of values does not imply the incommensurability of cultures. If it did, there would be nothing to distinguish pluralism from cultural relativism. To say that cultures are incommensurable with one another would be to say that cultures are infallible moral authorities, which is precisely the characteristic claim of cultural relativists (and strong multiculturalists). But pluralism and cultural relativism are distinct ideas, indeed opposed in crucial respects. A greater plurality of cultures may actually reduce value plurality, since not all cultures are equally welcoming to a multiplicity of goods. Moreover, pluralism is truer to our experience of universal goods that transcend cultural boundaries, and of conflicts and hard choices among these and other goods both across cultures and within them. Even if moral universals are highly generic, their universality makes them points of overlap for all or most cultures. Cultures, therefore, cannot be incommensurable in the same degree as values or goods.

Pluralism in the sense that concerns me here is primarily about the multiplicity and incommensurability of values or goods, not of whole cultures. This is not to say that pluralism does not have any connection with cultural diversity at all. On the contrary, pluralism does imply valid cultural diversity, within a certain range, since if goods are plural and incommensurable then there are many legitimate ways of ranking or combining them as general ideals or norms. In this sense, different rankings or combinations of goods yield different legitimate cultural patterns. The point I want to stress, however, is that this legitimate cultural diversity should be qualified by attention to the implications of *value* diversity.

What are those implications? The key line of thought here is one raised during my discussion of Berlin: the possibility that the concept of pluralism itself implies normative principles that apply across cultures. In that earlier discussion I questioned the particular argument proposed by Berlin. However, I also believe that Berlin's general line of argument can be restated more persuasively. The claim is that there are norms that are implicit in the concept of pluralism, and that they qualify or condition the kind of politics that pluralism endorses. These norms condition the pluralist response to multiculturalism.

The most general of these norms can be called 'respect for value plurality'. The idea of value pluralism means that there are multiple intrinsic goods. All must be taken seriously in the sense that pluralists must acknowledge the value of all genuine human goods, not just some rather than others. For the pluralist, no such good is inherently more or less valuable than any other. In that sense each has an equal status; each speaks with its own voice, one might say.

If that is so, then prima facie we should promote all goods in the human spectrum equally. But of course in practice that is not possible, since no single life, whether of an individual or of a whole society, is capacious enough to include the simultaneous pursuit of all possible human values to the same extent. In particular situations we have to make choices between alternative paths, and these involve either ranking or trading off the values involved. More liberty may necessitate less equality, for example.

But if we often have to choose against one value in order to pursue another, how can that be squared with the general principle of respecting all genuine goods equally? There is indeed a problem if we choose against a good simply by ignoring or blinding ourselves to it. We then fail to take that good seriously. However, we can respect a good even when we choose against it if we do so for a good reason – that is, if we can point to a persuasive reason, in context, for accepting less equality in order to achieve more liberty, for example. Respect for plurality points to the need for practical reasoning in context when basic goods conflict.

Respect for plurality also suggests three more specific norms. The first is value diversity. The general idea is captured by Bernard Williams: 'if there are many and competing values, then the greater the extent to which a society tends to be single-valued, the more genuine values it neglects or suppresses. More, to this extent, must mean better' (Williams 1980: xvii). The fundamentally equal status of basic goods means that although no society can promote them all to the same extent, it ought to enable its members to pursue as many as possible.[2] Again, this imperative cuts across respect for cultures, which promote the diversity of human goods to varying degrees. The principle of value diversity gives pluralists critical leverage against existing cultures; it does not underwrite their authority indiscriminately.

A second norm suggested by respect for plurality is summed up in Charles Larmore's phrase 'reasonable disagreement' (Larmore 1996: 122). This refers to the fact of widespread disagreement among human beings concerning the content of the good life. Reasonable disagreement may be especially evident in modern societies, but on the pluralist view the problem is rooted in the moral experience of humanity at large: it is a permanent possibility in all human societies because of the deep structure of human value. Conceptions of the good life are essentially generalized rankings of values, including incommensurable values. Although pluralists should not accept that all such conceptions are automatically on a moral par, nevertheless the wide range of genuine human goods implies a wide range of legitimate permutations of those goods, that is, of reasonable rankings. Many such rankings will be equally reasonable, and concerning these there is consequently room for people to disagree on reasonable grounds. Once more, this consideration overrides respect for cultures, which vary in the extent to which they permit disagreement about the good life.

What kind of politics is best fitted to satisfy the principles of value diversity and reasonable disagreement? Liberalism is the leading candidate in both cases. The diversity of values that can be pursued within a single society is likely to be maximized by the support that liberalism characteristically extends to individual rights and liberties. Individual liberty – which I conceive as having a positive or effective as well as a negative dimension – enables different people to follow many different paths. Of course a liberal political framework will not be without its costs in terms of significant values diminished or foregone. Certain kinds of equality, solidarity and certainty will not feature prominently in a liberal society. However, no social order is without costs. The liberal-pluralist claim is not that it promotes values without limit but only that its value diversity is superior to that of the alternatives.

Similarly, liberalism has a strong claim to providing the fullest possible political acknowledgement of reasonable disagreement. Where disagreements are reasonable in the relevant sense they are likely to be permanent. A realistic and prudent form of politics will accept and accommodate reasonable disagreement rather than trying to overcome it. Liberalism, its defenders may fairly claim, is just such a realistic and prudent form, its historical origins responding precisely to the problem of conflicting conceptions of the good in the European Wars of Religion. Again, this is not to say that there are no limits to the range of beliefs that a liberal society can accommodate, only that such a society is likely to be more accommodating than the alternatives.

The Centrality of Personal Autonomy

At this point pluralists have good reason to conclude in favour of a broadly liberal framework for value and cultural diversity. That conclusion will set them at odds with the anti-liberal or non-liberal thinkers I have discussed – namely, Taylor, Tully, Parekh, Young and Gray. These writers tend either to adopt relativist positions that are dangerous to individual liberties, or to rely tacitly on essentialist notions of culture, or to smuggle liberal values back into their arguments despite their claims to having rejected liberalism or transcended it.

But if multiculturalism has to be qualified by liberalism, what kind of liberalism will this be? In the terms introduced by Galston, will this be a Reformation liberalism based on toleration or an Enlightenment liberalism that emphasizes personal autonomy?

Here we should be guided by a third norm implicit in the concept of pluralism: that to choose well among conflicting incommensurables – that is, to choose for good reason – requires certain virtues or dispositions of character. These point to a distinctively Enlightenment liberal framework for multiculturalism, in which the promotion of personal autonomy is a goal of public policy.

This idea can be seen as a revival and development of Berlin's argument from choice (Chapter 7). That argument failed in its attempt to pass directly from the necessity of choice under pluralism to the valuing of choice under liberalism. But the argument can be restated to emphasize the inescapability not merely of choice but of the particular kind of choice imposed on us by value pluralism. Under pluralism we are confronted by choices not just among values but specifically among incommensurable values. As we have seen, these are characteristically hard choices, both in the sense that they involve unavoidable loss and in the sense that they must be made without reliance on monist rules. But we have also seen that reasoned choices in such cases, although hard, are not always impossible. We do often seem to arrive at decisive reasons for resolving these hard cases.

The process by which we do so cannot be reduced to a simple rule or formula, but is perhaps best approximated in moral theory by the Aristotelian model of practical reasoning as a skill developed from experience of dealing with concrete choice situations. Such a skill may be seen to have the following elements, which echo the principal features of the pluralist outlook.[3] First, pluralists must possess a degree of generosity or open-mindedness in order genuinely to appreciate the full range of human values and legitimate ways of life (Walzer 1995). Second, they should approach their task with what Berlin called 'a sense of reality', or feeling for the real costs of moral and political decisions, bearing in mind that the gain of one incommensurable good cannot wholly compensate for the loss of another (Berlin 2008: 127, 236). Third, pluralists' rejection of neat abstract rules and insistence on the particularity of moral solutions should make them attentive to the relevant details of the choice situation, including the claims and circumstances of those people affected by the choice (Nussbaum 1992: 101). Finally, in the absence of decisive monist rules, pluralists need to be flexible in tailoring their judgement closely to the situation at hand.

These pluralist virtues are likely to receive greater encouragement in some types of political society than in others. Once again, pluralism implies a set of norms that cut across, and that provide a critical benchmark for, the performance of particular cultures. Moreover, the benchmark will again be a distinctively liberal one, since the pluralist virtues are also characteristically liberal virtues. Generosity towards the human range of goods and lives is a recognizable trait of liberalism at its best (Galston 2002: 61–2). Realism in the face of unavoidable costs and conflicts is a theme which, as Berlin saw, separates liberals from their utopian opponents. Attentiveness is represented by the core liberal concern for the fate of individual human beings, as captured, for example, by Kant's doctrine of respect for the person.

Most importantly, pluralist flexibility converges with the Enlightenment-liberal commitment to personal autonomy. To judge flexibly in the light of value pluralism is to judge for one's own reasons in a strong sense – that is, autonomously. There is no alternative. For one thing, conflicts among incommensurable goods cannot be decided for good reason merely by the mechanical application of a standard monist rule such as utilitarianism. Such a rule, by definition, emphasizes one consideration at the expense of others regardless of the circumstances. The rational pluralist judgement cannot rely on any ready-made monist procedure but must go behind such perspectives to weigh the values they embody against other goods that may be relevant in the situation.

Nor can pluralists answer such questions merely by appealing to the authority of local tradition. For pluralists, tradition is an unreliable guide because reasonable disagreement concerning the good life is a permanent possibility in all human societies. This kind of moral conflict is experienced not only among cultural groups but also within them. Individuals, too, can experience the conflicting attractions of incommensurable goods not only interpersonally but also within themselves. Here again there is a link between value pluralism and personal autonomy. For, where the nature of the good life is subject to reasonable disagreement, conceptions of the good cannot be permanent bases for decision but must be subject to revision. Such revision is possible only through the exercise of independent, critical thinking. Pluralism, in short, imposes on us choices that can be made rationally only by autonomous agents. If pluralism is true, then the best lives will be characterized by personal autonomy.

Further, personal autonomy should be promoted by the state rather than simply left as a value to be pursued privately. The capacity for autonomy in this strong sense does not develop in people automatically; for most people it requires education and a social environment in which autonomy is widely valued. Neither cultural tradition alone nor the free market can be relied upon to provide those conditions. Rather, they require the deliberate policy of a state that is prepared to pursue explicitly liberal goals, especially in its oversight of education.[4]

Note, however, that this is not to say that the promotion of personal autonomy will become an overriding value. It is a central claim of value pluralism that no value is overriding. Rather, my argument is that liberal pluralism emphasizes personal autonomy in much the same way as Berlin emphasizes negative liberty – he allows that negative liberty, while especially important, especially as a political value, may sometimes be overridden or traded off in favour of other important or pressing goods (Berlin 2002: 46, 172). The stress on personal autonomy imparts a certain shape to a liberal-pluralist society without denying that a range of other goods is also important to it.

To sum up, the value-pluralist outlook draws us towards support for a polity that has the following general features. It will value a wide diversity of goods, not just a single good or narrow range. Subject to that prior concern for value diversity, it will make room for multiple cultures or ways of life. Further, it will actively promote personal autonomy, chiefly through the education system. Such a society will be a liberal society. More specifically, in its concern for personal autonomy, it will tend towards Enlightenment liberalism.

Public Recognition or Hands Off?

Will a liberal-pluralist society be committed to multiculturalism? It might seem from what I have said already that it must be. For example, the strong although qualified link between value pluralism and the positive value of cultural diversity may seem to point in that direction. Might it be the case, however, that the insights of pluralism would be just as well satisfied, perhaps more fully satisfied, by a more traditional form of liberalism in which minority cultures are left alone by the state rather than publically recognized and supported?

Recall the three elements of multiculturalism proper outlined in the Introduction: acknowledgement of the presence in modern societies of multiple cultures as an unavoidable fact; a commitment to the positive valuation (not merely toleration) of those cultures; and the politicization of that positive valuation through public recognition. How far does the value-pluralist outlook recommend multiculturalism thus understood?

The first two of these elements are clearly supported by liberal pluralists. Pluralists are just as capable as anyone else of appreciating the reality of contemporary globalization that makes domestic cultural diversity a fact of life. Further, the link between pluralism and the positive valuation of multiple cultures has been noted several times.

However, the question of whether pluralists ought to go further and support public recognition – the definitive component of multiculturalism proper – is harder to answer. Although we are drawn by pluralism beyond mere toleration of other cultures towards an attitude of positive valuation, it does not follow that such an attitude must be translated into political recognition. In principle it remains possible that the liberal-pluralist state should merely stand aside in the field of intercultural relations, leaving it to individuals and groups to respect and value one another. The state might enforce toleration yet refrain from promoting or sustaining either cultural diversity in general or any particular minority culture.

The strongest form of this 'hands off' approach is the extreme cultural laissez-faire championed by Kukathas in which there is no state support for cultural groups, nor any interference with them apart from guaranteeing their members a right of exit. In Chapter 2, I indicated some major difficulties with this view. Individuals have no protection from the oppressive practices of their own groups apart from their right of exit, and the right of exit on the laissez-faire account consists of a purely negative liberty of non-interference that will be useless in cases where the constraints on exit are economic, educational or psychological rather than directly coercive.

From a pluralist perspective, Kukathas's position is basically a monist view that accords overriding status to negative liberty. Whatever difficulties may arise, Kukathas's solution is that people should be free to leave. But clearly there are often considerations that weigh against such an answer, such as the value people place on their cultural membership. Shachar, for example, argues that people ought not, so far as possible, be forced to choose between their human rights and their cultural identity.

For these reasons the form of hands-off policy advocated by Kukathas looks ill-fitted to a liberal-pluralist approach. But what about Barry's more moderate 'privatization' strategy (Chapter 3)? Here, some state intervention is permitted in the internal affairs of cultural groups in order to protect the basic civil liberties of individuals, but otherwise the state neither hinders such groups nor helps them. Cultures are generally left to order their own affairs in private as long as they do not violate the most basic liberal norms.

The obvious reply to this is Kymlicka's critique of 'benign neglect' (Chapter 2). State non-intervention is never even-handed, since the dominant culture sets the institutional framework for the whole society through the official language, calendar and so forth. Minority cultures are inevitably at a disadvantage. However, is that disadvantage unfair? Barry's rejoinder is that any institutional framework or set of rules will tend to advantage one group over another but it does not follow that the advantage, and corresponding disadvantage, must be unjust. Complete neutrality of effect among cultures is impossible, so why should it be held up as a standard of fairness?

For Kymlicka, the answer to this depends on which of two main kinds of group we are talking about. First, immigrants are certainly at a disadvantage in relation to the dominant culture of their new country, but that in itself is not unfair because they have chosen freely to come. What would be unfair is their hosts doing nothing to help them to integrate into their new society, and so immigrants have limited 'polyethnic' rights to assistance – for example, with language-related matters and perhaps some legal exemptions.

From this position Barry's version of privatization is not far removed. He is generally opposed to the differentiation of welfare benefits along cultural lines, but insists that immigrants should be educated to speak the local language, which suggests special arrangements in that area at least. He is also hostile to legal exemptions as long as there is good reason for the relevant law in the first place, as in the case of motor-cycle helmet requirements. But by the same token he is willing to revise laws and practices that disadvantage immigrants where the rules have no adequate justification, as in the case of the banning of religious clothing in work situations where the clothing does not prevent the person doing the job. So far there is not much to choose between multiculturalist recognition and Barry's less interventionist form of egalitarian liberalism.

The case of national groups is different. Here we are usually talking about groups, such as indigenous peoples, that have not chosen to join the larger society but have been incorporated into it against their will, often violently. The disadvantage they suffer as a result is often very severe, and may involve the suppression or marginalization of their language and religion, the dismantling of their sovereign institutions and the taking of their land and other natural resources. It is in cases like these that Kymlicka's attack on benign neglect begins to bite. Privatization may help somewhat in the fields of language and religion – at least to the extent of preventing their deliberate destruction – but it will not be enough to recover or maintain self-determination, land and resources. For these goals it is hard to see how various forms of public recognition will not be necessary.

There will, of course, be limits to national cultural recognition in line with a liberal framework. Cultural practices will be protected on this view only to the extent that they comply with international human rights and domestic civil and political liberties. Kymlicka would add that recognition should also be framed by a concern for personal autonomy. Pluralists should agree, as I have argued, since they ought to acknowledge that it is only through independent critical thinking that people can navigate among conflicting incommensurable values in a way that does those values justice. From a pluralist perspective, individual autonomy is desirable for any good life. A view that acknowledges the centrality of autonomy must be preferred to one that does not.[5]

So, should liberal pluralists accept Kymlicka's case for recognition of national groups, subject to a framework of basic liberal values including personal autonomy? Not necessarily, because they will be concerned not only with the merits of multiculturalist recognition but also with its costs. For the pluralist, no gain is without loss, and the field of multiculturalism is no exception to that rule.

This concern is raised by Barry, who complains that cultural recognition distracts from or conflicts with the economic redistribution that ought to be the egalitarian liberal's primary goal. For example, policies aimed at sustaining a language may have the effect of preventing people from pursuing opportunities for mainstream employment. This objection was partly met by Fraser's response that redistribution and recognition are both important policies, pursuing equally legitimate and important goals. Fraser is wary of merely 'affirmative' recognition that perpetuates existing hierarchies, but that is not the kind of recognition that Kymlicka and other liberal multiculturalists would defend.

Pluralists will be only partly reassured. They will agree with Fraser that redistribution and recognition policies both pursue important ends, but they will be inclined to see those ends as incommensurable. Material well-being and collective self-determination are very distinct goods, and they may conflict. Hence, it may be harder than Fraser supposes to combine such purposes in a single account of social justice and a single practical programme. Much will depend on the details of particular cases. As we saw in Chapter 7, when incommensurables conflict a reasoned resolution is not out of the question, but it will appeal to contextual considerations. Liberal pluralism is a framework for choice, not a formula. Given the broad principles I have outlined it remains to determine policies in particular circumstances.

Perhaps in the end the most that can be concluded at this abstract level is that liberal pluralism tends to draw us beyond privatization and towards multiculturalist recognition, at least in the case of national groups, but which approach should prevail will depend on contextual details. One might go so far as to say that pluralism raises a presumption in favour of recognizing national claims (within the limits I have endorsed) that can be rebutted by an account of its costs in the relevant circumstances. Privatization may yet be the better policy in circumstances where the costs of recognition are too high.

It may help to consider an example: Fiji. Stephanie Lawson (1996) argues that in the case of Fiji policies designed to preserve traditional indigenous culture have had destructive and unjust consequences because the traditions in question are elitist and anti-democratic. Various constitutional provisions secure a privileged political position for a class of traditional chiefs (who are located mainly in one region of the islands), limit parliamentary representation for non-indigenous Fijians, make indigenous land inalienable and in general assert a doctrine of indigenous Fijian 'paramountcy'. These provisions are especially discriminatory in their effects on Fiji's largest minority group, the descendants of the indentured Indian labourers brought to the islands by the British colonial government in the nineteenth century. Indigenous Fijians have been encouraged in the belief that the Indian minority is entitled to no more than a token presence in Fijian politics. Fears of an 'Indian takeover' have led to four armed coups since 1987, the most recent in 2006 leading to the suspension of Fiji from the Commonwealth of Nations. Not only Indo-Fijians but ordinary indigenous Fijians, too, are ill-served by the preservationist policies, according to Lawson, since the continuation of such policies has resulted in a low level of economic development and the syphoning of such economic benefits as there are to the chiefly class and the region where they live. Moreover, it is doubtful that the practices enshrined in the constitution are genuinely traditional anyway, but rather inventions or manipulations inherited from the colonial administration that again serve the interests of certain groups and areas rather than others.

Of course, context is open to interpretation. Lawson's reading of the Fijian case is disputed by Joseph Carens (2000), who offers a qualified defence of the policy of preserving Fijian traditions. Carens concedes that there is force in Lawson's objections, but by way of reply he asks, what were the alternatives? When it comes to the land policy in particular, what would have happened if the land had been opened up for individual acquisition? The result would have been an influx of white settlement of the kind seen in Australia and New Zealand and the consequent dispossession of the indigenous population. The context of a policy, Carens argues, must include reference to its historical origins, which in turn involves an appreciation of the feasible alternatives available to policy makers at the time. At the time when Fiji became a colony in 1874 it was a reasonable, even enlightened policy to make the securing of native lands a priority. Similarly, the division of Fijian politics along ethnic lines and the emphasis on chiefly authority merely reflected local realities. It is true that the role of chiefs was in part a colonial creation, but all traditions are invented to some degree and in this case there was 'enough continuity' with what had gone before for the practice to count as meaningfully traditional. Although these policies have had costs, these have on the whole been worth paying bearing in mind the likely effect of the alternatives and the actual benefits in terms of the well-being of Fijians relative to other indigenous peoples.

Carens's view could, in turn, be contested at several points. Arguably he underestimates the costs of the Fijian policies and overestimates their benefits. Writing in 2000, he is satisfied that 'the democratic culture of Fiji may be more robust than Lawson supposed and the anti-democratic effects of the efforts to preserve Fijian culture far less severe' (Carens 2000: 253). This judgement looks less convincing after the coup of 2006 in which indigenous Fijians once again suspended democratic procedures. One may also ask about alternatives. It may be that the policies in question were reasonable in their original nineteenth-century context, but does that remain the case? The Victorian colonial administration seemed relatively unconcerned about the claims of the indentured Indian labourers, but that does not justify the continued abrogation of the rights of their descendants. Might it not be possible to ensure some protection for indigenous Fijians without going to the undemocratic extremes now in force?

However, my purpose here is not to settle the Fijian question but simply to illustrate the notion of contextual argument in the field of cultural recognition. Carens would agree with Lawson's broad approach to the Fijian issue by way of a careful examination of the social, political and historical background. For Carens, such an approach generally 'fits better with' recognition, as long as the latter is 'even-handed', because contextual particulars are usually inseparable from cultural commitments, but he also allows that circumstances sometimes suggest more of a 'hands-off' approach to culture (Carens 2000: 13–14). My proposal is in keeping with this view. The question of whether a cultural group should be accorded political recognition is one that ought to be framed and to some extent guided by the principles of liberal pluralism, which may be said to raise a presumption in favour of such a policy in the case of national groups. But in the end the matter can only be settled, so far as that is possible, by argument in context.[6]

Nationalism, Democracy and Global Cultures

Assuming, then, a framework of autonomy-based liberalism and the possibility of a contextual case for multiculturalist recognition, how should pluralists respond to the other main issues raised in this book? In all cases they will prefer a balanced approach that allows due weight to all relevant values in context while laying especial (but not overriding) emphasis on the value of personal autonomy. But how will this play out in relation to nationalism, democracy and 'global' cultures?

In the contest between nationalism and cosmopolitanism (Chapter 4), the leading candidates for such a balanced view are the liberal nationalism of Miller and Tamir on the one hand and the moderate cosmopolitanism of Appiah and Sen on the other. One would think that, from a pluralist perspective, it is the cosmopolitans who have the edge, with their stress on the extent to which modern identities are multiple, cross-cutting and not necessarily hierarchical within the same individual. This fits well with the central pluralist theme of plural, conflicting and incommensurable values. For cosmopolitans, as for pluralists, moral experience is more complex than allowed for by those nationalists (or communitarians or cultural relativists) who suppose it to be determined by a single overriding identity.

On the other hand it would be unwise to write off the nationalists completely. As Berlin points out, the continuing power of national identity remains a reality, even if one might wish it were otherwise.[7] The persistent power of nationalism comes from its capacity to answer to the human need for belonging and solidarity in the context of an impersonal modern world. Pluralists can acknowledge these as genuine human goods. But of course pluralists will also be wary of the historic danger of nationalism's turning into a grotesque form of monism if it is not balanced by other considerations. Liberal nationalism aims at achieving such a balance, and its proponents make a fair case that is not easy to dismiss.

Pluralists will also be sympathetic, to a degree, with calls for greater democracy in multicultural affairs (Chapter 6). In general, democracy will be attractive to pluralists because, at its best, it will introduce into the political process many different voices that will in turn express many different values. There is always a risk, however, that democracy will be turned into a vehicle for elite or populist leaders to promote their own views in the name of the group they claim to represent, or for groups that will take advantage of their power to the detriment of other groups. In pluralist terms the values of the powerful few will predominate over those of the disenfranchised or apathetic many. This is especially a problem for systems of group representation of the kind advanced by Young, which can so easily be captured by elite activists. But even Parekh's intercultural dialogue and the deliberative democracy exemplified by Benhabib can be distorted when the agenda is manipulated or access to dialogue or deliberation is monopolized.

Pluralists can still support democratic moves, but only on condition that these genuinely express a range of goods rather than just the monistic programmes of a few zealots or professional organizers. In particular, liberal pluralists will be concerned to ensure that the collective autonomy implicit in all democratic mechanisms is not permitted to eclipse the personal autonomy of the group's members. Indeed, the pluralist outlook may be useful in identifying the sort of constraints on dialogue that are necessary to make it more democratic. Plausible candidates for structuring multicultural dialogue include the four pluralist virtues: generosity, realism, attentiveness and flexibility. These dispositions intersect with the conditions for fair deliberation listed by deliberative democrats like Benhabib.

Finally, pluralists should take a similarly balanced view of the prospects for reconciling or accommodating the 'global' cultures within a liberal-democratic framework (Chapter 8). On the one hand, Islam and Confucianism must be acknowledged as embodying combinations of genuine human values that are entitled not merely to toleration but also to respect and even celebration. On the other hand there are undeniable points of tension between these worldviews and liberal pluralism.

The case of Islam raises the issue of the relation between a value-pluralist outlook and monotheism – although of course Islam is not the only world religion that raises this issue. Some pluralists would argue that pluralist and monotheistic views are diametrically opposed, since pluralists deny exactly what monotheists appear to assert, namely the absolute superiority of a single conception of the good or ranking of values (Hardy 2007). Others, however, see the relation in less intransigent terms, allowing that as world religions develop they tend to evolve multiple interpretations that reflect, within the religion, much of the value plurality of humanity in general (Galston 2007).

As for Confucianism, how can value pluralism be reconciled with the classical Confucian value of harmony? Pluralists typically emphasize the extent to which values come into conflict so that people have to make hard choices or messy compromises. Pluralism does not deny the possibility of goods harmonizing in some cases – justice does not always collide with mercy or loyalty, for example. But pluralists will not expect or look for harmony as a general goal in public (or even personal) affairs. Indeed, they will tend to see such an ideal as misleading and even dangerous, since it conceals the reality of value conflict that ought to be confronted honestly, and it may be used to disguise the true nature of biased or undemocratic decisions.

This is a question for Bell in particular, since he appears committed to both Confucian harmony and value pluralism. He might reply that the classical Confucian texts distinguish between harmony and conformity, recommending a tolerant form of politics in which 'the ruler should be open to different political views among his advisers' (Bell 2010: 172). However, to the extent that such differences are acknowledged, that leaves the question of how they can be 'harmonized' and what that means. It is one thing to acknowledge distinct ethical considerations but one of the central pluralist themes stresses the extent to which these are not only different but also in conflict with one another. Pluralists should not deny the possibility of rational resolution where incommensurable values collide, but this will usually take the form of ranking or trade-off, always carrying a sense of genuine loss. Harmony suggests the dovetailing of values without loss, and therefore remains a dubious aspiration from a pluralist point of view.

Nevertheless, there are also resources in both Confucianism and Islam that are favourable to the liberal-pluralist outlook, notably points at which both worldviews can be given relatively liberal interpretations. In Chapter 8 I indicated some possibilities along these lines. That there are such liberal dimensions within Islam and Confucianism shows that to commend liberal-democratic limits for multiculturalism is not necessarily to favour 'the West' against 'the rest'. Liberal democracy is not the exclusive property of the West (assuming that there is such an entity) but rather a desirable framework for managing the diversity of human values and cultures more generally.[8]

A Final Word

In a prominently published lecture, Timothy Garton Ash has recently joined those who would consign multiculturalism 'to the dustbin of history' (Garton Ash 2012). Part of the problem, he writes, is the uncertainty that has entered the term. In some versions multiculturalism 'has come close to official endorsement of cultural and moral relativism', resulting in the reinforcement 'of cultural norms that would be unacceptable in the wider society, especially in relation to women'. As for those versions that explicitly accept liberal constraints, these are merely redundant, since the liberal constraints are what really matter. 'Why not simply talk about the form of modern liberalism suited – meaning also, developed and adapted – to the conditions of a contemporary, multicultural society?' The idea of liberalism applied to current conditions is all we need. This is the kind of liberalism that results from 'the attempt by Isaiah Berlin and others to blend liberalism and pluralism'.

There is much in Garton Ash's analysis that should be accepted. He is correct that the term 'multiculturalism' has become a political and philosophical football. He is right to distinguish two tendencies in particular: a stronger, more relativist form, and a more moderate form hedged by liberal constraints. Again, the judgement is justified that the former, stronger kind of multiculturalism is flawed, dangerous and should be rejected, and that liberal limits must be supported.

However, it is another matter to claim that (in its liberal form) the notion of multiculturalism is altogether redundant. Here Garton Ash argues that when liberals extended their thinking to embrace the rights of workers and women, for example, they did not find it necessary to address 'multiclassism' or 'multigenderism'. So, why bother with 'multiculturalism'? But actually, liberals did adopt qualifying terms to mark the development of liberal thought in the directions mentioned. That is why theorists now distinguish between 'classical' and 'egalitarian' liberalism, for example, and why the term 'liberal feminism' seems to make sense. In the same way, the term 'liberal multiculturalism' marks a distinct step in the evolution of liberal thought, beyond the focus on economic injustice that was the central concern of egalitarian liberals such as Rawls and Dworkin, to include attention to the kind of injustice that can only be remedied or ameliorated by public recognition of a group's claims – the field illuminated by Kymlicka. 'Liberal multiculturalism' is not a redundant term, because it picks out a particular way in which liberal principles are being 'developed and adapted'.

So, when Garton Ash wants us to talk about the form of modern liberalism appropriate to a multicultural society, that is just what liberal multiculturalists are trying to do. Moreover, when he says that such an outlook can be formed from a blend of liberalism and Berlinian pluralism, that is exactly the claim of those multiculturalists who are also liberal pluralists.

Notes

Introduction

1 Concise treatments of multiculturalism in general can be found in Kivisto (2002); Modood (2007); and Rattansi (2011). The political-theory literature on the subject is surveyed by Kymlicka (2002: ch. 8); Kukathas (2004); and Murphy (2012). Significant collections of essays on multiculturalism by political theorists include Horton (1993); Joppke and Lukes (1999); Laden and Owen (2007).
2 On the alleged retreat of multiculturalism in the UK and the Netherlands see Entzinger (2003); Joppke (2004). France, Germany and the US are discussed by Brubaker (2003). On the Canadian experience see Kymlicka (1998a). On Australia see Levey (2008).
3 This list is based on that set out in Banting and Kymlicka (2006: 56–7).
4 See in this connection the 'curriculum' multiculturalism, especially prominent in the United States, which opposes the traditional dominance of 'Western civilization': Bloom (1987); D'Souza (1992); Schlesinger (1992); Hughes (1993); Friedman and Narveson (1995).
5 For further examination of the concept of culture see White and Dillingham (1973); Carrithers (1992); Scott (2003); Jenks (2004); Lawson (2006).
6 For a useful survey both of the distinct dimensions of identity and of the links among these see Preece (2005).
7 According to Stephen Castles and Mark Miller, between 1945 and 1975 the minority population of France increased in millions from 2.1 to 4.1, that of Germany from 0.5 to 4.0 and that of the UK from 1.5 to 4.1. By 2005 the foreign-born population of France was 4.9 million, that of Germany 10.6 and that of the UK 5.8. See Castles and Miller (2009: Tables 5.1 and 5.3).

8 The United Nations adopted a Declaration on the Rights of Persons Belonging to National or Ethnic, Religious and Linguistic Minorities in 1993. See the discussion by Kymlicka (2001: 120–32).
9 The following distinction between toleration, non-discrimination and multiculturalism is indebted to Raz (1995: 172–3).
10 For opposing views on this example see Kymlicka (1995a: 97) and Barry (2001: 44–5). I return to it in Chapters 2 and 3.

1 Universalism, Relativism and Culture

1 For a standard account of the nature and history of human rights see Donnelly (2003).
2 As an example of the former see Jeremy Bentham's utilitarianism, in which moral considerations are quantified as units of pleasure measured along various dimensions including duration, intensity and so forth (Bentham 1789 [1982]). Evolutionary biology is taken as the model by 'social Darwinists' such as Herbert Spencer: see Flew (1967).
3 Although these movements claim to supersede Marxism, their relation with Marxism is complex: see e.g. Smart (1992: ch. 6).
4 Ter Ellingson (2001) argues that the widespread attribution of 'the myth of the noble savage' to Rousseau is mistaken. According to Ellingson, the myth was in fact invented a century before Rousseau wrote, and was popularized only in the latter half of the nineteenth century. Still, there seems little doubt that indigenous peoples were often romanticized by Europeans in the eighteenth century, and that this tendency was influenced by reports from contemporary explorers such as James Cook and Bougainville.
5 See e.g. Herder (1774 [2004]). For differing interpretations of Herder see Berlin (2000b); Norton (1991); Spencer (2012).
6 However, Berlin retreated from this relativist interpretation of Herder in his later work: see the discussion of Berlin in Chapter 7.
7 See similarly Boas (1940); Herskovits (1955); Geertz (1973, 1989).
8 The merits of relativism are debated in Ladd (1973); Hollis and Lukes (1982); Krausz (1989); Levy (2002); Lukes (2008).
9 The example is taken from Rachels (1993: 23–5).
10 This is also an instance of the more general fallacy that values can be logically derived from facts. The rule that values cannot be derived from facts is sometimes known as 'Hume's Law', after David Hume (1739–40 [1978]: 469–70).
11 This contrast between negative (or 'formal') and effective freedom is one version of the standard distinction between negative and 'positive' freedom: see Swift (2006: 55–9).
12 Nussbaum's list has been supplemented by further capabilities identified by Wolff and De-Shalit (2007). Their contribution has been endorsed by Nussbaum (2011: 42–5).

13 Nussbaum also sees her position as accommodating diversity in other ways. For example, since 2000 she has emphasized that the capabilities are intended to apply only 'politically' in the sense defined by John Rawls's *Political Liberalism* (1993): see Nussbaum (2000: 74–5, 105; 2011: 89–93). Rawls's view is discussed in Chapter 2.
14 This item (along with item 7, 'affiliation') is given a special role in Nussbaum's list, since it is said to 'organize and suffuse all the others, making their pursuit truly human' (Nussbaum 2000: 82).
15 See e.g. Rawls (1993); Parekh (2006); Galston (2002).
16 See Nussbaum (2003) replying to Barclay (2003).
17 In particular, see the discussion of Parekh in Chapter 5.

2 Liberal Rights to Culture: Kymlicka's Theory

1 Kymlicka is a prolific writer, but his main works for our purposes are Kymlicka (1989; 1995a; 1998a; 1998b; 2001; 2007).
2 Helpful studies of liberalism include Manning (1976); Gray (1986); Bellamy (1992); Kelly (2005).
3 On negative vs positive liberty, see Gray (1991); Miller (1991); Berlin (2002); Crowder (2004: ch. 4); Swift (2006).
4 See in particular 'communitarian' writers such as Sandel (1982); MacIntyre (1985; 1988); Taylor (1985; 1989); Walzer (1983).
5 Kymlicka sometimes refers to 'equality between the minority and majority groups' (Kymlicka 1995a: 152), which seems different from, or even at odds with, the liberal equality that refers to relations among individuals. But, as before, Kymlicka sees groups as valuable only to the extent that they contribute to the well-being of individuals. For a critical discussion of the idea of equalizing groups, see Kukathas (2003: 229–36).
6 Personal autonomy is a stronger, more demanding form of freedom than the 'moral' autonomy mentioned earlier as the basis for equality of moral worth. A person could be morally autonomous, possessing a basic ability to understand and follow moral rules, without being able to reflect critically on those rules and consequently to revise his overall way of life. Moral autonomy is characteristic of all normal adults in any society, while personal autonomy is found more frequently, and is more often celebrated, in distinctively liberal societies. See Johnston (1994: 71–7).
7 See Robert Goodin (2006), who distinguishes between 'protective' and 'polyglot' multiculturalism. On this view Kymlicka's multiculturalism is protective rather than polyglot.
8 Another version of this popular argument sees cultural diversity as valuable 'in the quasi-aesthetic sense that it creates a more interesting world' (Kymlicka 1995a: 121). This, too, is different from Kymlicka's view, although he does concede that the cultural diversity argument, in

either version, carries somewhat more weight in the case of 'ethnic' minorities compared with 'national' minorities. That distinction is explained below.

9 See also the more comprehensive list of policies in Kymlicka (1998a: 42). Note, too, that some of Kymlicka's cultural rights are intended to be permanent, others only temporary: see Kymlicka (1989: 143–4).

10 Note that Kymlicka's case for national rights does not depend on an argument frequently offered in their defence – namely, that the group concerned has been treated unjustly in the past. Kymlicka agrees that 'indigenous people have suffered terrible wrongs in being dispossessed of their lands', and that these wrongs deserve compensation (Kymlicka 1995a: 220, note 5). But it does not follow that the compensation must take the form of national self-determination, which is the principal right Kymlicka is concerned to justify. Past injustice is 'neither necessary nor sufficient' to a claim for this most important right for national minorities. Further, the most straightforward remedy for historical dispossession, the return of the land to its original owners, may involve massive injustice to its current owners or occupiers, who know no other home. Historical injustice can be 'superseded' by changed circumstances (Waldron 1992).

11 Leading critical discussions of Kymlicka's theory include Kukathas (1992); Waldron (1995); Levey (1997); Walker (1997); Okin (1999); Carens (2000); Barry (2001); Festenstein (2005).

12 Another problem is that it is hard to see how Kukathas's freedom of exit can be effective if it is not guaranteed by a state, yet according to Kukathas the state is only one island among others in the archipelago, with no superior status or authority. I return to the issue of freedom of exit when I discuss Barry in Chapter 3, and again in my discussion of William Galston in Chapter 7.

13 But although Kymlicka is clear on the conditions for personal autonomy being possible at all in a community, he is in some doubt as to whether it should be insisted on in cases like that of the Amish, where the group has been given 'tacit or explicit assurances about their right to maintain separate [and restrictive] institutions' over a long period of time: Kymlicka (1995a: 170).

3 Liberal Critics of Cultural Rights

1 Other significant liberal approaches to multiculturalism include Spinner (1994); Raz (1995); Carens (2000); Levy (2000); Gill (2001); Festenstein (2005); Phillips (2007).

2 It follows that Kymlicka's demand that the relative positions of cultures be equalized is, for Barry, unrealistic and not required by justice: see Chapter 2, note 5 above.

3 For an indication of this range, see the articles collected in Banting and Kymlicka (2006) and Olson (2008).
4 Another problem with Fraser's view is her political conclusion in favour not only of deconstruction but also of socialism. According to Fraser, socialism is the transformative expression of redistribution, the merely affirmative form of which is 'liberal welfare'. So, the ideal combination of redistribution and recognition will be transformative in both dimensions, a mix of socialism and deconstruction. Quite apart from the conceptual question of how these will fit together, Fraser herself concedes that in both cases her ideal is 'far removed from the immediate interests and identities of most people' (Fraser 2008: 39).
5 Other discussions of the gender implications of multiculturalism include Deveaux (2006); Song (2007); Phillips (2010).
6 See the essays by Janet Halley, Joseph Raz and Yael Tamir in Okin (1999).
7 It is less clear what happens if there is disagreement between the parties over whether the present case constitutes a reversal point in the first place. Shachar says that the opt-out provisions 'cannot be used lightly'; individual applicants must show that the group has failed to provide a meaningful remedy (Shachar 2001: 135). So, the pro-group presumption at the negotiation stage is balanced by an emphasis on the vulnerable individual's choice at the application stage, but the latter itself has limits.
8 See also Joseph Raz (1986; 1995), whose work is discussed in Chapter 7, and my own position set out in Chapter 9.

4 Nationalists and Cosmopolitans

1 There is also a suspicion here that Kymlicka's position is coloured by a distinctively Canadian perspective, indeed driven by the specific political agenda of Quebec (Barry 2001: 310).
2 A related distinction is sometimes made between 'ethnocultural' and 'civic' forms of nationalism, although whether this can be strictly equated to the illiberal vs liberal division is questioned by David Brown (2000: ch. 3).
3 The distinction between integration and assimilation was touched on in Chapter 2. See Kymlicka (1995a: 78).
4 For a similar liberal acceptance of the current reality of nationalism but without any expectation of its being transcended in the future, see Isaiah Berlin, 'Nationalism: Past Neglect and Present Power', in Berlin (1979).
5 Mill's argument for individuality is linked to identity by Appiah (2005: ch. 1).
6 Miller is close to Kymlicka in several respects, although see below for some points of divergence. He also notes that he finds 'little to disagree

with' in Raz's liberal multiculturalism (Miller 1995: 131, note 17). I discuss Raz in Chapter 7.

7 The cases Tamir has in mind here include Estonia's exclusion from full citizenship of its Russian minority and Israel's treatment of its Palestinian minority (Tamir 1995: 158, 160).

8 In a later essay Tamir retreats from her 1995 enthusiasm for group rights, agreeing with Okin that these may protect patriarchal practices: see Tamir in Okin (1999). Of course, this concern applies to national as well as non-national identities.

9 See Soutphommasane (2012), who advocates a substantial 'patriotic' form of liberal nationalism, which he also sees as consistent with a defensible multiculturalism.

10 This and similar formulations of cosmopolitanism are discussed by Nussbaum (1996: 6–11). See also Appiah (2005: 217, 220).

11 Kant stops short of expecting or arguing for a world government, instead advocating a global society of republican nation-states. See his essay on 'Perpetual Peace' (Kant 1795 [1991]).

12 For the Kantian liberal response to this criticism see the discussion of Charles Taylor and communitarianism in Chapter 5.

13 Appiah might also have mentioned Rawls's notion of the overlapping consensus in this connection (Rawls 1993).

14 In this respect Appiah seems to have been influenced by Richard Rorty, who similarly advocates narrative over argument as a way of changing people's minds (Rorty 1989). Where Appiah differs from Rorty is in his insistence that such a view need not entail a wholesale abandonment of the principles of the Enlightenment. 'I prefer to speak *with* the Enlightenment: to think of dialogue . . . as a shared search for truth and justice' (Appiah 2005: 250).

15 Sen memorably illustrates the evils of solitarism with a recollection, from his own childhood experience, of the death of Kader Mia, a poor day-labourer killed by Hindu thugs who could see him only as a Muslim: Sen (2006: 170–2).

5 Beyond Liberalism?

1 For the leading communitarians see Chapter 2, note 4 above. An authoritative introduction to the 'liberal–communitarian debate' is provided by Mulhall and Swift (1996).

2 Notable examples include Kymlicka (1989; 2002: ch. 6); Caney (1992); Swift (2006).

3 On the question of masculinity, Tully endorses the view of feminist 'care' ethics that women have 'culturally different ways of engaging in a dialogue' that are suppressed in the language of liberal constitutionalism (Tully 1995: 52). For the pros and cons of care ethics see Gilligan (1982); Tronto (1993); Bowden (1997); Kymlicka (2002: 398–420).

4 See Tully (2002: 105). Here Tully is replying to Barry, but the same objection would apply to Kymlicka and other liberals.
5 Ironically, Tully's claim that 'customs and ways of peoples are a manifestation of their free agreement' (Tully 1995: 125) is akin to the notion of 'tacit consent' found in Locke – an instrument of imperialism, one would have thought, in Tully's terms. Indeed, Locke's notion of tacit consent is narrower than Tully's, since Locke makes it dependent on the enjoyment of property in land (Locke 1689 [1970]: sections 119–21). For Tully, by contrast, mere membership of a group seems to be evidence that one has freely agreed to its customs and ways.
6 However, on Parekh's account Hindu beliefs are so malleable that it is uncertain what a Hindu 'framework' would be (Parekh 2008: 150–1).
7 See the epic account of this process in Hegel (1821 [1956]).
8 Similarly, Parekh takes Samuel Huntington to task for the latter's blunt distinction between 'Western' and other cultures as part of his 'clash of civilizations' thesis (Parekh 2008: ch. 8). Huntington's view is discussed in Chapter 8.

6 Democrats

1 Group representation is also supported by Phillips (1998).
2 On 'whiteness', see Hill (1997); Bonnett (2000).
3 For this objection to 'mirror' representation in general, see Pitkin (1971).
4 In addition, Kukathas argues that Young's group representation policy will lead to destructive competition for public resources between rival minority groups, between minority groups and the mainstream and within groups (Kukathas 1997: 147–9).
5 We saw in Chapter 3 that this is not entirely true, although Benhabib could be forgiven for reaching this conclusion in the wake of Barry's anti-multiculturalist rhetoric.
6 There is now a vast literature on deliberative democracy. See e.g. Gutmann and Thompson (1996; 2004); Macedo (1999); Dryzek (2000); Fishkin and Laslett (2003).
7 On discourse or communicative ethics, see Habermas (1984). Readable introductions include Giddens (1985); Chambers (1995).
8 For ideas about how to institutionalize deliberative democracy in general, see Gutmann and Thompson (2004: 29–39, 59–63); Ackerman and Fishkin (2004).
9 A similar response to deliberative democracy in the context of cultural diversity can be found in the work of Monique Deveaux (2000; 2006).
10 For other criticisms of deliberative democracy along these lines see Williams (1998; 2000); Deveaux (2000). See also Walzer (1999), who objects that deliberation is not really central to political action.

11 See also Gutmann and Thompson (2004: 49–51).
12 See similarly Appiah's view discussed in Chapter 4.

7 Value Pluralists

1 On the case for the truth of value pluralism, see Raz (1986); Stocker (1990); Nussbaum (1992); Lukes (1991); Nagel (1991); Kekes (1993); Chang (1997); Crowder (2002).
2 See Allen (2007), who makes a case for a 'complex compromise' between considerations of justice and social unity in connection with the Truth and Reconciliation Commission in post-apartheid South Africa.
3 See 'Nationalism: Past Neglect and Present Power' in Berlin (1979); 'The Origins of Israel' and 'Jewish Slavery and Emancipation' in Berlin (2000a).
4 This case is far from conclusive for the reason that emerged in the discussion of Tamir in Chapter 4. Even if non-national identities have value, it does not follow that they have as strong a claim to public recognition as national identities.
5 At least this is true of Gray during what may be called his value-pluralist period. Formerly he had been a strong supporter of Mill and Hayek: see Gray (1983; 1984).
6 For further critical discussion of Gray see Crowder (2006).
7 Gray may respond that totalitarian political regimes can be ruled out by the 'minimal standards of decency and legitimacy' that he says are consistent with pluralism (Gray 2000: 109). This claim is hard to test because he says little about what the minimal standards are. In any case, even if pluralism does rule out totalitarian politics, Gray is clear that it is consistent with a more broadly 'authoritarian' or 'non-liberal' politics. The question remains how far that kind of regime is capable of accommodating cultural diversity.
8 Confusingly, Parekh labels this position 'pluralism' or (somewhat less confusingly) 'culturalism'.
9 Parekh seems to appreciate this point when he is criticizing the cultural pluralism of Herder. There he distinguishes between 'diversity of cultures' and diversity 'within' them, complaining that Herder's pluralism is inadequately sensitive to the latter (Parekh 2006: 73). But he fails to see the significance of this insight for his own treatment of liberalism.
10 It is possible that one culture may exhibit certain universals while another enjoys a different set altogether with no commonalities at all, but this is improbable. Good human lives are likely to have at least some overlapping features. Again, Nussbaum's list of human capabilities is a plausible account of what those commonalities may be.
11 Parekh stops short of allowing the judgement that one culture is superior or inferior to another all things considered. Such a judgement he

regards as 'logically incoherent' (Parekh 2006: 173). But it may be possible to argue that culture X is superior to culture Y along all dimensions of comparison, or within a particular context, or in accordance with the norms outlined in Chapter 9.

12 Galston does, in one place, describe his position as 'a politics of recognition', but in context this does not imply the kind of active state support for cultures usually meant by that phrase: see Galston (2005: 41).

13 See note 11 above.

14 There is a degree of ambiguity in Raz's comments on this point, since the 'protection of freedom' that he envisages here does not necessarily include the promotion of personal autonomy that he advocates elsewhere (and which is endorsed by Kymlicka). Thus, the first of his 'concrete policies' entitles people to educate their young in the culture of their group, subject only to a requirement for instruction in 'the history and traditions of all the cultures in the country, and an attitude of respect for them' (Raz 1995: 189). There is no requirement for education in autonomy or critical thinking. This is surprising in view both of the centrality of autonomy in Raz's thinking overall, and of the prominence of personal autonomy as an issue in multicultural education: see Levinson (1999); Brighouse (2000); Reich (2002).

8 Global Cultures

1 Huntington takes care to distinguish 'civilization in the singular' from 'civilization in the plural' (Huntington 1996: 40–1). Civilization in the singular has usually been contrasted with 'barbarism' to imply 'a single standard for what is civilized'. But that usage has fallen out of favour in recent times and been replaced by reference to civilizations (plural), suggesting that there are 'many civilizations, each of which was civilized in its own way'. On the concept of civilization in the singular see Bowden (2009).

2 According to Huntington, the only major world religion without its own major civilization is Buddhism, which was extinguished in the land of its origins, India, and which took root elsewhere only by adapting to the local culture. In particular, Huntington seems to regard Buddhism as failing to establish a major civilization because it lacks the support of sufficiently powerful 'core states' (Huntington 1996: ch. 7). To count as 'major' on his view, a civilization needs to be centred upon one or more 'core states' dedicated to advancing the culture and interests of that civilization – for example, China for Sinic civilization, the United States and the leading states of Europe for the West. Islam possesses no single acknowledged core state, although there are several candidates among which competition for the lead is a source of instability.

3 For similar views see Weber (1965); Wittfogel (1957); Lewis (2002).

4 See the discussion of postmodernism in Chapter 1. For other criticisms of Said see Irwin (2006); Warraq (2007). A mirror-image of the orientalism thesis, investigating tendentious 'occidentalist' accounts of 'the West' (although without the postmodernist apparatus), is presented by Buruma and Margalit (2004).
5 See e.g. the approach taken in Esposito (1999).
6 See also An-Na'im (2010). An-Na'im frequently acknowledges that his work is based on the thought of his former teacher, Mahmoud Mohamed Taha, an outspoken critic of the Sudanese government who was executed by that regime in 1985.
7 For other attempts to find common ground between liberal democracy and Islam, see Hashmi (2002); Safi (2003); Azra and Hudson (2008); Ramadan (2009; 2010).
8 Discussions of the Asian values debate include Davis (1995); de Bary (1998); Langlois (2001); Avonius and Kingsbury (2008).
9 However, Bell seems to take a more orthodox Western view of democracy when he is discussing Singapore (Bell 2000: ch. 4).
10 This is similar to a standard objection brought against Huntington, with whom Bell appears to have some sympathy when it comes to distinguishing different 'civilizations': see Bell (2000: 175–6).
11 See also Nisbett (2003); Shin (2011).
12 Bell argues, however, that in the Confucian tradition critical thinking should be preceded by understanding and empathy (Bell 2010: ch. 7).
13 For a more pessimistic assessment of the prospects for minority group rights in China, in the face both of Confucian tradition and recent globalization, see He (2005).

9 A Liberal-Pluralist Approach

1 This view is developed in greater detail in Crowder (2002; 2004; 2007a; 2007b; 2008).
2 The principle of maximizing diversity needs to be qualified by various considerations, most notably by a concern for coherence, since values can come into conflict (Crowder 2002: 139–40; 2007b: 221–2).
3 See the discussion of 'pluralist virtues' in Crowder (2002: ch. 8).
4 Further arguments in favour of education for autonomy as a public goal are presented by Levinson (1999); Brighouse (2000); Reich (2002).
5 Also, as I argued in response to Galston (Chapter 7), autonomy is necessary to give substance to the right of exit that non-intervention theorists rely on so heavily (see also Crowder 2007a). So, although toleration theorists purport to reject autonomy as a leading value, they implicitly commend it through their stress on exit.
6 For another contextual analysis of a multicultural issue see Jeff Spinner-Halev, who argues that Okin's feminist critique of group rights does not take into account situations where the group is oppressed by the

surrounding state, as in the case of Muslims in India and Israel. In such cases the injustice of discrimination against women can be outweighed by 'the injustice of imposing reform on oppressed groups': Spinner-Halev (2001: 86). The general notion of 'contextual multiculturalism' is discussed by Murphy (2012: ch. 9).

7 Berlin, 'Nationalism: Past Neglect and Present Power', in Berlin (1979).

8 See also the argument for the universality of personal autonomy in response to Parekh in Chapter 5.

References

Abbey, Ruth (2000) *Charles Taylor*. Princeton University Press, Princeton.
Ackerman, Bruce and James Fishkin (2004) *Deliberation Day*. Yale University Press, New Haven, CT.
Allen, Jonathan (2007) 'A Liberal–Pluralist Case for Truth Commissions: Lessons from Isaiah Berlin', in George Crowder and Henry Hardy (eds), *The One and the Many: Reading Isaiah Berlin*. Prometheus Books, Amherst, NY.
An-Na'im, Abdullahi Ahmed (1990) *Toward an Islamic Reformation: Civil Liberties, Human Rights, and International Law*. Syracuse University Press, Syracuse, NY.
An-Na'im, Abdullahi Ahmed (2010) *Islam and the Secular State: Negotiating the Future of Shari'a*. Harvard University Press, Cambridge, MA.
Anderson, Benedict (2006) *Imagined Communities*, new edn. Verso, London.
Appiah, Kwame Anthony (2005) *The Ethics of Identity*. Princeton University Press, Princeton.
Appiah, Kwame Anthony (2006) *Cosmopolitanism: Ethics in a World of Strangers*. Norton, New York.
Aquinas, St Thomas (1959) *Selected Political Writings*, ed. A. P. D'Entrèves, trans. J. G. Dawson. Basil Blackwell, Oxford.
Aristotle (n.d. [1962]) *The Politics*, trans. T. A. Sinclair. Penguin, Harmondsworth.
Avonius, Leena and Damien Kingsbury (eds) (2008) *Human Rights in Asia: A Reassessment of the Asian Values Debate*. Palgrave Macmillan, New York.
Ayer, A. J. (1936) *Language, Truth and Logic*. Gollancz, London.
Azra, Azyumardi and Wayne Hudson (eds) (2008) *Islam Beyond Conflict: Indonesian Islam and Western Political Theory*. Ashgate, Aldershot.

Banting, Keith and Will Kymlicka (eds) (2006) *Multiculturalism and the Welfare State: Recognition and Redistribution in Contemporary Democracies*. Oxford University Press, Oxford.

Barber, Benjamin (1995) *Jihad vs McWorld*. Ballantine, New York.

Barclay, Linda (2003) 'What Kind of Liberal is Martha Nussbaum?' *Sats – Nordic Journal of Philosophy*, 2 (2): 5–24.

Barry, Brian (2001) *Culture and Equality*. Polity, Cambridge.

Barry, Brian (2002) 'Second Thoughts – and Some First Thoughts Revived', in Paul Kelly (ed.), *Multiculturalism Reconsidered:* Culture and Equality *and its Critics*. Polity, Cambridge.

Bayle, Pierre (1702 [1991]) *Historical and Cultural Dictionary: Selections*, trans. R. Popkin. Hackett, Indianapolis, IN.

Bell, Daniel A. (2000) *East Meets West*. Cambridge University Press, Cambridge.

Bell, Daniel A. (2006) *Beyond Liberal Democracy*. Cambridge University Press, Cambridge.

Bell, Daniel A. (2010) *China's New Confucianism: Politics and Everyday Life in a Changing Society* new edn. Princeton University Press, Princeton.

Bellamy, Richard (1992) *Liberalism and Modern Society: A Historical Argument*. Pennsylvania State University Press, University Park, PA.

Benedict, Ruth (1935) *Patterns of Culture*. Routledge & Kegan Paul: London.

Benhabib, Seyla (2002) *The Claims of Culture*. Princeton University Press, Princeton.

Benn, Stanley (1988) *A Theory of Freedom*. Cambridge University Press, Cambridge.

Bentham, Jeremy (1789 [1982]) *An Introduction to the Principles of Morals and Legislation*, ed. J. H. Burns and H. L. A. Hart. Methuen, London.

Berlin, Isaiah (1979) *Against the Current: Essays in the History of Ideas*, ed. H. Hardy. Hogarth, London.

Berlin, Isaiah (1990) *The Crooked Timber of Humanity: Chapters in the History of Ideas*, ed. H. Hardy. John Murray, London.

Berlin, Isaiah (2000a) *The Power of Ideas*, ed. H. Hardy. Chatto & Windus, London.

Berlin, Isaiah (2000b) *Three Critics of the Enlightenment: Vico, Herder and Hamann*. Princeton University Press, Princeton.

Berlin, Isaiah (2002) *Liberty*, ed. H. Hardy. Oxford University Press, Oxford.

Berlin, Isaiah (2008) *Russian Thinkers*, revised edn, ed. Henry Hardy and Aileen Kelly. Penguin, London.

Berlin, Isaiah and Bernard Williams (1994) 'Pluralism and Liberalism: A Reply', *Political Studies*, 42: 306–9.

Bloom, Allan (1987) *The Closing of the American Mind*. Simon & Schuster, New York.

Boas, Franz (1940) *Race, Language, and Culture*. Macmillan, New York.

Boghossian, Paul (2006) *Fear of Knowledge: Against Relativism and Constructivism*. Clarendon Press, Oxford.

Bonnett, Alastair (2000) *White Identities: Historical and International Perspectives*. Longman, London.

Bowden, Brett (2009) *The Empire of Civilization: The Evolution of an Imperial Idea*. University of Chicago Press, Chicago, IL.

Bowden, Peta (1997) *Caring: Gender-Sensitive Ethics*. Routledge, London.

Brighouse, Harry (2000) *School Choice and Social Justice*. Oxford University Press, Oxford.

Brown, David (2000) *Contemporary Nationalism: Civic, Ethnocultural and Multicultural Politics*. Routledge, London.

Brubaker, Rogers (2003) 'The Return of Assimilation? Changing Perspectives on Immigration and its Sequels in France, Germany, and the United States', in C. Joppke and E. Morawska (eds), *Toward Assimilation and Citizenship: Immigrants in Liberal Nation-States*. Palgrave Macmillan, Basingstoke.

Burke, Edmund (1790 [1970]) *Reflections on the Revolution in France*, ed. C. C. O'Brien. Penguin, Harmondsworth.

Buruma, Ian and Avishai Margalit (2004) *Occidentalism: The West in the Eyes of its Enemies*. Penguin, New York.

Cameron, David (2011) 'Speech on Radicalisation and Islamic Extremism'. *New Statesman*, 5 February http://www.newstatesman.com/blogs/the-staggers/2011/02/terrorism-islam-ideology Accessed 15 May 2012.

Caney, Simon (1992) 'Liberalism and Communitarianism: a Misconceived Debate', *Political Studies*, 40 (2): 273–89.

Carens, Joseph (2000) *Culture, Citizenship, and Community: A Contextual Exploration of Justice as Evenhandedness*. Oxford University Press, Oxford.

Carrithers, Michael (1992) *Why Humans Have Cultures: Explaining Anthropology and Social Diversity*. Oxford University Press, Oxford.

Castles, Stephen, and Mark J. Miller (2009) *The Age of Migration: International Population Movements in the Modern World*, 4th edn. Guilford Press, New York.

Chambers, Simone (1995) 'Discourse and Democratic Practices', in Stephen K. White (ed.), *Cambridge Companion to Habermas*. Cambridge University Press, Cambridge.

Chang, Ruth (ed.) (1997) *Incommensurability, Incomparability, and Practical Reasoning*. Cambridge University Press, Cambridge.

Christman, John (1991) 'Liberalism and Individual Positive Freedom', *Ethics*, 101 (2): 343–59.

Cohen, G. A. (1978) *Karl Marx's Theory of History: A Defence*. Clarendon Press, Oxford.

Connor, Michael (2005) *The Invention of Terra Nullius*. Sydney: MacLeay Press.

Crowder, George (1994) 'Pluralism and Liberalism', *Political Studies*, 42 (2): 293–305.

Crowder, George (2002) *Liberalism and Value Pluralism*. Continuum, London and New York.

Crowder, George (2004) *Isaiah Berlin: Liberty and Pluralism*. Polity, Cambridge.
Crowder, George (2006) 'Gray and the Politics of Pluralism', in J. Horton and G. Newey (eds), *The Political Theory of John Gray*. Routledge, London and New York.
Crowder, George (2007a) 'Two Concepts of Liberal Pluralism', *Political Theory*, 35 (2): 121–46.
Crowder, George (2007b) 'Value Pluralism and Liberalism: Berlin and Beyond', in G. Crowder and H. Hardy (eds), *The One and the Many: Reading Isaiah Berlin*. Prometheus Books, Amherst, NY.
Crowder, George (2008) 'Multiculturalism: a Value-Pluralist Approach', in G. B. Levey (ed.) *Political Theory and Australian Multiculturalism*. Berghahn, New York.
Dalacoura, Katerina (2003) *Islam, Liberalism and Human Rights: Implications for International Relations*, revised edn. I. B. Tauris, London and New York.
Danley, John (1991) 'Liberalism, Aboriginal Rights and Cultural Minorities', *Philosophy and Public Affairs*, 20 (2): 168–85.
Davies, Nigel (1981) *Human Sacrifice: In History and Today*. Macmillan, Basingstoke.
Davis, Michael C. (ed.) (1995) *Human Rights and Chinese Values: Legal, Philosophical and Political Perspectives*. Oxford University Press, Oxford.
de Bary, William Theodore (1998) *Asian Values and Human Rights: A Confucian Communitarian Perspective*. Harvard University Press, Cambridge, MA.
Defoe, Daniel (1719 [1985]) *Robinson Crusoe*, ed. A. Ross. Penguin, Harmondsworth.
d'Entrèves, A. P. (1951) *Natural Law: An Introduction to Legal Philosophy*. Hutchinson University Library, London.
Deveaux, Monique (2000) *Cultural Pluralism and Dilemmas of Justice*. Cornell University Press, Ithaca.
Deveaux, Monique (2006) *Gender and Justice in Multicultural Liberal States*. Oxford University Press, New York.
Donnelly, Jack (2003) *Universal Human Rights in Theory and Practice*, 2nd edn. Cornell University Press, Ithaca.
Dryzek, John (2000) *Deliberative Democracy and Beyond: Liberals, Critics, Contestations*. Oxford University Press, Oxford.
D'Souza, Dinesh (1992) *Illiberal Education: The Politics of Race and Sex on Campus*. Vintage Books, New York.
Dworkin, Ronald (1977) *Taking Rights Seriously*. Duckworth, London.
Dworkin, Ronald (1981) *A Matter of Principle*. Harvard University Press, Cambridge, MA.
Dworkin, Ronald (1984) 'Rights as Trumps', in J. Waldron (ed.), *Theories of Rights*. Oxford University Press, Oxford.
Dworkin, Ronald (1985) *A Matter of Principle*. Harvard University Press, Cambridge, MA.

Dworkin, Ronald (2000) *Sovereign Virtue: The Theory and Practice of Equality*. Harvard University Press, Cambridge, MA.

Ellingson, Ter (2001) *The Myth of the Noble Savage*. University of California Press, Berkeley, CA.

Entzinger, Han (2003) 'The Rise and Fall of Multiculturalism: The Case of the Netherlands', in C. Joppke and E. Motawska (eds), *Toward Assimilation and Citizenship: Immigrants in Liberal Nation-States*. Palgrave Macmillan, Basingstoke.

Esposito, John L. (1999) *The Islamic Threat: Myth or Reality?* 3rd edn. Oxford University Press, Oxford.

Fabre, Cecile and David Miller (2003) 'Justice and Culture: Rawls, Sen, Nussbaum and O'Neill', *Political Studies Review*, 1 (1): 4–17.

Festenstein, Matthew (2005) *Negotiating Diversity: Culture, Deliberation, Trust*. Polity, Cambridge.

Fishkin, James and Peter Laslett (eds) (2003) *Debating Deliberative Democracy*. Blackwell, Oxford.

Flew, Anthony (1967) *Evolutionary Ethics*. Macmillan, London.

Foucault, Michel (1977) *Discipline and Punish: the Birth of the Prison*, trans. A. Sheridan. Penguin, Harmondsworth.

Fraser, Nancy (2008) 'From Redistribution to Recognition? Dilemmas of Justice in a "Postsocialist" Age', in Kevin Olson (ed.), *Adding Insult to Injury: Nancy Fraser Debates Her Critics*. Verso, London.

Fraser, Nancy and Axel Honneth (2003) *Redistribution or Recognition?: A Political-Philosophical Exchange*. Verso, London.

Friedman, Marilyn, and Jan Narveson (1995) *Political Correctness: For and Against*. Rowman & Littlefield, Lanham, MD.

Fukuyama, Francis (1992) *The End of History and the Last Man*. Penguin, Harmondsworth.

Galligan, Brian and Winsome Roberts (2004) *Australian Citizenship*. Melbourne University Press, Melbourne.

Galston, William (2002) *Liberal Pluralism: The Implications of Value Pluralism for Political Theory and Practice*. Cambridge University Press, Cambridge.

Galston, William (2005) *The Practice of Liberal Pluralism*. Cambridge University Press, Cambridge.

Galston, William (2007) 'Must Value Pluralism and Religious Belief Collide?', in George Crowder and Henry Hardy (eds), *The One and the Many: Reading Isaiah Berlin*. Prometheus Books, Amherst, NY.

Gardels, Nathan (1991) 'Two Concepts of Nationalism: An Interview with Isaiah Berlin', *New York Review of Books*, 21 November.

Garton Ash, Timothy (2012) 'Freedom and Diversity: A Liberal Pentagram for Living Together', *New York Review of Books*, 22 November.

Geertz, Clifford (1973) *The Interpretation of Cultures: Selected Essays*. Basic Books, New York.

Geertz, Clifford (1989) 'Anti Anti-Relativism', in Michael Krausz (ed.) (1989) *Relativism: Interpretation and Confrontation*. University of Notre Dame Press, Notre Dame, IN.

Gellner, Ernest (1983) *Nations and Nationalism*. Cornell University Press, Ithaca.

Giddens, Anthony (1985) 'Jürgen Habermas', in Quentin Skinner (ed.), *The Return of Grand Theory in the Human Sciences*. Cambridge University Press, Cambridge.

Gill, Emily (2001) *Becoming Free: Autonomy and Diversity in the Liberal Polity*. University Press of Kansas, Lawrence, KS.

Gilligan, Carol (1982) *In a Different Voice: Psychological Theory and Women's Development*. Harvard University Press, Cambridge, MA.

Glazer, Nathan (1997) *We Are All Multiculturalists Now*. Harvard University Press, Cambridge, MA.

Goodin, Robert (2006) 'Liberal Multiculturalism: Protective and Polyglot', *Political Theory*, 34 (3): 289–303.

Gray, John (1983) *Mill on Liberty: A Defence*. Routledge, London.

Gray, John (1984) *Hayek on Liberty*. Routledge, London.

Gray, John (1986) *Liberalism*. Open University Press, Milton Keynes.

Gray, John (1995a) *Berlin*. HarperCollins, London.

Gray, John (1995b) *Enlightenment's Wake: Politics and Culture at the Close of the Modern Age*. Routledge, London and New York.

Gray, John (2000) *Two Faces of Liberalism*. Polity, Cambridge.

Gray, Tim (1991) *Freedom*. Humanities Press, Atlantic Highlands, NJ.

Green, Leslie (1995) 'Internal Minorities and Their Rights', in Will Kymlicka (ed.), *The Rights of Minority Cultures*. Oxford University Press, Oxford.

Green, Thomas Hill (1881[1991]) 'Liberal Legislation and Freedom of Contract', in D. Miller (ed.), *Liberty*. Oxford University Press, Oxford.

Griffin, Roger (ed.) (1995) *Fascism*. Oxford University Press, Oxford.

Guthrie, W. K. C. (1960) *The Greek Philosophers: From Thales to Aristotle*. Harper & Row, New York.

Gutmann, Amy and Dennis Thompson (1996) *Democracy and Disagreement*. Belknap, Cambridge, MA.

Gutmann, Amy and Dennis Thompson (2004) *Why Deliberative Democracy?* Princeton University Press, Princeton.

Habermas, Jürgen (1984) *The Theory of Communicative Action*, vols 1 and 2, trans. Thomas McCarthy. Beacon, Boston, MA.

Hardy, Henry (2007) 'Taking Pluralism Seriously', in George Crowder and Henry Hardy (eds), *The One and the Many: Reading Isaiah Berlin*. Prometheus Books, Amherst, NY.

Hashmi, Sohail (ed.) (2002) *Islamic Political Ethics: Civil Society, Pluralism and Conflict*. Princeton University Press, Princeton.

Hayek, Friedrich (1944) *The Road to Serfdom*. Routledge, London.

He, Baogang (2005) 'Minority Rights with Chinese Characteristics', in Will Kymlicka and Baogang He (eds), *Multiculturalism in Asia*. Oxford University Press, Oxford.

Hegel, Georg Wilhelm Friedrich (1821 [1956]) *The Philosophy of History*, trans. J. Sibree. Dover, New York.

Held, David (1980) *Introduction to Critical Theory: Horkheimer to Habermas*. University of California Press, Berkeley, CA.

Herder, Johann Gottfried (1774 [2004]) *Another Philosophy of History and Selected Political Writings*, trans. I. Evrigenis and D. Pellerin. Hackett Publishing Company, Indianapolis.

Herder, Johann Gottfried (1969) *On Social and Political Culture*, ed. F. M. Barnard. Cambridge University Press, Cambridge.

Herodotus (n.d. [1972]) *The Histories*, trans. A. de Selincourt, revised A. R. Burn. Penguin, Harmondsworth.

Herskovits, Melville J. (1955) *Cultural Anthropology*. Knopf, New York.

Hill, Mike (ed.) (1997) *Whiteness: A Critical Reader*. New York University Press, New York.

Hobhouse, Lionel Trelawny (1911 [1964]) *Liberalism*. Oxford University Press, Oxford.

Hobsbawm, Eric (2012) *Nations and Nationalism Since 1780: Programme, Myth, Reality*, 2nd edn. Cambridge University Press, Cambridge.

Hollis, Martin and Steven Lukes (eds) (1982) *Rationality and Relativism*. MIT Press, Cambridge, MA.

Horton, John (ed.) (1993) *Liberalism, Multiculturalism and Toleration*. St Martin's Press, New York.

Hughes, Robert (1993) *Culture of Complaint: The Fraying of America*. Oxford University Press, New York.

Hume, David (1739–40 [1978]) *A Treatise of Human Nature*, ed. L. A. Selby-Bigge, 2nd edn. Revised by P. H. Nidditch. Clarendon Press, Oxford.

Huntington, Samuel (1996) *The Clash of Civilizations and the Remaking of World Order*. Simon & Schuster, New York.

Irwin, Robert (2006) *Dangerous Knowledge: Orientalism and its Discontents*. Overlook, London.

Ivison, Duncan (2002) *Postcolonial Liberalism*. Cambridge University Press, Cambridge.

Ivison, Duncan, Paul Patton and Will Sanders (eds) (2000) *Political Theory and the Rights of Indigenous Peoples*. Cambridge University Press, Cambridge.

Jayasuriya, Laksiri (2007) 'White Australia Policy', in Brian Galligan and Winsome Roberts (eds), *Oxford Companion to Australian Politics*. Oxford University Press, Oxford.

Jenkins, Roy (1970) *Essays and Speeches*. Collins, London.

Jenks, Chris (2004) *Culture*. Routledge, London.

Johnston, David (1994) *The Idea of a Liberal Theory: A Critique and Reconstruction*. Princeton University Press, Princeton.

Joppke, Christian (2004) 'The Retreat of Multiculturalism in the Liberal State: Theory and Policy', *British Journal of Sociology*, 55 (2): 237–57.

Joppke, Christian and Steven Lukes (eds) (1999) *Multicultural Questions*. Oxford University Press, Oxford.

Kant, Immanuel (1785 [1956]) *The Moral Law* (*Groundwork of the Metaphysic of Morals*), trans. H. J. Paton, 3rd edn. Hutchinson University Library, London.

Kant, Immanuel (1795 [1991]) 'Perpetual Peace', in *Political Writings*, ed. H. Reiss. Cambridge University Press, Cambridge.
Kedourie, Elie (1961) *Nationalism*, revised edn. Hutchinson University Library, London.
Kekes, John (1993) *The Morality of Pluralism*. Princeton University Press, Princeton.
Kelly, Paul (2005) *Liberalism*. Polity, Cambridge.
Kipling, R. (1897 [2003]) 'Recessional', in *Selected Poems*, ed. Peter Keating. Penguin, London.
Kivisto, Peter (2002) *Multiculturalism in a Global Society*. Blackwell, Oxford.
Krausz, Michael (ed.) (1989) *Relativism: Interpretation and Confrontation*. University of Notre Dame Press, Notre Dame, IN.
Kukathas, Chandran (1992) 'Are There Any Cultural Rights?', *Political Theory*, 20 (1): 105–39.
Kukathas, Chandran (1997) 'Liberalism, Multiculturalism and Oppression', in Andrew Vincent (ed.), *Political Theory: Tradition and Diversity*. Cambridge University Press, Cambridge.
Kukathas, Chandran (2003) *The Liberal Archipelago*. Oxford University Press, Oxford.
Kukathas, Chandran (2004) 'Nationalism and Multiculturalism', in Gerald Gaus and Chandran Kukathas (eds), *Handbook of Political Theory*. Sage, London.
Kymlicka, Will (1989) *Liberalism, Community, and Culture*. Oxford University Press, Oxford.
Kymlicka, Will (1992) 'The Rights of Minority Cultures: Reply to Kukathas', *Political Theory*, 20 (1): 140–6.
Kymlicka, Will (1995a) *Multicultural Citizenship: A Liberal Theory of Minority Rights*. Oxford University Press, Oxford.
Kymlicka, Will (1995b) 'Introduction' to W. Kymlicka (ed.), *The Rights of Minority Cultures*. Oxford University Press, Oxford.
Kymlicka, Will (1998a) *Finding Our Way: Rethinking Ethnocultural Relations in Canada*. Oxford University Press, Oxford.
Kymlicka, Will (1998b) 'Introduction: An Emerging Consensus', *Ethical Theory and Moral Practice*, 1 (2): 143–57.
Kymlicka, Will (2001) *Politics in the Vernacular*. Oxford University Press, Oxford.
Kymlicka, Will (2002) *Contemporary Political Philosophy: An Introduction*. Oxford University Press, Oxford.
Kymlicka, Will (2007) *Multicultural Odysseys*. Oxford University Press, Oxford.
Ladd, John (ed.) (1973) *Ethical Relativism*. Wadsworth, Belmont, CA.
Laden, Anthony Simon and David Owen (eds) (2007) *Multiculturalism and Political Theory*. Cambridge University Press, Cambridge.
Lamey, Andy (1999) 'Francophonia Forever', *Times Literary Supplement*, 23 July.

Landes, David (1999) *The Wealth and Poverty of Nations: Why Some are so Rich and Some are so Poor*. Norton, New York.
Langlois, Anthony (2001) *The Politics of Justice and Human Rights: Southeast Asia and Universalist Theory*. Cambridge University Press, Cambridge.
Larmore, Charles (1996) *The Morals of Modernity*. Cambridge University Press, Cambridge.
Lawson, Stephanie (1996) *Tradition Versus Democracy in the South Pacific: Fiji, Tonga and Western Samoa*. Cambridge University Press, Cambridge.
Lawson, Stephanie (2006) *Culture and Context in World Politics*. Palgrave Macmillan, Basingstoke.
Levey, Geoffrey Brahm (1997) 'Equality, Autonomy and Cultural Rights', *Political Theory*, 25 (2): 215–48.
Levey, Geoffrey Brahm (2008) 'Multicultural Political Thought in Australian Perspective', in Geoffrey Brahm Levey (ed.), *Political Theory and Australian Multiculturalism*. Berghahn Books, New York.
Levinson, Meira (1999) *The Demands of Liberal Education*. Oxford University Press, Oxford.
Levy, Jacob T. (2000) *The Multiculturalism of Fear*. Oxford University Press, Oxford.
Levy, Neil (2002) *Moral Relativism: A Short Introduction*. Oneworld, Oxford.
Lewis, Bernard (2002) *What Went Wrong? Western Impact and Middle Eastern Response*. Weidenfeld & Nicolson, London.
Lingle, Christopher (1996) *Singapore's Authoritarian Capitalism: Asian Values, Free Market Illusions, and Political Dependency*. Edicions Sirocco, S. L., Barcelona, and The Locke Institute, Fairfax, VA.
Locke, John (1689 [1991]) *A Letter Concerning Toleration*, ed. J. Horton and S. Mendus. Routledge, London.
Locke, John (1689 [1970]) *Two Treatises of Government*, ed. P. Laslett. Cambridge University Press, Cambridge.
Losurdo, Domenico (2011) *Liberalism: A Counter-History*. Verso, London.
Lukes, Steven (1985) *Marxism and Morality*. Oxford University Press, Oxford.
Lukes, Steven (1991) 'Making Sense of Moral Conflict', in *Moral Conflict and Politics*. Clarendon Press, Oxford.
Lukes, Steven (2003) *Liberals and Cannibals: The Implications of Diversity*. Verso, London.
Lukes, Steven (2008) *Moral Relativism*. Picador, New York.
Lyotard, Jean-François (1984) *The Postmodern Condition: A Report on Knowledge*. University of Minnesota Press, Minneapolis, MN.
Macedo, Stephen (ed.) (1999) *Deliberative Politics: Essays on Democracy and Disagreement*. Oxford University Press, New York.
MacIntyre, Alasdair (1985) *After Virtue*, 2nd edn. Duckworth, London.
MacIntyre, Alasdair (1988) *Whose Justice? Which Rationality?* Duckworth, London.

Manning, D. J. (1976) *Liberalism*. Dent & Sons, London.
Margalit, Avishai and Joseph Raz (1995) 'National Self-Determination', in Will Kymlicka (ed.), *The Rights of Minority Cultures*. Oxford University Press, Oxford.
Mazzini, Giuseppe (1907 [1966]) *The Duties of Man and Other Essays*, trans. Thomas Jones. Dent, London.
Mehta, Uday Singh (1999) *Liberalism and Empire*. Chicago University Press, Chicago, IL.
Mendus, Susan (2002) 'Choice, Chance and Multiculturalism', in P. Kelly (ed.), *Multiculturalism Reconsidered:* Culture and Equality *and its Critics*. Polity, Cambridge.
Mill, John Stuart (1859 [1974]) *On Liberty*, ed. G. Himmelfarb. Harmondsworth, Penguin.
Mill, John Stuart (1861 [1958]) *Considerations on Representative Government*, ed. Currin V. Shields. Bobbs-Merrill, Indianapolis, IN.
Miller, David (ed.) (1991) *Liberty*. Oxford University Press, Oxford.
Miller, David (1993) 'In Defence of Nationality', *Journal of Applied Philosophy*, 10 (1): 3–16.
Miller, David (1995) *On Nationality*. Oxford University Press, Oxford.
Miller, David (1999) 'Communitarianism: Left, Right, and Centre', in Dan Avnon and Avner De-Shalit (eds), *Liberalism and its Practice*. Routledge, London.
Miller, David (2002) 'Liberalism, Equal Opportunities and Cultural Commitments', in P. Kelly (ed.), *Multiculturalism Reconsidered:* Culture and Equality *and its Critics*. Polity, Cambridge.
Mitter, Rana (2004) *A Bitter Revolution: China's Struggle with the Modern World*. Oxford University Press, Oxford.
Modood, Tariq (2007) *Multiculturalism*. Polity, Cambridge.
Momigliano, Arnaldo (1976) 'On the Pioneer Trail', *New York Review of Books*, 11 November.
Montesquieu, Charles-Louis de Secondat (1721 [1973]) *Persian Letters*, trans. C. J. Betts. Penguin, Harmondsworth.
Moore, Margaret (2001) *The Ethics of Nationalism*. Oxford University Press, Oxford.
Mulhall, Stephen and Adam Swift (1996) *Liberals and Communitarians*, 2nd edn. Blackwell, Oxford.
Murphy, Michael (2012) *Multiculturalism: A Critical Introduction*. Routledge, London and New York.
Muthu, Sankar (2003) *Enlightenment Against Empire*. Princeton University Press, Princeton.
Nagel, Thomas (1991) 'The Fragmentation of Value', in *Mortal Questions*. Canto: Cambridge.
Nisbett, Richard (2003) *The Geography of Thought: How Asians and Westerners Think Differently . . . and Why*. Free Press, New York.
Norton, Robert (1991) *Herder's Aesthetics and the European Enlightenment*. Cornell University Press, Ithaca.
Nozick, Robert (1974) *Anarchy, State, and Utopia*. Basic Books, New York.

Nussbaum, Martha (1990) 'Aristotelian Social Democracy', in R. B. Douglass, G. M. Mara and H. S. Richardson (eds), *Liberalism and the Good*. Routledge, New York.
Nussbaum, Martha (1992) *Love's Knowledge: Essays on Philosophy and Literature*. Oxford University Press, Oxford.
Nussbaum, Martha (1996) 'Patriotism and Cosmopolitanism', in Martha Nussbaum with Respondents, *For Love of Country: Debating the Limits of Patriotism*, ed. Joshua Cohen. Beacon Press, Boston, MA.
Nussbaum, Martha (2000) *Women and Moral Development: the Capabilities Approach*. Cambridge University Press, Cambridge.
Nussbaum, Martha (2001) *The Fragility of Goodness: Luck and Ethics in Greek Tragedy and Philosophy*, 2nd edn. Cambridge University Press, Cambridge.
Nussbaum, Martha (2003) 'Political Liberalism and Respect: A Response to Linda Barclay', *Sats – Nordic Journal of Philosophy*, 2 (2): 25–44.
Nussbaum, Martha (2011) *Creating Capabilities: The Human Development Approach*. Belknap Press, Cambridge, MA.
Nussbaum, Martha and Amartya Sen (eds) (1993) *The Quality of Life*. Clarendon Press, Oxford.
Okin, Susan (1999) *Is Multiculturalism Bad for Women?* (with respondents), ed. J. Cohen, M. Howard and M. Nussbaum. Princeton University Press, Princeton.
Okin, Susan (2002) '"Mistresses of Their Own Destiny": Group Rights, Gender, and Realistic Rights of Exit', *Ethics*, 112 (2): 205–30.
Olson, Kevin (ed.) (2008) *Adding Insult to Injury: Nancy Fraser Debates Her Critics*. Verso, London.
Parekh, Bhikhu (1992) 'The Cultural Particularity of Liberal Democracy', *Political Studies*, 40, Special Issue: 160–75.
Parekh, Bhikhu (1994) 'Superior People', *Times Literary Supplement*, 25 February.
Parekh, Bhikhu (2006) *Rethinking Multiculturalism: Cultural Diversity and Political Theory*, 2nd edn. Palgrave, London.
Parekh, Bhikhu (2008) *A New Politics of Identity: Political Principles for an Interdependent World*. Palgrave, London.
Phillips, Anne (1998) *The Politics of Presence*. Oxford University Press, Oxford.
Phillips, Anne (2007) *Multiculturalism Without Culture*. Princeton University Press, Princeton.
Phillips, Anne (2010) *Gender and Culture*. Polity, Cambridge.
Pitkin, Hanna (1971) *The Concept of Representation*. University of California, Berkeley, CA.
Pitts, Jennifer (2005) *A Turn to Empire: the Rise of Liberal Imperialism in Britain and France*. Princeton University Press, Princeton.
Preece, Jennifer Jackson (2005) *Minority Rights: Between Diversity and Community*. Polity, Cambridge.
Rabinow, Paul (ed.) (1984) *The Foucault Reader*. Penguin, Harmondsworth.

Rachels, James (1993) *The Elements of Moral Philosophy*, 2nd edn. McGraw-Hill Inc., New York.
Ramadan, Tariq (2009) *Radical Reform: Islamic Ethics and Liberation*. Oxford University Press, Oxford.
Ramadan, Tariq (2010) *What I Believe*. Oxford University Press, Oxford.
Rattansi, Ali (2011) *Multiculturalism: A Very Short Introduction*. Oxford University Press, Oxford.
Rawls, John (1971) *A Theory of Justice*. Oxford University Press, Oxford.
Rawls, John (1985) 'Justice as Fairness: Political Not Metaphysical', *Philosophy and Public Affairs*, 14 (3): 223–51.
Rawls, John (1993) *Political Liberalism*. Columbia University Press, New York.
Raz, Joseph (1986) *The Morality of Freedom*. Clarendon Press, Oxford.
Raz, Joseph (1995) 'Multiculturalism: A Liberal Perspective', in *Ethics in the Public Domain*. Clarendon Press, Oxford.
Reich, Rob (2002) *Bridging Liberalism and Multiculturalism in American Education*. University of Chicago Press, Chicago, IL.
Richardson, Henry S. (1997) *Practical Reasoning about Final Ends*. Cambridge University Press, Cambridge.
Rodan, Garry (2004) *Transparency and Authoritarian Rule in Southeast Asia: Singapore and Malaysia*. RoutledgeCurzon, London and New York.
Rorty, Richard (1989) *Contingency, Irony, and Solidarity*. Cambridge University Press, Cambridge.
Rowse, Tim (2001) 'Terra Nullius', in Graeme Davidson, John Hirst and Stuart MacIntyre (eds), with the assistance of Helen Doyle and Kim Torney, *The Oxford Companion to Australian History*, revised edn. Oxford University Press, Melbourne.
Safi, Omid (ed.) (2003) *Progressive Muslims: On Justice, Gender and Pluralism*. Oneworld, Oxford.
Said, Edward (1978) *Orientalism: Western Conceptions of the Orient*. Routledge & Kegan Paul, London.
Said, Edward (2001) 'Clash of Ignorance', *The Nation*, 4 October.
Sandall, Roger (2001) *The Culture Cult: Designer Tribalism and Other Essays*. Westview, Boulder, CO.
Sandel, Michael (1982) *Liberalism and the Limits of Justice*. Cambridge University Press, Cambridge.
Scheffer, Paul (2011) *Immigrant Nations*, trans. Liz Waters. Polity, Cambridge.
Schlesinger, Arthur M. (1992) *The Disuniting of America: Reflections on a Multicultural Society*. Norton, New York.
Scholte, Jan Aart (2000) *Globalization: A Critical Introduction*. Palgrave, Basingstoke.
Scott, David (2003) 'Culture in Political Theory', *Political Theory*, 31 (1): 92–115.
Scruton, Roger (2002) *The West and the Rest: Globalization and the Terrorist Threat*. Continuum, London.

Sen, Amartya (1992) *Reexamining Inequality*. Oxford University Press, Oxford.
Sen, Amartya (2001) *Development as Freedom*. Alfred A. Knopf, New York.
Sen, Amartya (2005) *The Argumentative Indian: Writings on Indian History, Culture and Identity*. Farrar, Straus & Giroux, New York.
Sen, Amartya (2006). *Identity and Violence: The Illusion of Destiny*. Norton, New York.
Sen, Amartya (2009) *The Idea of Justice*. Belknap Press of Harvard University Press, Cambridge, MA.
Shachar, Ayelet (2001) *Multicultural Jurisdictions*. Cambridge University Press, Cambridge.
Shin, Doh Chull (2011) *Confucianism and Democratization in East Asia*. Cambridge University Press, Cambridge.
Smart, Barry (1992) *Modern Conditions, Postmodern Controversies*. Routledge, London.
Smith, Adam (1776 [1970]) *The Wealth of Nations*, ed. A. Skinner. Harmondsworth, Penguin.
Song, Sarah (2007) *Justice, Gender, and the Politics of Multiculturalism*. Cambridge University Press, Cambridge.
Soutphommasane, Tim (2012) *The Virtuous Citizen: Patriotism in a Multicultural Society*. Cambridge University Press, Cambridge.
Spencer, Vicki (2012) *Herder's Political Thought: A Study on Language, Culture and Community*. University of Toronto Press, Toronto.
Spinner, Jeff (1994) *The Boundaries of Citizenship: Race, Ethnicity, and Nationality in the Liberal State*. Johns Hopkins University Press, Baltimore.
Spinner-Halev, Jeff (2001) 'Feminism, Oppression, and the State', *Ethics*, 112 (1): 84–113.
Stocker, Michael (1990) *Plural and Conflicting Values*. Clarendon Press, Oxford.
Sunstein, Cass (1995) 'Incompletely Theorised Agreements', *Harvard Law Review*, 108 (7): 1733–72.
Swift, Adam (2006) *Political Philosophy: A Beginners' Guide for Students and Politicians*, 2nd edn. Polity, Cambridge.
Tamir, Yael (1995) *Liberal Nationalism*, revised edn with new Preface. Princeton University Press, Princeton.
Taylor, Charles (1985) 'Atomism', in *Philosophy and the Human Sciences: Philosophical Papers*, vol. 2. Cambridge University Press, Cambridge.
Taylor, Charles (1989) 'Cross-Purposes: The Liberal-Communitarian Debate', in Nancy Rosenblum (ed.), *Liberalism and the Moral Life*. Harvard University Press, Cambridge, MA.
Taylor, Charles (1994) 'The Politics of Recognition', in A. Gutmann (ed.), *Multiculturalism: Examining the Politics of Recognition*. Princeton University Press, Princeton.
Tomlinson, J. (1995) 'Homogenisation and Globalisation', *History of European Ideas*, 20 (4–6): 891–7.

Trevor-Roper, Hugh (1992) 'The Invention of Tradition: The Highland Tradition of Scotland', in Eric Hobsbawm and Terence Ranger (eds), *The Invention of Tradition*. Canto, Cambridge.

Tronto, Joan (1993) *Moral Boundaries: A Political Argument for an Ethic of Care*. Routledge, New York.

Tully, James (1995) *Strange Multiplicity*. Cambridge University Press, Cambridge.

Tully, James (2002) 'The Illiberal Liberal: Brian Barry's Polemical Attack on Multiculturalism', in Paul Kelly (ed.), *Multiculturalism Reconsidered:* Culture and Equality *and its Critics*. Polity, Cambridge.

Vertovec, Steven (2007) 'Super-Diversity and its Implications', *Ethnic and Racial Studies*, 30 (6): 1024–54.

Vincent, Andrew (2002) *Nationalism and Particularity*. Cambridge University Press, Cambridge.

Waldron, Jeremy (1992) 'Superseding Historic Injustice', *Ethics*, 103 (2): 4–28.

Waldron, Jeremy (1995) 'Minority Cultures and Cosmopolitan Alternatives', in W. Kymlicka (ed.), *The Rights of Minority Cultures*. Oxford University Press, Oxford.

Walker, Brian (1997) 'Plural Cultures, Contested Territories: A Critique of Kymlicka', *Canadian Journal of Political Science*, 30 (2): 211–34.

Walzer, Michael (1983) *Spheres of Justice*. Blackwell, Oxford.

Walzer, Michael (1988) *The Company of Critics*. Basic Books, New York.

Walzer, Michael (1995) 'Are There Limits to Liberalism?' *New York Review of Books*, 19 October.

Walzer, Michael (1999) 'Deliberation, and What Else?', in Stephen Macedo (ed.), *Deliberative Politics: Essays on Democracy and Disagreement*. Oxford University Press, New York.

Warraq, Ibn (2007) *Defending the West: A Critique of Edward Said's Orientalism*. Prometheus, Amherst, NY.

Waters, Malcolm (2000) *Globalization*, 2nd edn. Routledge, London.

Weber, Max (1965) *Sociology of Religion*, trans. E. Fischoff. Methuen, London.

White, Leslie A. and Beth Dillingham (1973) *The Concept of Culture*. Burgess, Minneapolis, MN.

White, Stephen K. (1991) *Political Theory and Postmodernism*. Cambridge University Press, Cambridge.

Williams, Bernard (1972) *Morality*. Cambridge University Press, Cambridge.

Williams, Bernard (1979) 'Conflicts of Values', in Alan Ryan (ed.), *The Idea of Freedom: Essays in Honour of Isaiah Berlin*. Oxford University Press, Oxford.

Williams, Bernard (1980) 'Introduction' to *Isaiah Berlin, Concepts and Categories*, ed. Henry Hardy. Oxford University Press, London.

Williams, Melissa (1998) *Voice, Trust, and Memory: Marginalized Groups and the Failings of Liberal Representation.* Princeton University Press, Princeton.

Williams, Melissa (2000) 'The Uneasy Alliance of Group Representation and Deliberative Democracy', in Will Kymlicka and Wayne Norman (eds), *Citizenship in Diverse Societies.* Oxford University Press, Oxford.

Wittfogel, Karl (1957) *Oriental Despotism: A Comparative Study of Total Power.* Yale University Press, New Haven, CT.

Wolff, Jonathan, and Avner De-Shalit (2007) *Disadvantage.* Oxford University Press, Oxford.

Wong, David (1993) 'Relativism', in P. Singer (ed.), *A Companion to Ethics.* Blackwell, Oxford.

Young, Iris Marion (1990) *Justice and the Politics of Difference.* Princeton University Press, Princeton.

Young, Iris Marion (2000) *Inclusion and Democracy.* Oxford University Press, Oxford.

Index